COMMITMENT IN MODERN
FRENCH LITERATURE

COMMITMENT IN MODERN
FRENCH LITERATURE

Politics and Society in
Péguy, Aragon, and Sartre

M. ADERETH

SCHOCKEN BOOKS · NEW YORK

To Linda and Victor

FOREWORD

This book is intended for the general public. As one of the main purposes of commitment is to bring together literature and life, it is fitting that a discussion of modern committed writers should not be confined to a narrow circle of specialists but should aim at all those who care about the problems and hopes of the modern world. The following pages are offered as a contribution to such a discussion. This does not mean that literary and aesthetic issues have been avoided or vulgarized. On the contrary, I am convinced that these issues are by no means remote from ordinary life and that the greater the number of people who take an informed interest in them, the better it will be both for the public at large and for literature itself.

The aims of this essay can be briefly summed up. First, to try to define "littérature engagée", which is the French version of commitment, but whose achievements and difficulties have a significance which extends well beyond the confines of a single country; secondly, to trace the emergence of the committed outlook in the life and works of three writers as strikingly different as Péguy, Aragon and Sartre[a] and to show that commitment has created great similarities among them; thirdly, to introduce the English reader to Aragon as a committed writer[b]; and lastly, to examine the contribution that he, together with Péguy and Sartre, has made towards clarifying such issues as literary realism and the nature of poetry.

The selection of Péguy, Aragon and Sartre deserves an additional word of explanation. Initially, it was simply dictated by the desire to include a representative from each of the main currents of our time. Later, however, it became clear that a parallel study of their work could throw more light on the concept of commitment by showing that over and above ideological

[a] This book is obviously not an attempt to present a complete picture of these writers. Anything which is not directly relevant to their committed outlook has been deliberately left out.

[b] Péguy and Sartre are already well known on both sides of the Channel but Aragon has not yet attracted the same attention in this country. This is largely due to political prejudice and is rather unfortunate, for he is one of France's leading poets, novelists and critics.

differences, writers who commit themselves to the cause of helping their fellow men through the medium of art approach a number of basic problems in the same spirit. When Paul Eluard gathered a few extracts for an anthology on art and literature, he explained that the only link between the writers he had selected was that they had regarded themselves as "men among men" and that, whether they had taken "the divergent paths of faith, dreams or reasoning", they had all rejected the barren concept of art for art's sake.[a] This actually constitutes the guiding spirit of committed literature and also, by welcome coincidence, it seems to justify the choice of Péguy, Aragon and Sartre as men who have endeavoured to serve through "faith, dreams and reasoning"—the faith of the Catholic poet, the dreams of the revolutionary artist, and the reasoning of the Existentialist philosopher.

[a] Cf. T. S. Eliot's statement that ". . . pure poetry is a phantom" and that ". . . both in creation and enjoyment, much always enters which is from the point of view of 'Art' irrelevant". This of course does not represent acceptance of commitment, but it does expose the fallacy that aesthetic considerations can be artificially isolated from moral and ideological reactions. And this is one of the first contentions of commitment—it claims that art, and more particularly literary art which is expressed through the social phenomenon of language, is a form of communion with other men, and that this communion involves all aspects of human personality.

CONTENTS

NOTE ON QUOTATIONS

All quotations from French sources have been translated by me, unless otherwise stated, and I take full responsibility for the English version. This does not apply to titles of books by Péguy, Aragon and Sartre, when these are available in English, although I have drawn attention to some unfortunate renderings.

All page references are to the French original, unless otherwise stated. Editions used are indicated in the Bibliography at the end.

M. A.

INTRODUCTORY

CHAPTER I

WHAT IS "LITTÉRATURE ENGAGÉE"?

THE CONCEPT OF "littérature engagée" emerged as a result of the impact of modern ideologies on literature. These ideologies, in spite of their diversity, have one thing in common— they reflect the deep and rapid social changes of our time. Because of this, they compel each one of us to re-examine critically his position in the world and his responsibility to other men. Under their influence the writer in particular approaches his work in a new way, he commits himself. This simply means that he becomes aware that the real nature of his art is to focus attention on an aspect of reality and thus, inevitably, to pass judgement on it. The greatest originality of the modern conception of commitment is that it claims to be inseparable from literature itself. It does not merely repeat the pious platitude that there should be room in art for the big world of reality outside, but asserts almost aggressively that a writer is great only to the extent that he can provide society in general (or the reading public of the time) with a true mirror of itself, of its conflicts and its problems. His success in this respect is determined by the fact that he himself is no mere spectator in the drama he depicts, he is also an actor. What is required of him is that he should be a conscious actor.

The idea is not specifically French, but if it received its first coherent expression in post-war France, it is probably because the years of Occupation and Resistance had made Frenchmen more keenly aware of the need for a complete reassessment of all values. In the late forties, the part which literature could play in the world came in for particular attention, and the idea of commitment arose quite naturally, both as an answer to the problems of art and as a contribution to the requirements of society. That the movement survived those specific circumstances and moreover spread to other lands is proof enough that its vitality does not rest on the conditions which helped to give it birth. The emergence of commitment in the twentieth century rather suggests that it corresponds to the needs of the present age. There are two main reasons for this. We are faced today with a reality which is moving so fast that it is difficult to understand it, even partly, without being to some extent involved in it. Standing by the wayside condemns one to missing the essence of life. It may not necessarily spell the doom of art (for native talent usually finds more than one way of asserting itself), but it almost certainly limits its appeal and its human greatness. In the past, it was possible for artists to delude themselves into believing that their art was a thing apart. If in fact very few of them did, it was precisely because they had genius and could see beyond superficial appearances. Today, no one can hide even behind such appearances. We know only too well that the province of art is not a so-called unchangeable human nature but a contemporary situation which has its own unique features, and that it is only through this highly original situation that one can express the lasting and universal emotions which give art its permanent appeal. The paradox that eternal issues have a temporal shell has ceased to be a paradox for our generation because life has repeatedly proved it in practice. To ignore the temporal shell is to deal with lifeless abstractions.

Closely connected with a sense of the present is another objective factor peculiar to our age—the profound crisis of modern civilization. Not only have two world wars shattered most of our illusions, but we are now compelled to choose between life and death for our species. In the age of nuclear energy this is the dilemma which faces us. How can sensitive men escape from it? Some writers affect to be quite cynical about it, others tend to dismiss the issue as too big and too remote for them, but both their attitudes could well be a form of protest or an expression of suffering and anxiety. Moreover, their refusal to face reality, whether it is deliberate or cowardly, does not make contemporary reality disappear. Far from it! The latter manages to sneak in through the back door and leave its mark on thinkers and artists who think they have turned their backs on it. For example, it is doubtful whether an age less given to turmoil and violence could have witnessed such movements as the revolt of the "angry young men", the theatre of the absurd, or the impersonal objectivity of the Robbe-Grillet type of "nouveau roman", this last feature being almost certainly an echo of the inhuman world in which individuals are crushed. Committed writers do not despise any of those trends, but they believe that an open acknowledgement of the links between the writer and society would be more honest and more profitable. This is the path of commitment, a path bristling with hardships and setbacks, but difficult to avoid.

THE CASE AGAINST COMMITMENT

As the committed writer must begin by discarding many cherished notions and habits, it may not be a bad idea to examine very briefly some of the most important objections which have been put forward against commitment. This will clarify the true nature of committed literature and help us to avoid possible misconceptions about its aims. A frequent criticism is that "littérature engagée" gives too big a place to politics. The objection has been expressed time and again and it is not uncommon to find that people reduce committed writing to political writing or, at best, to books whose main interest is political. Even a subtle critic like R. Albérès complains that committed writers have paid too much attention to politics.[1]

The committed reply would start by pointing to the fact that the political crisis is the most acute expression of the general crisis of our time. Our moral and ideological conflicts all have a political background and there are hardly any aspects of our private lives which are not tangled with the political battle, in one way or another. Aragon and Sartre often illustrate the point in their novels. For example, in Aragon's *Passengers of Destiny* the central character is a man who prides himself on deliberately ignoring the political events of his day, refusing even to read the newspapers except for the financial columns. In the end, however, as a result of an accident, he finds himself partly paralysed. By a supreme irony of fate, he loses the use of speech, except for one word which is now the only one he can utter: "politique"! And so it is with the help of this one word that he makes all his wants known to the woman who looks after him—hunger, thirst, sleep, etc. This is a particularly forceful allegory to suggest that in the twentieth century human destiny is decided through politics. (Napoleon called politics "la forme moderne du destin".) The same lesson emerges from Sartre's novel *Reprieve*. The action takes place at the time of the Munich crisis in 1938, and the fate of each character is influenced by Hitler's decisions and by Chamberlain's and Daladier's capitulation before his demands. A really pathetic figure is that of Gros Louis, an illiterate peasant who would do no harm to anyone and yet finds himself, very much against his will, transported from place to place and finally locked up in jail, all because of "politics" of which the poor fellow is quite ignorant. The inescapable moral is that even if we ignore politics, politics will not ignore us.

This does not mean that politics is the only theme, or even the most important one, in committed works of art. In some of them, it seems to be almost absent, as for example in the lyrical poems of Péguy and Aragon. In "engagé" novels, particularly in those of Aragon, the story concerns private individuals, busily trying to solve their personal problems and usually unaware of the part played by politics in shaping their destinies. Most of the heroes of Sartre's *Roads to Freedom* are in the same position. But the novelists themselves never forget that their characters are firmly rooted in the society of their time, with the result that the message about the importance of political problems is conveyed precisely by showing the little impact they make on the heroes' conscious minds. The political moral is seldom artificially or pompously laid down—it is implied without being openly suggested. One can say that in committed fiction, politics is literally the background—a vital one, but only a background.

Moreover, "littérature engagée" does not believe that complete individual freedom is achieved outside or against society. It rather takes the view that outside society man ceases to be a human being altogether and is reduced to the level of the brute, and, as such, subject to the most relentless determinism. Human freedom is a social conquest. Neither is it true, committed writers would add, that society cripples the free instincts of the individual. Social institutions may, and often do, stand in the way of individual self-expression, but the remedy is to attack and abolish those institutions; simply to ignore them does not remove their harmful effects, any more than the ostrich kills its enemy by pretending not to see him.

What applies to the characters of committed literature applies with even greater force to the committed artist himself. There is a reciprocal and fruitful exchange between his creative activity and his life as a man of action. The latter provides him with rich material for his art; as he mixes with people, he shares their difficulties and learns about their feelings. In return, his works can help his fellow men to understand themselves. Péguy probably provides the most convincing illustrations of this fact because the spiritual truths which he discovered were the result of his deep involvement in the struggles of his time: it was in the course of fighting for the innocence of Dreyfus that he came face to face with the issues involving "the eternal salvation" of man.

Lastly, according to Sartre, "metaphysical anguish" (i.e. the attempt to grasp the full meaning of life) is a "luxury" in which the vast majority of mankind can ill afford to indulge so long as their social problems still clamour for solution, but he adds that the search for the ultimate significance of existence will eventually become the main concern of man "when men have made themselves truly free".[a] As for commitment, it involves giving "a complete picture of the human condition".[2] In fact, we shall see that Péguy, Aragon and Sartre have always endeavoured not to "mutilate" man in any essential respect. For example, Péguy held that "spiritual salvation" was an extension of "temporal" (i.e. political) salvation; Aragon always links the quest for personal happiness with political activity, and sees in love the finest *individual* expression of the committed approach because in love each partner prefers the other to himself; and Sartre attaches great importance to the study of "mediations", i.e. of the concrete, specific ways in which society exerts an influence on individuals (e.g. family relationships, etc.).

A second objection is that modern society has made commitment obsolete, for there are supposedly no causes left to which it is worth committing oneself. This is the really sophisticated objection against commitment, the one which is usually accompanied by the condescending admission that the idea could have been useful in the thirties, a bygone era for our critics, but that today no serious literature can be based on such primitive notions. The rejection of the traditional novel which is basically constructed around the conflict between the individual and

---

[a] Sartre makes this point in an essay devoted to the Jewish question in which he explains why modern Jews are more prominent in the field of politics than in philosophy. This, according to him, is due to their feeling of insecurity, for, he adds, "one must be quite sure of one's rights in society to be able to concern oneself with the fate of man in the universe", so that, for the time being, metaphysics is bound to remain "the privilege of an Aryan ruling class". (*Réflexions sur la question juive*, p. 174.)

society, and its replacement by the *objective* type of fiction, are advanced as proof that commitment is dead.

The committed reply is that this objection is not really "literary" but is based on a very debatable assessment of the present time. There is no doubt that life in the sixties is very different from what it was twenty or thirty years ago, but the work of committed writers illustrates the change remarkably well. The Sartre who wrote the autobiographical essay *Words* in 1963 has obviously learnt from his own mistakes and he can describe his childhood as well as his early illusions with greater lucidity. As for Aragon, the majority of the books he has published in the last ten years give a privileged place to subjective elements, much to the surprise and chagrin of some of his friends. Actually, this new approach, far from being accidental or due to the author's personal whims, corresponds much better to the stage our society has reached: on the one hand, the increased complexity of life makes greater demands on personal initiative whereas, on the other, the danger of technology reducing us to mere robots is sufficiently real to warrant a vigorous reaction from the artist—in *Les Poètes* (1960), Aragon tries to visualize the new world which is being built and he makes the following passionate plea:

In that world I claim room for poetry[a]

With regard to the assumption that there are no suitable conflicts to inspire today's writers, it is contradicted by the existence of at least four major sources of tension. First, writers and artists are the last people who should be taken in by the assertion that we've "never had it so good". Whether this is true on the purely material level or not, the sad fact is that modern life is dull and oppressive. Against such a background it may be difficult to write the type of poignant fiction which was inspired by the Spanish Civil War, for example, but for a sensitive artist, there is rich material to be found in a society which has manifestly failed to provide its members with a sense of purpose and a true appreciation of the joys of life. And as the remedy involves more than strictly cultural measures, as it is bound up with political and moral decisions, it requires commitment. A two-way process is involved here: on the one hand, modern man

[a] "Je réclame dans ce monde-là une place pour la poésie", op. cit., p. 145.

needs artists to depict his life to him without illusions or complacency and suggest a way out; but on the other hand, the
artist can find in the tragedy of modern man a challenging
source of inspiration precisely because so much of contemporary
life is vulgar and cheap.

This is closely connected with another conflict peculiar to
our age, the acute and disturbing contrast between "pop"
culture and traditional culture. Without examining all the
implications of this issue, perhaps a few questions should at least
be raised. Is "pop" culture the inevitable price we have to pay
for the extension of political and social democracy, i.e. is it the
only type of culture one can expect the broad masses to enjoy—
or does it rather illustrate the fact that we are still very far from
having achieved democracy and that the tendency of our
modern masters is to prevent most of us from engaging in the
eternally dangerous activity of thinking clearly and deeply? Is
"pop" culture entirely negative, or does it, in spite of all efforts
to commercialize it, express in its own way the anguish of our
generation and its pathetic search for new values? What, in
any case, is the real dividing line between the two cultures?
These and similar questions are the concern of all those who feel
that "man does not live by bread alone" and that cultural and
ideological poverty is at least as bad as material poverty, if not
worse. They affect each one of us, and not just a handful of
"intellectuals". As one of Arnold Wesker's heroines says, "The
whole stinkin' commercial world insults us and we don't care a
damn . . .—it's our own bloody fault."[3] Commitment does not
claim to have all the answers to the above questions, nor does it
suggest there cannot be more than one answer. What it does say
is that they are bound up with one's philosophy of life and that
the writers and artists whose obvious right and duty it is to
contribute to their solution can hardly do so without taking
sides in the political and moral debates of their times, in other
words *without committing themselves*!

Another aspect of modern culture is the frightening increase
of pornography. I use the word "frightening", not in a puritanical sense, but because there is a real danger of losing one's
sense of perspective in approaching this issue. Very few people
would deny that the open and frank discussion of sex by present-
day writers is a welcome reaction against Victorian prudery and
hypocrisy and, moreover, that an artist worthy of the name

should not recoil from describing all aspects of human behaviour, including those which bring into play our most primitive and animal instincts. Such an approach is rightly regarded
as realistic art and not as pornography at all. The difference
between the two lies in the intention of the artist and consequently in the effect produced. It is one thing to describe sex
without any squeamish disgust, and as *part*, but only part, of
human life, and quite another to aim simply at being crude for
no other reason than the belief that most of us are sure to like it
anyway. This cheapens sex and insults man; it degrades both
author and public instead of producing an uplifting effect, as
genuine art usually does. It is necessary to emphasize that the
uplifting effect is not achieved by the convenient suppression of
what is sordid and crude in human life, nor even by relegating
these aspects to a secondary place. Paradoxical though it may
sound, it can be achieved by giving pride of place to such elements, provided the object is to increase our human understanding and sympathy. Once again, this requires more than
mere technical skill, it requires a definite philosophy to which
the writer is genuinely *committed*. The novels of Sartre are a case
in point. There is much in his trilogy *Roads to Freedom* which
could rival any "Fanny Hill" type of fiction when it comes to
crudity and obscenity, but these aspects are never isolated and
presented for their own sake. It is impossible, for example, not
to be genuinely moved (as opposed to morbidly excited) after
reading the pathetic scene where two cripples attempt to make
love and can only achieve an orgasm by the combined use of
their hands and imagination. The luxury of details has the
effect of increasing the poignancy of the situation and certainly
not of titillating our sexual hunger.

A third modern conflict is provided by the contrast between
the potential advantages and the real dangers of scientific
advances. The discovery of nuclear energy has given this issue
an urgent and compelling character and made the question of
war and peace one of the most vital questions of our time. That
it has not left artists indifferent is shown by the number of
songs, plays and novels which actually deal with the topic, to
say nothing of all those which would be unintelligible if one did
not take this background into account. Furthermore, at the
time of writing, the war in Vietnam is eliciting in the West the
same kind of responses as did the struggle against Fascism

thirty years ago in the sense that it is providing a comparable polarization of opinions and attitudes[a]—this tends to disprove the supposedly outmoded character of commitment, for there are still many vital choices before us, and we still need the inspiring help of art and literature in facing them. Aragon's poem *Les Yeux et la mémoire* (Eyes and Memory), which appeared in 1954, was written as a sort of counterpoint to one of his wife's novels (Elsa Triolet's *Le Cheval roux*—The Red Horse)[b] in which she visualized the destruction of mankind by H-bombs. Not that the novel was pessimistic: it was rather intended to make us aware of the nuclear threat so that we should act in time. The poet supplements the lesson by showing with great simplicity and sincerity all the things it is worth preserving and fighting for. He concludes with a poem on peace (inspired by the end of another Vietnam war, the war between the Vietnamese and the French) of which the last two lines read:

> Be silent ye atoms and ye guns cease spluttering
> Cease fire on every front on every front cease fire[c]

Lastly, there is the eternal conflict between ideals and reality, the kind of conflict which led Péguy to remark bitterly at the beginning of this century that a "mystique" usually degenerates into a "politique", by which he meant, as we shall see later, that it is a normal fate for a pure ideal to deviate from its original noble purpose and become exploited for selfish ends. Such a conflict is particularly acute for those who are politically committed because the world of politics is often a world of "dirty hands", as the title of a Sartrian play suggests. A recent example was afforded by the shock in Communist

---

[a] This does not mean that we can, or should, expect to be flooded with books dealing directly with the Vietnam conflict. It means rather that the Vietnam war, like the Spanish Civil War before it, is one of those concrete issues which compel us periodically to re-examine our basic principles. So long as this war continues, and threatens to turn into a world war, the whole question of man's inhumanity to man remains an acute, practical problem.

[b] An allusion to the Red Horse in the Book of Revelation, which is a symbol of war.

[c] "Tais-toi l'atome et toi canon cesse ta toux/Partout cessez le feu cessez le feu partout"—op. cit., p. 163. Aragon's lack of punctuation is intentional. Its aim is to compel the reader to regard each line of poetry as a complete unity where no artificial divisions can be made.

ranks after the 20th Congress of the C.P.S.U. had revealed the mistakes and the crimes of Stalin. But it is not only for Communists that there are rude awakenings in the modern world. All those who seek to improve conditions for others are bound to realize sooner or later that the pace of change is seldom as fast as they had hoped; and it is not very long before they discover that as soon as an ideal begins to be translated into practice, there are many unexpected difficulties which suddenly spring up and call for an "agonizing reappraisal". The danger in such cases is that people tend to hide their disappointment behind a blasé and cynical façade. Great committed art can save us from this fruitless attitude, because the artist's vision helps us to see beyond temporary setbacks and defeats. Another of Wesker's heroines comes to mind, the valiant Sarah Kahn who stubbornly refuses to follow her friend Monty along the road of betrayal and her son Ronnie along the path of despair:

> If the electrician who comes to mend my fuse blows it instead, so I should stop having electricity? I should cut off my light? Socialism is my light, can you understand that? A way of life. A man can be beautiful.[4]

In a recent poem (*Elégie à Pablo Neruda*, 1966) Aragon described poets as "creatures of the night" who nevertheless "carry the sun within themselves".[a] The background to the poem is the 1965 earthquake in Chile which destroyed Pablo Neruda's house. After expressing sympathy for his friend, Aragon went on to accuse the earth itself of betraying the poets, and he widened his theme by showing that there is an even worse calamity for an artist when he realizes the gap between his generous dreams of justice and happiness and the obstacles which must be overcome before men turn those dreams into realities. The poet's message is not that we should give up the struggle, but fight with our eyes open and be vigilant:

> Oh what did we allow Pablo my friend
> Pablo my friend what of our dreams what of our dreams[b]

---

[a] "Nous sommes les gens de la nuit qui portons le soleil en nous".

[b] "Qu'avons-nous permis Pablo mon ami/Pablo mon ami nos songes nos songes"—op. cit., p. 26.

The above examples do not seem to bear the contention that the days of commitment are numbered because there are no real conflicts in modern society. Committed writers believe that present-day conflicts are less "obvious" and probably more "sophisticated" than those of two or three decades ago; this simply means that commitment must express itself differently, not that it is obsolete. It would be a great pity if the conflicts of our time found their sole expression in the modern protest songs and failed to inspire the writer. It would be a tragedy, not for the writer "as a citizen", but "as a writer"!

We owe the above distinction to George Orwell. According to him,

> When a writer engages in politics he should do so as a citizen, as a human being, but not AS A WRITER. . . . He should make clear that his writing is a thing apart.[5]

This is the "liberal" objection to commitment. It does not refuse commitment as such—for Orwell admits that ". . . to lock yourself up in the ivory tower is impossible and undesirable"—but it insists that there is no place for it in literature, for the latter is "a thing apart". The French "new novelists" take the same view. Robbe-Grillet, in particular, repeats Orwell almost word for word when he writes,

> It is not reasonable . . . to claim to serve a political cause in our novels, even a cause that seems to us a just one, even if, in our political life, we fight for its triumph.[6]

For the writers of the "nouveau roman", there is only one possible commitment—literature itself, and Robbe-Grillet adds,

> . . . commitment for the writer is a full awareness of the problems of his own language, his conviction of their extreme importance, and his determination to resolve them from within.[7]

According to "littérature engagée", such an opinion rests on the fallacy that artistic problems arise outside society and can be looked upon as technical issues exclusively. A committed writer like Aragon, without in the least playing down the importance of language and the need to master it, stresses that language is a means of communication and that all creative attempts aimed at improving such a medium have been linked with a philosophy of life. In literature, "technical" change is never an end in itself, but a way of conveying more adequately, more powerfully, the artist's experiences and views. Robbe-Grillet himself admits that the "new novel" is a valid experiment because it can express the realities of the modern age better than traditional fiction. Does not this contradict his own assertion that a work of art has no purpose and that an artist creates "for nothing"?

Moreover, if Orwell is right in thinking that there is a Chinese wall between art and life, one would have to assume that the same individual is entitled to get out of his ivory tower when he behaves "as a citizen", but should immediately return to it when he is about to perform his duty "as a writer", and presumably forget all he has learnt in the course of his brief encounter with lesser mortals. Admittedly, Orwell himself never went to such ridiculous lengths, but does not his statement lend itself to a treatment of this kind? The expression "a thing apart" is, to say the least, very vague and can be made the excuse for all sorts of irresponsible attitudes which Orwell would certainly condemn. If he simply meant that one cannot issue orders in art as one does in politics, no committed writer would disagree with him. (Mistakes made by religious and political leaders represent a distortion rather than a genuine application of the committed outlook.) But if Orwell or anyone else is prepared to go further and assert that a writer is independent from all authority, he is, in the view of "littérature engagée", treading on dangerous grounds. The writer's so-called independence is a myth because no literature can avoid being, implicitly or explicitly, a critical evaluation of contemporary values. Sartre even says that abstention is a form of commitment because it implies acceptance of the status quo. Moreover, does the idea of independence mean that an author is not accountable to anyone for what he writes because it is his privilege as an artist to be above normal human restrictions? Committed writers would strongly criticize this view. Irresponsibility, they would point out, is not an indispensable ingredient of art, and few masterpieces, if any, have been produced by disregarding the needs of society. What Orwell feared is that the writers would be *told* of those needs instead of discovering them for themselves, and it cannot be denied that his fears strike a sympathetic chord in all those who have been pained and horrified by past events in the Soviet Union and more recently in China. But because Orwell was right to sound the alarm, does it mean that he found the correct solution to the problem? Committed writers do not think so.

They admit that there are dangers in their approach and that it is not enough to dismiss sensitive critics as "petty bourgeois".[a] Sticking a label on your opponent is not the best way of silencing him. The real answer is not to deny that one is taking risks, but to ask oneself if they are worth taking and the extent to which they can be minimized. No great task can be accomplished without taking certain risks, and commitment does not claim it is an insurance policy against all dangers. It rather feels that it contains the seeds of its own purification because it generally implies greater acceptance on the writer's part of the opinions of other people. The committed writer is not alone, he is a "man among men", as Sartre repeatedly emphasizes.

The main danger he must guard against is that of bias, one-sidedness and dogmatism. It is a very real one, but it is inherent in any human enterprise, and no writer has ever been free from it. In fact, the non-committed writer, who tends to recognize no other authority than himself, is more vulnerable to the danger. One of the cardinal requirements of commitment, on the other hand, is that a writer should not regard himself as the sole judge of truth, but should be willing to seek the truth alongside the members of a wider group, a church or a party. Will this

[a] Incidentally, there is little doubt that Orwell himself approached politics in a "petty bourgeois" way, if by this one means that he had more faith in the middle classes than in the organized workers. But these pages are not an attempt to discuss, however briefly, Orwell's personal contribution (his views have been mentioned simply because they sum up rather well what I termed the "liberal" standpoint), particularly as such a discussion exists already in John Mander's *The Writer and Commitment* (Secker and Warburg, 1961). The reader will find that "Orwell's thinking is frequently contradictory. He is quite capable of saying that propaganda is the ruin of art one day, and on the next that all art must have a political purpose" (p. 84). As for the meaning attached to the expression "art is a thing apart", Mr Mander thinks that for Orwell, "a writer can never become a good party-liner; if he introduces politics into his writing he will become a pamphleteer" (p. 112). May I add that no serious reader of Péguy, Aragon and Sartre could possibly describe them as "pamphleteers".

lead to the "regimentation" which Orwell feared so much? Here, we touch upon one of the dangers which is most frequently associated with commitment, although, in fact, it does not constitute a criticism of commitment at all. It may be a valid criticism of the Communist Party (or of any other group for that matter), but not of commitment as such. The regimentation of writers is detrimental to art and, in the long run, to the cause one serves. It gives an entirely distorted image of what commitment really is by confusing two vastly different things, the desirability of the writer's descending into the arena (which is a personal decision for him to make), and the administrative measures which a ruling party or an established church may take against him if he does not toe the line. The latter must be thoroughly condemned, but it cannot be done effectively by retiring into the wilderness. Whether the writer decides to combat narrow-mindedness inside his own party, like Aragon,[a] or to retain the critical independence of the friendly outsider, like Sartre,[b] or to give up for ever "the god that failed", the fact is that each of these positive stands represents more commitment, not less. One could venture to express the following paradox: in order to present a thorough case against commitment as it is being practised, one has to be thoroughly committed!

Moreover, the excesses of what came to be known as Zhdanovism in the Stalin era were due to an abusive interpretation of a correct principle, in this case the principle that the writer has a responsibility towards society. The Zhdanov mistake, it is worth stressing, was to approach the issue of responsibility in an *administrative* way and to forget that the methods

[a] Aragon's independence of mind was recently brought to the attention of a large public when he roundly condemned the Soviet decision to sentence two writers for publishing their books abroad, but this does not represent a new departure for him. In the post-war era, particularly, he has associated himself with the fight against "dogmatism" and "sectarianism".

[b] Sartre's refusal to join a political party is not regarded by him as a virtue but as a regrettable necessity so long as he feels unable to endorse the methods of the French Communist Party. He realizes that his position is neither fully consistent nor comfortable, but he believes it is the only one open to him at the moment. (For his attitude to Communism, see pp. 131–36.) Sartre's Communist critics naturally stress the weakness of his stand and some even accuse him of having produced a "non-militant" version of literary commitment. Does not this betray a rather restrictive conception of militancy?

which work in the field of politics do not necessarily apply to the field of aesthetics. (Lenin himself had a much healthier view of the matter when he wrote that "literature is the last thing in the world to lend itself to mechanical levelling and uniformity, to the subjection of the minority by the majority . . . in this field, great freedom must be assured to individual initiative".) This does not excuse social or political irresponsibility in the writer, but the point is that a correct approach cannot be imposed on him. Administrative measures lead to an impoverishment of art; literature which is written "to order" is a caricature of committed literature, if only because it utterly fails to achieve its object. Instead of instilling enthusiasm in the reader, it leaves him cold and unmoved. An artist must listen to the voice of his own conscience, not because he is always sure to be right, but because if he does not, his work would immediately reveal the presence of a foreign, spurious element and would cease to be *effective*. It is on behalf of commitment itself rather than in the name of "pure" art that regimentation must be opposed. "Littérature engagée" has always emphasized that an ideology cannot be artifically introduced into a work of art. It should come from within the artist himself and be inseparable from his own personality. Although it believes that all art is a form of "propaganda" in the sense that it is a criticism of life and expresses a particular point of view,[a] if propaganda is superimposed on the work of art, the artist has failed. Péguy never allowed anyone, not even the Church, to tell him how or what to write, and when he could not publicly defend a Catholic decision, he either kept quiet or courted ecclesiastical disapproval by speaking his own mind. (The Church's attitude to Bergson is a case in point: Péguy, always a great admirer of Bergson, continued to express his support for the master even when there were moves denouncing him from Rome.) Sartre goes further than Péguy and refuses to join any political party, although this is not really consistent with his understanding of a committed writer's duty. As for Aragon, who cannot be suspected of any "individualistic deviation" in view of his unbroken membership of the French Communist Party over a

[a] People usually call "propaganda" (in a derogatory sense) the defence of ideas with which they disagree, but they would never dream of describing their own unquestioned assumptions or their own acceptance of certain values as "propaganda"!

period of forty years, he utterly rejects the idea of "directives" in literature and speaks instead of an "inner necessity" which makes the artist echo in his work ideas and trends with which he is in agreement. His own war-time poetry, which constitutes a vivid illustration of the Communist "line" in those days, manages at the same time to retain an unmistakable personal flavour, without which it would have failed to move millions of Frenchmen from all parties.

In spite of all this, it would be idle to deny that the greatest danger facing "littérature engagée" is that of forgetting "literature" for the sake of "engagement",[a] or to claim that the correct relationship between these two aspects has either been successfully established in practice or easily defined in theory. We are dealing here with one of the most difficult issues connected with commitment. All that one can add to what committed writers have said on the subject is that the idea of commitment is still a young idea; as it matures, it will be enriched by experience and gradually discard excesses and misconceptions. Already, the personal evolution of Péguy, Aragon and Sartre (described more fully in the next chapters) is instructive in this respect. The unexpected autobiographical revelations made by Aragon and Sartre in very recent years[b] show that neither of them has been entirely free from "mauvaise foi" (i.e. self-deception), but also that both of them place sincerity and truth above everything else—to use a favourite expression of Aragon's, they are determined to leave of themselves "une image vraie", a true image.

THE CASE FOR COMMITMENT

The case for commitment rests on two simple propositions. One is that interest in one's own time is a great source of inspiration for art, and the other that creative freedom for the writer is inseparable from a sense of social responsibility. With regard to the first point, the example of the past tends to show

---

[a] Cf. Sartre's famous dictum: "Dans la littérature engagée, *l'engagement* ne doit en aucun cas faire oublier *la littérature*" (*Situations II*, p. 30). Cf. also his article on *Nationalisation de la littérature* (op. cit., pp. 35–53) where he warns that a novel, committed or not, is primarily an individual work, ". . . l'entreprise hasardeuse d'un homme seul". (43) Readers and critics must agree to be mutually involved—literature is a gamble, and without this element of risk, art dies.

[b] See below, Chapters III and IV.

that the lasting value of a literary masterpiece often derives from its topical character at the time of publication and that the greater the artist's involvement in his own age, the deeper is his understanding of permanent human characteristics, and consequently, the more lasting and universal his appeal. This illustrates a thesis which is common to Péguy, Aragon and Sartre and can be summed up by saying that eternal issues express themselves through concrete and specific circumstances. According to Aragon, great poetry is eternal *because* it is dated, "éternelle d'être datée", as he puts it.[8] Sartre extends this to all literature, claiming that eternity is the reward of those who take sides in the "peculiarity of our time" ("la singularité de notre époque").[9] Finally, Péguy puts the matter in a nutshell when he writes,

And Eternity itself belongs to the temporal world.[10]

If we leave aside the theological aspect of the notion of *eternity*, what men, as finite beings, call "eternal" is that which survives passing circumstances; but according to "littérature engagée", the paradox of human affairs is that this lasting quality demands, in addition to artistic genius, that one should enter into the concrete life of a transient epoch. Although love, hatred, anger, etc., are of all times, they move us only when they are embodied in creatures of flesh and blood, in men and women who belong to a real human age and are rooted in a real corner of the planet. For example, before Romeo and Juliet could symbolize, as they do, the lovers of all time, they had first to be lovers of their own day and age; in Shakespeare's play, their love is not thwarted by vague "eternal" obstacles, but by contemporary social values, and although these have long ceased to have any meaning for us, it is in the course of their fight against such *dated* values that Romeo and Juliet are able to express those basic human emotions in which men and women of all ages recognize their kith and kin. Another example is provided by the patriotic poetry written in France during the years of German Occupation.[a] There is little doubt that future generations will forget the precise incidents which aroused the anger of Resistance poets, but so long as there are national

[a] A good account of Aragon's contribution in those years may be found in *Aragon, Part of Resurgent France.*

tragedies, their protest will keep a permanent quality and inspire those who are waging the unending battle against injustice. Aragon remarks that such was indeed the fate of Hugo and Péguy, whose patriotic writings took on a special significance in 1940 although they had been inspired by other defeats and other circumstances.

But the crux of the matter, so far as commitment is concerned, lies in the relationship between creative freedom and social responsibility. Broadly speaking, the opinion of "littérature engagée" is that the writer is entitled to expect freedom from any given society, but that society is entitled to expect a sense of social responsibility in the writer. *The recognition of this double demand and of this dialectical process is at the heart of commitment.* It is important to insist on the social aspect of responsibility in French "littérature engagée" because in his book on English committed writers,[11] John Mander, after rightly saying that "commitment is grounded . . . in responsibility", suggests that it is nothing more than a "moral concept". This is either too wide or too restrictive a view. It is too wide in so far as there is no work of art which does not display *some* moral attitude, so that all one has to do, as Mander puts it, is to determine, in each case, "the quality" of the writer's commitment. I believe that to talk of commitment in such broad terms is misleading and that INVOLVEMENT would be a much better word, a point to which I intend to return when I discuss Sartre's definition of commitment. But involvement is not a literary method at all— it is simply a fact from which no writer (and no man) can escape. On the other hand, Mr Mander's definition means too little because it reduces commitment to devotion to an *idea*, whereas French "engagés" insist on the militant and practical character of their writing. Péguy, for example, was never content with generalities of a socialist or a Christian nature; his works untiringly discuss the events of the day as seen by a Socialist and a Christian, and more particularly the Dreyfus Affair. One critic describes him as "a journalist who looks upon current happenings 'sub specie aeterni' ".[a] Most of Sartre's works also have this militant character. Sometimes the author intervenes directly in topical controversies, and sometimes he

[a] "Il peut apparaître comme un journaliste qui examinerait les faits du jour 'sub specie aeterni'." (Maurice David, *Initiation à Charles Péguy*, pp. 21-22.)

raises fundamental moral issues *in the light of present-day problems*. As for Aragon, he described his work as a permanent song to help us keep our faith in human happiness:

> To sing to sing to sing
> So that the shadow becomes human
> As Sunday blesses the week
> And as hope sweetens truth[a]

All this represents much more than a vague "moral concept". It involves a definite social point of view, not necessarily a right one, but one which is inseparable from commitment and without which the latter simply does not make sense. It should be stressed that social responsibility is not synonymous with the defence of a social system, even when one happens to agree with it, as this often leads to the type of insipid and nauseating literature which unconvincingly sings the praises of the Establishment, such as the happily-forgotten edifying fiction written in Victorian England or in Third Republic France, or more recently in Stalinist Russia. A sense of social responsibility should be, according to "littérature engagée", a *critical* sense, for the aim of commitment is not to foster illusions but rather to destroy them. The debunking of false values is an important characteristic of its approach. In this respect, Aragon's attitude to changing cultural developments in the Communist Movement is not without significance. To his credit, he did not wait until Stalin's death in order to support the timid but genuine attempts to bring more constructive criticism into Soviet art instead of confining it to the stereotyped glorification of the system. In more recent years, he went much further and openly sided with the more daring and unorthodox Soviet trends. In a speech he made in 1959 to a group of Young Communists, he reminded his audience that "there is no light without a shadow" and that a book in which there are no conflicts or in which they are conveniently settled at the end "does not deserve to be opened". Then he went on to say,

> If you expect to be supplied with beautiful and reassuring pictures which do not raise any problems in your minds and with which you are bound to agree beforehand, don't rely on

[a] ". . . chanter chanter chanter/Pour que l'ombre se fasse humaine Comme un dimanche à la semaine/Et l'espoir à la vérité"—*Les Poètes*, p. 161.

me. The kind of literature which settles all the hard issues of life in a few hundred pages belongs to the kind of activity generally known as *utopia*. Nothing is so dangerous as utopia. It lulls people to sleep and when they are awakened by reality, they are like sleep-walkers on the top of a roof—they suddenly find themselves tumbling down to the ground.[a]

Lastly, is it true that in order to maintain his integrity the artist must refuse to "compromise" and have no truck whatever with non-literary bodies? This point of view, with which we have become increasingly familiar since the second half of the last century, arose in a divided society, torn by class conflicts, and it contains within itself contradictory features. On the one hand, it expresses a critical refusal of the world as it is, an honest reluctance to become the accomplice of a lying, ruling clique; but on the other hand, it represents an individualistic protest which is, at best, highly ineffectual. By stressing the close relationship between literature and the public for whom it is meant, commitment helps to overcome the contradiction: the committed writer knows that in modern society he must side *with* certain social forces *against* injustice. He refuses to compromise with the Establishment, but his rebellion is part of a wider movement. For him, literature becomes what Sartre calls an "*integrated* and militant function" ("une fonction intégrée et militante"[12] (my italics).

SARTRE'S DEFINITION OF COMMITMENT

According to Mr Mander, we in England "have adopted Sartre's term, and largely ignored its theoretical basis". I am not sure that I agree with him when he adds that our neglect "...may prove to have been a blessing in disguise".[13] Although Sartrian theories are often debatable, and although the "theoretical basis" is not as fixed as the phrase suggests—for it is being modified by Sartre all the time, sometimes in a dramatic

---

[a] *J'abats mon jeu*, p. 136. Cf. also his forceful denunciation of utopia at the end of *History of the U.S.S.R.*, and in particular the passage where he states that utopia "is noxious because of the possibilities of disillusionment it carries within it, because at every step it holds up a false image in contrast to reality, because it leads to discouragement through the want of proportion between the hoped-for prospect and the work to be done; it might be said that utopia is 'a terrible strike-breaker' and even more a terrible seducer of the working class" (op. cit., p. 647, Engl. edn. Weidenfeld & Nicolson).

fashion—it is not good enough to be content with what Mr Mander calls "Anglo-Saxon empiricism". One of the purposes of the present essay is to suggest that commitment is not a haphazard or instinctive reaction, but a valid and challenging *method* of approaching artistic creation and that we can learn a good deal from the French example, both from the literary theories, for what they are worth, and from the works which endeavour to illustrate them.

According to Sartre, commitment is inherent in the act of writing. To write, he says, is to talk, and to talk is to reveal an aspect of the world, in order to change it. Literature is therefore the result of an attitude, conscious or unconscious, towards the world. The committed writer is different from others, not because he is involved in the world, but because he is aware of it, because ". . . he endeavours to acquire the most lucid, most complete awareness of being involved,[a] i.e. because he transfers his commitment from the level of the immediately spontaneous to the level of consciousness."[b]

The main weakness of this otherwise excellent definition is that it does not draw a sufficiently clear distinction between INVOLVEMENT (which no writer can avoid) and COMMITMENT proper (which is the conscious acknowledgement of the involvement). The distinction is all the more important inasmuch as it helps to explain an apparently strange contradiction in the crusade undertaken by Sartre and others in favour of commitment: if the latter is so common, so "inevitable", why waste ink and energy to preach about it? The answer, of course, is that it is involvement, not commitment, which is inevitable, and furthermore that writers are not automatically aware of their involvement (hence, the need to remind them of it). Sartre lays the blame at their door and speaks of "mental laziness", refusal to face facts, etc. That may be true in some cases, but by and

[a] The French word which Sartre uses is "embarqué", as he has just been discussing Pascal's famous saying, "Nous sommes embarqués" (We're all in the same boat). I have translated "embarqué" by "involved" (not a great liberty in this context, I believe) in order to introduce the important distinction between involvement and commitment which is made in the next paragraph.

[b] "Je dirai qu'un écrivain est engagé quand il cherche à prendre la conscience la plus lucide et la plus entière d'être embarqué, c'est à dire quand il fait passer . . . l'engagement de la spontanéité immédiate au réfléchi." (*Situations II*, p. 124.)

large confusion on this issue has precise historical roots. It is part of the general onslaught on the critical character of literature which began in the nineteenth century and is based on the fallacy, no matter how differently expressed, and no matter how sincerely accepted by many, that art is "a thing apart". Those who fear the effects of a truthful portrayal of reality would like nothing better than to spread the notion that art moves in a province of its own. The value of the committed concept is that it rejects this facile and escapist explanation and reminds writers that they cannot help belonging to the world of men. Commitment thus implies the debunking of a hypocritical lie as well as the acceptance of an obvious truth, deliberately blurred or hidden away by certain social forces. The practical consequence is that the writer looks upon his activity "as a citizen" as an essential part of his job "as a writer", and is in a better position to will the effect of his work instead of leaving it to chance. (It does not necessarily mean that he will invariably be successful; it will depend on the degree and on the quality of his commitment.) The "project" of writing becomes a lucid project.

The originality of Sartre's concept of commitment is not that it puts forward a new definition of literature but rather that it claims to be the only form of literature devoid of self-deception. It is an impressive challenge. For the writer, the challenge implies a new approach to his responsibility and to the issue of liberty. Sartre believes that the committed writer openly faces the two basic questions implied in literary creation—namely, *why* does one write? *for whom* does one write? Incidentally, these are the titles of two sections in *What is Literature?* Moreover, because he speaks to free men, the committed writer, according to Sartre, can only have one theme—Liberty. Not Liberty in general (which is a meaningless abstraction), but the concrete liberties which men try to win and preserve at each stage of their historical development. To illustrate his meaning, Sartre gives an example which is probably more topical today than when he first gave it: he says that a good book cannot be written to justify lack of liberty and that, consequently, a good novel against the Jews or the Negroes is impossible. Iris Murdoch takes him to task for this statement. She thinks he has been carried away by his own enthusiasm when he implies that only a "progressive" writer can produce good literature. It is true that Sartre has often tended to overstress his case and that he did, at one time, hold the extreme view ascribed to him by Miss Murdoch. But it is not necessary to go to the same lengths in order to grant that an avowedly anti-Semitic or anti-Negro novel can hardly be a great work of art. Whatever the theoretical value of the Sartrian analysis, his *practical* challenge (". . . show me a single good novel written against the Jews, etc.") has never been successfully taken up. Furthermore, although a writer may well be an arch-reactionary, his artistic work is certain to give the lie to his one-sided private opinions: a novelist who would describe Jews or Negroes as mere villains would fall *on aesthetic grounds* because his characters would be crude caricatures, devoid of any credibility; on the other hand, if he depicts them as real human beings, with their virtues as well as their faults, he is ipso facto destroying the case for racialism which rests on the irrational belief that "inferior" races have no virtues at all.

Iris Murdoch's criticism does, however, help to remind us that there are two ways of interpreting "littérature engagée": a narrow one, which consists in denying that art can have any real value unless it carries "good" ideas, and a broader one, which stresses that art, by its very nature, has the positive effect of making us think and look at reality in a different way, and that committed art has only one superiority—that of fulfilling the function of *all art* in a conscious way. Sartre himself began with the former outlook, but there has been in recent years a very significant and, in my opinion, very welcome, change in his approach.[a] *Commitment is no longer looked upon as a categorical imperative which all writers are in duty bound to embrace, but rather as a quality which adds awareness and lucidity to literature*

FROM 'WHAT IS LITERATURE?' TO 'WORDS'

No introduction to "littérature engagée" would be adequate if it did not attempt a brief discussion of Sartre's *What is Literature?*, for despite its many faults and the partial rejection

---

[a] As usual with him, one should not speak of change but of a radical shift of emphasis. For example, his present open-minded attitude is already contained in embryo in *What is Literature?*, particularly in such statements as those which assert that the description of *any* aspect of human behaviour increases our understanding and thus has a "liberating effect". (Cf. *Situations II*, pp. 143 and 185.)

of some of its theses by the author, this essay is rightly regarded as the Bible of French commitment. Even if some of its answers are unsatisfactory or insufficiently worked out, the book has the merit of being the first serious attempt to define "engagement". To regard it as final, however, is to forget that Sartre is still alive and can, at any time, enlarge upon it, if not disown it altogether, and—more important still—to ignore his plea that each of his works must be seen as a stepping-stone on the path to further progress.[a] It is therefore necessary to examine *What is Literature?*, first as it stands, and then in the light of later works on the subject, the most important of which is *Words*. Although commitment is by no means an exclusively Sartrian concept, its changes of meaning in the course of Sartre's own development reveal its living character—for it is under the influence of life that Sartre has amended and enriched his views—as well as its practical quality—for it is as the result of his own commitment that Sartre has made new discoveries.

What is Literature? can be divided into two parts, theoretical and historical, of which the former is by far the more stimulating. Its first major argument is that writing is a social act because it rests on the will to communicate with other people and on the resolve to change the world. It is difficult to disagree with the first part of the statement, which is almost an elementary truism. In fact, Sartre often bases his whole argument on such apparently axiomatic truths, with the object of drawing the logical and practical consequences which are implied in them. Therein lies his genius. He compels us to go back to first principles, as it were, and to make a permanent reassessment of what is involved in the truths which we take for granted. In the present case, the reminder that language is a means of communication naturally leads to the question of content (what to communicate?) and of responsibility, both of which are of crucial importance for "littérature engagée".

The aim of language, [Sartre writes], is to communicate . . .

---

[a] He says in *Words*, "My best book is the one I am in the process of writing", and he defines his aim as "doing better tomorrow, and better still the day after tomorrow". (French edn, pp. 200 and 201.)

Cf. Aragon's statement that each of his new books disappoints some of his friends. "It is against them that I write," he adds; "my purpose is not so much to write a new book, but rather to make people forget the books I have written." (*Entretiens avec Francis Crémieux*, p. 141.)

to impart to others the results one has obtained. . . . As I talk, I reveal the situation . . . I reveal it to myself and to others *in order* [Sartre's italics] to change it.[14]

Unfortunately, it is not enough to appreciate this point in order to disclose the nature of writing. Is it really true, as Sartre suggests, that literature communicates "results", or should one look upon it as a writer's *appeal*, as his defence of certain *values*? Later in the book, we are told that

A work of art is an end in itself . . . a work of art is a value because it is an appeal.[15]

There is perhaps a slight contradiction between the two statements quoted, and the ambiguity of Sartre's position leads him to assert, rather one-sidedly, that prose alone can be committed, all other arts, including poetry, being declared unfit to fulfil a revolutionary function because they approach reality through obscure and devious ways, instead of directly coming to grips with it through the medium of words. (It is ironic that the title of the book in which Sartre radically criticizes his former views should be just *Words*!) According to this argument, when the poet uses words, he treats them as ends in themselves, just as the musician handles sounds, or the painter colours and shapes. For the prose writer, on the other hand, words are merely *signs* which help us to stick labels on the objects around us so that we may easily act upon them. Prose alone can lead to action, because it is a rationalization of human activity (which Sartre often likes to endow with the Greek name of "praxis"); it clarifies the issues which modern man has to face, with the result that our will to act is considerably increased.[a] In subsequent articles, as we shall see later, Sartre modified his views, and described the art of painting as a form of human "praxis". This constitutes a remarkable advance on *What is Literature?*

As for the claim that the purpose of writing is "to change the world", it might have gained, I feel, from a more precise formulation.[b] Would it not be better to speak of the impact of

[a] For a further discussion of this point, see Chapter VI (Poetry and Commitment).

[b] The expression "to change the world" which Sartre often uses is an echo of Marx's famous saying that "philosophers have hitherto interpreted the world in various ways—the point, however, is to change it". By "change", Sartre occasionally means a political and social revolution in the Marxist sense, and sometimes a more modest and partial reform.

literature instead of its aim, and to state that the *effect* of great art is that it compels us to remould our lives?[a] Such a proposition could be proved both inductively and deductively. The inductive proof is that history provides us with convincing examples. Sartre himself mentions the writers of the Enlightenment, whose influence on their time was so obvious and so direct that it constitutes almost too good an illustration of the point; but in dealing with other periods, he seems more intent on passing wholesale condemnation on his predecessors than on making an objective assessment of the part they actually played in reflecting and criticizing their time. His description of the French seventeenth century in particular is based on the traditional notion of the period as one of order and stability, a view which no one accepts today. Similarly, his accusation that the nineteenth century no less than "betrayed" literature (he graciously makes an exception in the case of Victor Hugo!) cannot be taken seriously. In both cases, his opinion rests on inadequate historical knowledge (a really unforgivable sin in a thinker who never tires of talking of the importance of history), and on the debatable view that unless commitment takes at all times the same form of direct and militant participation in political events, it is not commitment at all.[b] The historical part of *What is Literature?* is one of the weakest (the author is not unaware of this[c]) and it would be wrong to regard it as the perfect example of committed literary criticism. Sartre's own study of Flaubert (in which he shows the various ways in which the individual Flaubert was influenced by the ideology of his time), Aragon's study of Stendhal (in which the political character of *Le Rouge et le Noir* is particularly well brought out),

[a] The *aim* of committed literature is certainly to "change the world", but this is not true of all art. The point which Sartre himself makes is that "littérature engagée" sets itself the *conscious* purpose which is always *implied* in a work of art.

[b] Commitment, one must repeat, is a twentieth-century concept because it corresponds to the specific conditions of our time. It is quite unrealistic to expect the writers of previous epochs to have developed such a concept, for which conditions were far from ripe. The similarities between the eighteenth century and the present are due precisely to the fact that both epochs are epochs of great changes.

[c] He admits that his historical analyses are hasty and superficial, but claims that this is because he had a more *urgent* task—that of *defining* literature. (Notice how this unwittingly proves that Sartre's approach is basically *not* historical.)

and, in a different way, Péguy's remarks on Corneille (whom he regards as one of the few great poets who managed to mix philosophy and poetry) are, fortunately, among the many interesting illustrations of the way in which a committed critic can arrive at a better understanding of the authors he is studying.

As for the deductive proof, it is also Sartre who supplied it—but much later, when he said at an international Writers' Congress that the artist is a witness of his time to the extent that he reflects the *totality* of its problems.

> In such conditions [he added], it matters little whether literature calls itself committed, for committed it is bound to be inasmuch as *totality* nowadays consists, among other things, in the fact that we are all threatened with the possibility of dying in a nuclear war. . . . This does not mean that the writer must necessarily deal with nuclear war; it rather means that a man who is afraid of dying like a rat cannot be wholly sincere if he confines himself to writing poems about birds. Some aspects of the times must, in one way or another, be reflected in a work of art.[16]

The notion of *totality* enables Sartre to make commitment implicit in all literature instead of restricting it to an explicit ideological point of view as he did in 1947.

But the main theoretical argument in *What is Literature?* is that there is no literature without a public.[a] The character of a work of art is determined by its public, and if we do not write today as in the time of Shakespeare or Racine, it is because the twentieth-century public is different, both historically and socially. Moreover, the writer, Sartre reminds us, is a consumer, not a producer. He is maintained by society, which, in class societies, means that he is maintained by the ruling class. He comes into conflict with the latter when he reveals the truth about the world. It is therefore imperative for him to decide *for whom* he is going to write. This choice is forced upon him, not by moral or ideological considerations, but by the requirements of his art. When the social conflict is particularly acute and when the alternatives are far from clear (at least for the writers themselves), literature inevitably reflects the tension by

[a] Once again, we have here an apparent truism from which Sartre is able to draw practical and logical conclusions.

acquiring a tragic character. (The nineteenth-century Romantics are a case in point.)

But even in 1947 the choice of public presented difficulties, according to Sartre, and he spoke of a "virtual public" for the committed writer. This represented a rationalization of his own uneasy position at the time as a critic of the bourgeois order who could not bring himself to support the Communist Party. If neither exploiters nor exploited, he argued, are ready to hear the committed message, then "littérature engagée" must speak to an imaginary public, the public it hopes will exist some day, either when the working class has given up Communist indoctrination, or when the exploiting class has been abolished. The necessarily utopian character of such a "virtual public" led Sartre to evolve a predominantly speculative conception of commitment, which he was later to modify as he grew more involved in social and political struggles without losing his independence in any way. In a recent interview, he expressed pleasure at being read by the common people:

I have changed my public. . . . Now, I receive letters from workers, from secretaries. They are the most interesting ones.[17]

The main weakness of *What is Literature?*, in my opinion, is that the approach is often based on an abstract conception of the nature of writing, or, to put it in Sartrian terminology, that essence seems to precede existence. Although Sartre's starting-point is the social character of literature, he tends to deduce the literary "project", not from the writer's concrete social situation, but from the ideal essence of literature. This leads him to over-estimate its value. He rightly says that writing is a "social function", but one has the impression at times that he is not far from believing that it is *the* social function par excellence. The danger of such an approach is, firstly, that it weakens the value of commitment by implying that the writer does not have to change his whole life, since the main thing for him is to handle words successfully, and, secondly, that it can easily lead to the opposite extreme of thinking that literature has no value at all, as soon as its real limitations are discovered in practice. It is just what happened to Sartre. There have been times when, not content with denouncing the illusion of literature as a *priesthood*, as he does specifically in *Words*, he has allowed himself to be carried away much further, even to the point of asserting that in a world where hunger prevails, most of Western art and literature is a waste of time![a] It is piquant to find a Marxist like Ernst Fischer replying indirectly to this outburst when he states in *The Necessity of Art* that although literature cannot side-step such issues as famine, poverty and ignorance, it would be wrong to expect a purely aesthetic attitude towards these problems, for it would amount to either an over-estimation or an under-estimation of the power of art. What Fischer means is that the solution to the world's problems is the concern of all men, writers included, but that theirs is not a privileged role. It is not merely "as writers" that they will change the world (this is the over-estimation Fischer has in mind), but as writers who *add* their contribution to a wider struggle; neither is their job an idle game with words (here we have the under-estimation Fischer denounces), because the task of changing the world requires many-sided activities, including talking, singing, writing and painting. It is no less piquant to find under the pen of another Marxist critic the accusation that Sartre is guilty of "aesthetic leftism", an expression which recalls that of political "leftism" which was coined by Lenin to describe an over-simplification of reality and a narrow-minded condemnation of all those who do not follow the "right" path. The critic in question is Christine Glucksmann who writes in *Nouvelle Critique*[18] that Sartre's leftism lies in his confusion of the *deed* with the *literary* deed and in his naïve belief that revolution will take place through language. This, she claims, led him to base commitment on avowed ideological content exclusively and to dismiss as unworthy all art which is not consciously "engagé". It is probably unfair to suggest that Sartre was ever as naïve and sectarian as that, even in *What is Literature?*, but when the critic goes on to state that he remains fundamentally a "leftist" despite the real changes which have taken place in his thought, it is hard to agree with her.[b] Is she

---

[a] Cf. his statement that "over against a dying child *La Nausée* [Sartre's first major novel] cannot act as a counterweight", and his challenge, "Do you think I can read Robbe-Grillet in an under-developed country?" (*Encounter*, No. 129, June 1964.)

[b] She accuses him, for example, of not having really changed because although his answers are no longer the same, he continues to ask the same questions (e.g. what is the place of literature in an under-developed

not making too much of Sartre's occasional, but uncharacter-
istic, moods of despair, in the course of which he condemns
literature to being "nothing", as a reaction against his former
belief that it was "everything"? Above all, is she not under-
estimating the significance of *Words*?

This little booklet, which came out as a literary bombshell at
the end of 1963,[19] dramatically destroys the image of Sartre as a
High Priest of Commitment, and reveals instead his bitter
scepticism concerning the all-powerful character of words and
his ironical onslaught on the so-called "mandate" of literature.
Although it is largely an account of the author's childhood, the
last few pages are a mercilessly frank commentary on the
relationship between his childish illusions and his adult attitude
until quite recently. He shows that little Jean-Paul's faith in
the magical revolutionary power of words was not really given
up by Sartre the man but was merely endowed with a new look.
His presentation of Commitment as a Moral Absolute was due
to the persistence of a deeply religious outlook, now subtly
disguised as a social and political philosophy. He had given up
God the Father and God the Son, but the Holy Spirit had
managed to keep a hold on him and inspire him with false ideas
about a special "mandate" and the "priesthood" of literature.
After describing how long he remained a prisoner of these
fallacies, Sartre says quite simply, "I have changed." Then, he
adds the significant explanation,

> I have given up the priesthood of literature, but not the
> frock. . . . I am still writing books and I shall go on doing so;
> they are needed; they have their uses after all. Culture does
> not save anything nor anybody, one cannot be justified
> through it. But it is a product of man . . . in this critical
> mirror alone does he find his own image.[a]

This shows that commitment has not been thrown overboard
but has been purified of illusions in order to become more

world?). But are not Sartre's questions inescapable, and is it not the very
opposite of "leftism" to have the courage to heed the lessons of experience
and life?

    [a] The French text (p. 211) actually says, "J'ai désinvesti mais je n'ai pas
défroqué." Notice Sartre's intentional retention of religious terminology.
His wording suggests that he has given up all ideas of wearing the "vest-
ment" of a High Priest of literature, but that he still believes in wearing the
ordinary cassock of the rank-and-file clergyman.

effective. (It is impossible not to be struck by the fact that the shedding of illusions also characterizes Aragon's recent evolution. Although the comparison must not be pushed too far, as the circumstances are different, it does reveal an unmistakable trend towards sober realism in this second half of the twentieth century.) In a recent interview, Sartre emphasized that for him, the writer's duty was still to place his pen at the service of the oppressed, but he added, ". . . this is the writer's task, and if he fulfils it as he should, he acquires no merit from it. Heroism is not to be won at the point of a pen. What I ask him is not to forget the reality and the fundamental problems that exist."[20] There is no going back on the essential aspect of *What is Literature?* The value of this early essay can be appreciated all the better in the light of Sartre's further development. In particular, it is no mean achievement to have raised the issue of commitment for the first time and have attempted to define it, to have stressed forcefully the writer's responsibility in the modern world (irrespective of the somewhat weak theoretical foundations on which it is based), to have analysed with great clarity (albeit insufficiently) the social character of literature and the importance of the public, and lastly to have posed a number of questions, whose answers we are still seeking, but without which it is impossible to evolve a modern theory of aesthetics.

ARAGON'S "REJECTION" OF "ENGAGEMENT"

It is impossible to close this chapter without mentioning Aragon's attitude to the concept of commitment. In a book published in 1946, he protested, almost laughingly, against the expression "poésie engagée" on the grounds that poetry was not a maid whom one can "engage" or dismiss at will. This was not an amusing sally or a facetious pun on the meaning of the word "engagée", but a spirited attack on the view which assimilates commitment to the toeing of a "party line" and the committed writer to a sincere but naïve sycophant. Twenty years later, Aragon was even more specific, and he vigorously called the critic Jean Sur to task for sticking the label "engagé" on to his person and his work. He argued that he had done more than "escape from" the Sartrian challenge that literature must be either "engagée" or "dégagée" (committed or detached), for he had denied that such a dilemma existed:

It is not so much that I escape from it, but that I violently deny its necessity. . . . One generally says that people like myself are *committed*, to signify that they say what they really think. I find this neologism quite unnecessary.[21]

When, later in the book, Jean Sur described him again as a "committed man", he hastened to assert that he would always categorically reject "not only the word but the concept of commitment", and he warned against the danger of using meaningless "labels".[22]

In the face of such unambiguous statements, has one the right to speak of Aragon as a committed writer and to take no notice of what he says? I suggest that one may do so, without necessarily rejecting his warning. Of course, commitment is only a label, and all labels are limiting, but can the literary critic do without them altogether? Aragon's own admission that he "says what he really thinks" is both a valid description of commitment and of his own approach, so that, in spite of his understandable reluctance to be labelled, it is legitimate to go on considering him as a committed writer. One should, however, bear in mind that commitment, whether it is an awful "neologism" or not, does not involve giving up the writer's freedom, but rather represents that rare and valuable quality of telling the truth as one sees it, a quality which Aragon shares with Péguy and Sartre. We may, and indeed we must, accept his criticism of the narrow conceptions with which commitment was unfortunately associated in its early years; but this should lead, not to the outright rejection of the label (unless a better one is substituted), but to a permanent attempt on the part of committed writers to seek a broadening of the concept. There is every indication that this is taking place, and Aragon's own effort is among the most valuable in this respect.

Moreover, Aragon is a man who would describe himself as a "socialist realist", a phrase which indicates that his literary activity is guided by Marxism. We shall examine later his specific contribution to the issues raised by socialist realism, but what can be stressed immediately is that he takes a passionate interest in the problems of his time and that his work is openly coloured by his philosophy of life. The concept of commitment implies nothing more—and nothing less.

Lastly, it was none other than Elsa Triolet, Aragon's wife,

who stated in a little book published in 1948 that it was permissible to use the word "committed" in the case of Mayakovsky, for example, because such a word "corresponds to something real in the minds of people today".[23] She emphasized that a committed work of art had value only to the extent that it expressed the "flesh and blood" of the artist and that it cannot be written to order. It is in this sense that I speak here of Aragon as a committed writer—his realism and his socialism are indeed his "flesh and blood".

SOME CONCLUSIONS

The concept of commitment, although it is particularly well illustrated in the field of literature, is not in itself a purely literary concept but a philosophical one. In broad terms, commitment is the acceptance of an outlook on life, a Weltanschauung, which is "defended and illustrated" to the best of one's ability in everything one undertakes.[a] Although Sartre has given it an atheistic content and has even measured the progress of his own commitment by his ability to discard religious patterns of thought, it does not necessarily follow that there is no such thing as a Christian commitment—the example of Péguy disproves such a contention. A committed man is primarily a man who feels a sense of responsibility to his fellow men and who takes practical steps to help them. No single ideology can claim that it alone is capable of arousing such an attitude among its followers. One of the most encouraging trends in recent years is the gradual breaking down of barriers of mistrust and incomprehension among people of the most diverse ideologies, and, more particularly, between believers and unbelievers. Neither side is giving up its own principles, but each has agreed to join in a *dialogue* in order to find possible areas of agreement, both on the theoretical and on the practical levels. This welcome way of interpreting "peaceful co-existence" in the field of ideas is still in its infancy, but it *is* taking place, in England as well as in many other countries. In France, the dialogue has already had important internal repercussions within the two most important

---

[a] The difference between a worker and a writer in this respect is that the former cannot express his commitment in his actual job—there is no committed way of making tools, for example—but that the latter finds his creative work acquires new meaning in the light of commitment. (Cf. *Que peut la littérature?*, p. 34.)

ideological groups involved, the Catholic Church and the Communist Party. Some Christians have been re-examining in a new light the old question of whether man can lead a good life without believing in God; and a lively debate has started among Marxists concerning the role of religion in society, with one group asserting that progressive Christians are progressive in spite of their faith, and the other suggesting that religious faith can under certain conditions actually inspire and support fighters for justice and liberty.

Perhaps the correct answer to these problems, both for Christians and for Marxists, is to recognize that there are two stages of development. The first stage is the desire to take part in the battle for human betterment, to commit oneself. The second stage is determined by a great number of circumstances, such as background, upbringing, personal experience, etc., and involves embracing a particular ideology. The committed approach is not the result of an ideology, but rather the step which precedes it and leads to it. It is not so much the particular ideology which matters but the *spirit* in which it is taken up. There will always be far more in common between a *committed* Christian and a *committed* Communist than between either of them and the Pharisees of his own church or party. Both Péguy and Aragon divined this important truth and voiced it in their works. For example, Péguy once wrote that "all is not lost—far from it—in the case of revolutionary atheism," because it contains "sparks of charity", but he added that "reactionary, bourgeois atheism" was an "atheism without charity, . . . an atheism without hope".[a] For his part, Aragon often expressed his respect for genuine Christians, as when he wrote his wartime poem, *La Rose et le réséda* (The Rose and the Mignonette), dedicated to Catholic and Communist patriots who were shot by the Germans. Devotion to the motherland, says the poet, matters more than an ideology:

> It matters little what you call
> The light which guided their steps
> Or that one would go to church
> While the other would stay away

[a] Significantly, this comes from an essay in which Péguy attacks an orthodox theologian of his time. (*Un Nouveau Théologien* in *Œuvres en Prose*, 1909–14, p. 893.)

He who believed in Heaven
And he who did not
Both of them were faithful[a]

Péguy and Aragon believe that people are usually better (or worse) than their ideologies. This does not mean that ideologies are not important and that pragmatism is the answer. On the contrary, if commitment is not given solid foundations, it is in danger of remaining vague and ineffectual. It would not be complete unless it were commitment to a specific cause, and it is perfectly legitimate to expect each ideology to state its claim for being a better guide than any other, provided that by doing so it does not close the door upon the possibility of co-operation with other men of good will. I suggest that commitment is the unifying link because, whatever his philosophical or political allegiance, a committed person knows that he is "a man among men".[b] Moreover, as commitment requires a realistic approach to life the better to change it, it can help to discard, not so much religion, as Sartre would have it, but dogmatism, which is—as recent events have shown—a disease which can disgrace any organized ideology. The rejection of routine and the tyranny of convention, which Sartre so eloquently proclaims, is not necessarily the prerogative of atheists and humanists, although it must be admitted they have done more than anybody else to spread these virtues. But a Catholic like Péguy spent his whole life denouncing the "bien-pensants"[c] and drawing a radical distinction between "respectable" Christianity—which accepts things ready-made ("du tout fait")

[a] *La Rose et le réséda* in *La Diane française.*

> Qu'importe comment s'appelle
> Cette clarté sur leur pas
> Que l'un fût de la chapelle
> Et l'autre s'y dérobât
> Celui qui croyait au ciel
> Celui qui n'y croyait pas
> Tous les deux étaient fidèles

[b] This favourite expression of Sartre's occurs frequently in his essays as well as in his novels and his plays. It sums up the basically human content of commitment.

[c] This expression describes "right-thinking" people who are uncritical in their acceptance of convention and orthodoxy. Péguy always hinted that the "bien-pensants" were smug, self-satisfied Pharisees, and he attacked them bitterly both before and after his own return to Christianity.

—and "revolutionary" Christianity—which is based on things in the making ("du se faisant").

"Littérature engagée" is the application of commitment to the special field of literature. Its one and only requirement is that the writer should take part in the struggles of the age,[a] and it urges him to do so, not because it is presumptuous enough to decree where his artistic duty lies, but, more modestly, because it knows the value of such a source of inspiration. Committed literature has no special themes, styles or methods—it is distinguished only by greater realism[b] and by the author's attitude to life. These do not, by themselves, create a work of art, but they do enhance its quality. They help literature to make us aware of our true condition and to increase our sense of responsibility. In addition to providing aesthetic enjoyment, "littérature engagée" fulfils a "social function". Is not the blending of these two aspects characteristic of all great art? This is probably what Bernard Shaw had in mind when he ridiculed "the parrot-cry that art should never be didactic" and defiantly proclaimed that "great art can never be anything else".[24]

NOTES

1. Cf. his *Bilan littéraire du vingtième siècle*.
2. Cf. *Situations II*, p. 251.
3. Beatie Bryant in *Roots*, p. 150 of Wesker's *Trilogy*, Jonathan Cape.
4. *Chicken Soup with Barley* in *Trilogy*, p. 75.
5. *Writers and Leviathan* in *England, Your England*, p. 25.
6. Article in the *Revue de Paris*, September 1961, p. 121.
7. *Pour un nouveau roman*, pp. 46–47.
8. *Chroniques du Bel Canto*, p. 25.
9. *Situations II*, p. 15.
10. *Œuvres poétiques complètes*, p. 813.
11. *The Writer and Commitment*.
12. *Situations II*, p. 185.
13. op. cit., p. 11.
14. *Situations II*, pp. 72–73.
15. Ibid., p. 98.

[a] The next three chapters will show how Péguy, Aragon and Sartre, through their own involvement in their time, arrived at the concept and the issues to which they committed themselves.

[b] The relationship between realism and commitment, as well as the precise meaning of the former, are discussed in Chapter V.

16. Statement made at the Writers' International Congress held in Leningrad in 1963.

17. Interview given to *Le Monde*, reproduced in *Encounter*, No. 129, June 1964 (pp. 61–63).

18. *La Nouvelle Critique*, No. 173–74 (March 1966).

19. It appeared first in two consecutive numbers of *Temps modernes* (October and November 1963) and was later published in book form by Gallimard (1964).

20. Interview to *Le Monde* mentioned above.

21. Jean Sur, *Aragon, le réalisme de l'amour* (with marginal comments by Aragon).

22. Ibid., p. 147.

23. *L'Ecrivain et le livre* (Editions Sociales), pp. 38–39.

24. Preface to *Pygmalion* (Penguin edn, p. 9).

PART I
DESCRIPTIVE

ORIGIN AND DEVELOPMENT OF "LITTÉRATURE
ENGAGÉE" IN THE LIFE AND WORKS OF PÉGUY,
ARAGON AND SARTRE

CHAPTER II

PÉGUY

THE INCLUSION OF Péguy in this study of *contemporary* literature (he was born in 1873 and died in 1914 at the battle of the Marne) may strike the reader as an anomaly. It is not really so, for Péguy, in addition to paving the way for the present "aggiornamento"[a] of the Roman Catholic Church, happens to be more keenly discussed and appreciated today than in his own life-time. He began to attract his countrymen's serious attention[b] long after his death, in fact almost at the same time as Sartrian existentialism was having its strongest appeal. In the early forties, many Frenchmen turned eagerly to Sartre and Péguy in their search for new ideals and new methods of thought.[c] That they should have looked up to a young living writer such as Sartre, who had just shared their own tragedy, was not really surprising, but what did they hope to find—and actually did find— in the message of a man whose death occurred in the early days of the first world war? The answer to this question is bound up, in my opinion, with Péguy's commitment. One may not care very much today about the issues which to him seemed of paramount importance, but it is hard not to feel inspired by his example, for in grappling with the temporal problems of his time, he discovered certain *spiritual* truths which are still meaningful to our generation. What makes him truly relevant to the present age is not so much what he says (his conclusions are often debatable) but

[a] The Italian word "aggiornamento" means "bringing up to date" and is currently used to describe the new approach by which the Church seeks to adapt itself to the modern world.

[b] In the last few years, interest in Péguy has also begun to spread to this country. The sympathetic studies of Alexander Dru (1956), Marjorie Villiers (1965) and N. Jussem-Wilson (1965) (see Bibliography at the end) represent an encouraging start.

[c] In 1941, the Vichy authorities tried to enlist Péguy as an ancestor of the so-called National Revolution, but the attempt boomeranged against them, for those who were rediscovering Péguy found that his burning patriotism and his hatred of "capitulators" could in fact inspire the fighters of the Resistance Movement.

his basic approach. This was dominated by his acute understanding that there is no future for man if he dissociates the
spiritual from the temporal, the eternal from the topical. In
one of his most significant works, he uttered a serious warning
which it is still vital to heed, whether one's view of the "eternal"
(another word for the ultimate destiny of man) is religious or
exclusively humanistic:

> The eternal has been temporarily suspended because those
> charged with power, those in whom the power of eternity
> is founded have scorned and forgotten and misunderstood
> the temporal.[1]

Although he never used the expression "littérature engagée",
his works stand out as one of the earliest and finest illustrations
of the modern committed outlook.

In order to understand Péguy's path to commitment, it is
important to start with a brief examination of the times in which
he lived and of his personal background. Not that these factors
are sufficient to explain Péguy: they are no more than the
situation which confronted him, but our task is to find out how
he met this particular situation, or, to put the matter differently,
to discover his own original response to the problems which his
time had set before him. Charles Péguy grew up in a country
which was still smarting under the humiliation of defeat
in the 1870–71 war against Prussia. He often laid great stress
on the fact that his generation was a "sacrificed generation"
because it had to live "after the defeat", and he thought that
its behaviour as well as its thinking were not unconnected
with that disaster on the battlefield. Instead of living in an
epoch, when great things were happening, they had to be
content with belonging to a *period*, a time devoid of ideals and
any sense of purpose.[a] One need not agree with his analysis.
As Paul Valéry once pointed out, war is easily considered as a
cause, in view of its spectacular nature, but in fact it is just a
symptom of a deeper *malaise*. The truth is that the 1870–71
war had merely brought to the forefront the general crisis of
modern civilization. It had helped to sharpen the social conflict, already acute enough, and had finally led to the Civil

---

[a] The years of the Dreyfus Affair were an outstanding exception, according to Péguy, for then it was really possible to witness history in the making:
the Affair was an *epoch*.

War of 1871, when the Parisian workers, refusing to accept the government's capitulation, set up their short-lived proletarian state, the Paris Commune, which was overthrown by Thiers after two-and-a-half months of existence, and was followed by bloody reprisals against its supporters. This setback was largely caused by the lack of unity between the working class on the one hand, and the peasants and middle classes on the other. Such lack of unity was itself due to the slower pace of development in the countryside, as well as to the views of some early Socialists who considered all classes other than the proletariat as "one reactionary mass". It explains the hesitations and contradictions within the French Socialist Party, and why it was torn between a sectarian faction (led by Jules Guesde) which tended to preach "splendid isolation" for the working class, and a liberal faction (led by Jean Jaurès) which tended to play down the independent role of the industrial workers and to rely increasingly on successful parliamentary manœuvres. This, of course, is not the whole truth and it considerably over-simplifies the matter, but it goes a long way to explain why a man like Péguy, who was anxious to seek a way out of the maze of social and political contradictions, found it so difficult to remain a loyal supporter of the Socialist Party for which he he had at first a strong sentimental attachment.

He himself was born among peasants (a fact which he tire-lessly recalls with great pride) and his earliest recollections are associated with poverty and hard toil. What he saw, learned and experienced in his childhood was to be of decisive importance in determining the ideas and the outlook he adopted in later years. In his case, the child was certainly father to the man, and as he says in one of the last works he wrote, *L'Argent* (Money) (1913), everything was decided for him before he reached the age of twelve.[2] The great event in his life, for himself as well as for his family, was that he was sent to school and that, unlike his illiterate ancestors and semi-literate mother, he was able to drink from the Fount of Knowledge. Not only did he learn to read, write and add up, but he was encouraged by a kindly teacher[a] to proceed to a secondary school, or "lycée", and to master the mysteries of Latin. It was, however, his primary school education which left the

[a] His name was Théodore Naudy, and Péguy paid him a grateful tribute in *L'Argent*—op. cit., pp. 1045–77.

deepest impression on him, both what he learnt when he was at
school and when he visited the parish priest on a Thursday
afternoon to be instructed in the Catechism. He accepted
grammar and the Scriptures with equal enthusiasm and with
equal naïve respect. Moreover, he found no conflict then
between what the schoolmaster and the priest had to tell him,
for both were men of "honour", uncontaminated by the vices
of the "modern world". They taught him the great dignity
of human labour, the difference between right and wrong, and
the need to look upon life as a serious business. He insisted later
that he could never have received such values from the industrial workers because they had been corrupted by the bourgeoisie. It was the small bourgeoisie which, in his view, had
"preserved the virtues of working men",[3] which they themselves
had lost.

How did Péguy react to the situation of his country and the
influences of his childhood? He reacted as a *poet*. Alexander
Dru is quite right when he says that "the key to Péguy is the
poetry, and it alone supplies the point of view for everything
he said and did".[4] This does not mean that his prose works are
unimportant, but rather that his approach to life is always
poetic.[a] The word "poet" is used here to describe a man
endowed with two essential qualities, a powerful imagination,
capable of going beyond what is immediately accessible (hence
the prophetic character of much of Péguy's message), and the
ability to grasp a whole situation or a whole problem in a
condensed form and to communicate this vision adequately. The
two qualities are naturally closely connected, and they manifest
themselves through poetic imagery, images being the special
way in which the poet sees the world as well as his most vivid
way of condensing reality. To these qualities, one might perhaps
add a striving for the absolute in all things, what Aragon calls
"le goût de l'absolu", which is the hall-mark of a great poet.
Péguy was such a man. His commitment was the devotion of a
poet to an ideal for which it is worth living—and dying.
For the sake of convenience, one can isolate five great

---

[a] This accounts for his style, for the special way in which he uses accepted
words and phrases—he sees them differently (in particular words such as
"moderne", "mystique" and "politique"), and for his unusual titles. (His
titles seldom bear *direct* relation to the topic he develops, but they represent
the initial inspiration which started his thinking.)

"moments" in his career, five encounters with reality, and
see how he applied his poetic vision and enthusiasm to each
one of them.

FIRST ENCOUNTER WITH REALITY:
THE ECOLE NORMALE

It was at the Ecole Normale[a] that Péguy first discovered
what he later denounced as a typically modern evil, "intellectualism". French university thought in those days was
dominated by a barren and uninspiring positivism. In philosophy and in literature, facts alone seemed to matter, whilst
the spirit of a thinker or the beauty of a work of art lay hidden
beneath an impressive mass of so-called objective scholarship.
Péguy was horrified, and his hatred for the Sorbonne, the first
of many lasting hatreds which he developed, dates from this
early experience. From then onwards, the "intellectuals"
became the special target of his attack and his abuse. Although
one may find that some of his later remarks on the subject are
marred by passion, it should be admitted that, as a young man,
eager to commune with the living thoughts of the great masters,
he must have found the meticulous dissecting of artistic masterpieces fruitless and irksome and the whole intellectual atmosphere quite stifling.[5] He was also profoundly disturbed by the
system of state grants which were awarded on the basis of
competitive examinations. To achieve success at these examinations, one did not need talent or an original mind, but an
infinite capacity for memorizing as many facts as possible. Thus
did the bourgeoisie deprive those who had a lively enquiring
mind from the benefits of a higher education, whilst at the
same time preserving a pretence of democracy through a
system which claimed that university places were given to
those who "deserved them". This led to the formation of an
intellectual "aristocracy" and to a divorce between culture
and the common people. Péguy immediately associated this
aspect with the previous one and believed that the false scientific
façade of modern culture stemmed from the fact that it was
the culture of a privileged minority, that the so-called devotion
to facts and nothing but facts betrayed a passive acceptance of the
status quo. He suggested that the remedy lay in the intellectual's

[a] The "Ecole Normale" referred to is the Teachers' Training College of
the *rue d'Ulm* which turned out most of France's university professors.

commitment, for this would bring him into contact with the living needs of the people and would turn him away from the goal of specialization, whose aim was not culture for its own sake, but the securing of comfortable sinecures in "the temporal world". He had no time for those who made a living out of the cause they were supposed to serve, be they university professors or professional politicians. When he later founded his own review *Les Cahiers de la Quinzaine* (Fortnightly Notebooks) he thought little of financial rewards, but was mainly concerned with the value of a regular periodical dedicated to Truth.[a] It was in this spirit that Péguy turned to socialism. The poverty of his childhood and his hatred of injustice had already convinced him that something must be done in the economic and social sphere; now, his recent intellectual experience suggested to him that a radical change was also needed in order to bring about a "harmonious society" in which art and culture might blossom. He started a small circle of socialist propaganda and told his friend Challaye that a socialist paper was needed, whose contributors would be dedicated people, living *for* the paper, not making a living *out of* it.[6]

The year 1897 marks the beginning of Péguy's literary career. He published five articles in the *Revue Socialiste*, of which the most important was *De la cité socialiste*, a kind of blueprint of the future socialist state in which he predicted that the "administration of things" would replace the "government of men" (a formula borrowed from Saint-Simon, the nineteenth-century thinker) and where the means of production would become collective property, "that is to say, returned to the city, to all citizens".[7] This was followed a year later by *Marcel, premier dialogue de la Cité Harmonieuse* (Marcel—First Dialogue of the Harmonious City), in which Péguy stressed that the purpose of a "harmonious" organization of material life was to ensure the full and free development of spiritual life. The latter, he said, must be quite free, and no man, not even the "Cité" itself (the socialist state) could give orders in this essentially individual province.

---

[a] It is true that the *Cahiers* became Péguy's livelihood, for someone had to assume full-time responsibility for the undertaking, but his life-long poverty bears eloquent testimony to his unselfish spirit. He made many a financial sacrifice for the *Cahiers* and never allowed commercial considerations to determine their content or policy.

The poet was already fighting for the freedom of poetry.

It was also in 1897 that Péguy's first major work, *Jeanne d'Arc* (which he had taken two years to write), was published at his own expense. Péguy was always interested in Joan of Arc, and in his last years, she became his model in all things. Yet when he began to write about her, he was not a Christian. He was regarding himself as an anti-clerical atheist. This was partly due to his socialism. The French Socialist Party fought the Church both as a political institution which defended the privileges of the rich and as a spiritual body whose "obscurantist" philosophy contradicted progress and humanism. The English reader must bear in mind that the friendly relations between the Labour movement and organized religion which accompanied the birth of the Labour Party in this country, were quite unknown in France; there, from the eighteenth century onwards, the Church played an open political role and opposed all movements for political reform and social advance. To be a Christian and a socialist at the same time was almost a contradiction in terms. There were, however, other reasons for Péguy's rejection of the faith of his childhood. They concerned primarily his horror at the doctrine of eternal damnation, an issue which never ceased to torment him, even after his conversion, perhaps even more so then. In his youth, he considered the doctrine as "odious" and "barbarous" and he proclaimed his solidarity with both the "damned of the earth"[a] and those who were damned eternally.[8] His interest in Joan of Arc, although it foreshadows his return to Catholicism, was mainly due at that time to the fact that she was a simple peasant girl who had shaken her countrymen out of their cowardice. She had intervened in the human battle—and fought. For Péguy, who was dreaming of doing just that, she symbolized courage and feeling for the suffering of others, the qualities of his own commitment, and he naturally endowed her with many of his personal characteristics. He dedicated his *Jeanne d'Arc* to all those who had fought against "the universal human evil" and for the establishment of "the universal socialist republic".[9] The work itself consists of three plays. The first one, *A Domrémy*, describes Joan's childhood and tells how deeply

[a] In French, the first line of the revolutionary anthem, *L'Internationale*, reads as follows: "Debout, les damnés de la terre!" (Arise, ye damned of the earth.)

sad she was because of the misery around her, the ruins of war and the general passivity of the people. These were Péguy's own preoccupations at the time. Joan is seen arguing at length with two of her friends, and eventually with God Himself. The second play, *Les Batailles* (Battles), stresses the hostility Joan encountered everywhere except among simple folk, an obvious echo of Péguy's own feelings of isolation in a society which spurned his values. In the last play, *Rouen*, the theme is the trial of Joan and her condemnation by the "doctors" of the Church. We are reminded that her judges were all "learned" men (the ancestors of the present Sorbonne, in other words!) and Péguy makes one of them say, with heavy sarcasm, that with all their degrees in theology, in Canon Law and in Civil Law, they formed a "real fine assembly" ("une bien belle assemblée").[10] After the verdict, Joan is left alone and she gives vent to her doubts and despair,

> I should really like to know
> Oh my God if it be true that I have damned my soul.[a]

It is only at the very end that she reasserts her belief in her mission.

Péguy's *Jeanne d'Arc* is not a historical work. Its author certainly never claimed that it was one, although he had made an extensive study of available sources. He was more interested in the spirit of his heroine and in making her message relevant to modern times. His was a poetic evocation of a great patriot and a great fighter, as well as a committed appeal for militancy and action.

Meanwhile, in the big world outside the University, a momentous storm was gathering which was to turn Péguy's dream of militant action into reality—the Dreyfus Affair had exploded.

SECOND ENCOUNTER WITH REALITY:
THE DREYFUS AFFAIR AND ITS AFTERMATH

The facts of the Dreyfus Affair are now common knowledge, but what is not always realized is the frenzy of passion it

---

[a] Je voudrais bien savoir
O mon Dieu s'il est vrai que je me sois damnée.
(*Œuvres poétiques complètes*, p. 1193.)

produced. Around the struggle between Dreyfus's supporters and his opponents, a much more fundamental fight was being waged, the fight between the Republic and its enemies. The Establishment itself was divided, for what was at stake was nothing less than the control of the state machine. The conflict spread to all aspects of life. It ended life-long friendships, divided families and broke the strongest ties of loyalty and affection: one was either on one side of the fence or the other. Péguy describes how he once took a stroll with a fellow student, but had to leave him after twenty minutes because "the Dreyfus Affair was walking between us".[11]

From the start, Péguy had believed in Dreyfus's innocence and he was astounded by the Socialist Party's attitude. In the early days of the Affair, the socialists had tended to ignore all the fuss and to dismiss it as a mere squabble among bourgeois. Péguy went to see Jaurès and argued that it was a socialist duty to defend Dreyfus, on the moral grounds that socialism is against all injustices, and on the tactical grounds that people who were discovering the iniquity of the state for the first time would become easily converted to the cause. Jaurès was quite receptive to such arguments, as they corresponded to his own feelings in the matter. In the end, his policy won the day, and the Socialist Party sided with Dreyfus.

The importance of the Affair for Péguy went far beyond the immediate issues involved. He saw it as a unique opportunity for putting his moral principles into practice. At last, the hour had struck when one could *do* something really great, instead of talking endlessly and fruitlessly. Poetry had descended into the street. To fight for the release of Dreyfus was to fight for the triumph of an ideal of Absolute Justice in human affairs. This is why he was so shocked when politicians tried to "use" the Affair for ends which had nothing to do with it and which, moreover, contradicted its moral principles. He had in mind the laws against religious bodies (such as the Jesuit *congrégations*) which were voted after the innocence of Dreyfus had been recognized and after the shameful role of the Church, among others, had been exposed. Péguy's argument was simply that two wrongs don't make a right, and that it was impossible to demand justice for one's friends alone. Justice, he argued, was the inalienable right of all. In this, he was supported by a Jewish friend, the journalist Bernard

Lazare, to whom he was to devote many a moving page in *Notre Jeunesse* (Our Youth). What neither of them was prepared to accept was the spectacle of politicians (who had usually remained in the background when it was safer to do so) trying to exploit the success of the Dreyfus cause in order to settle old scores with their opponents. The poetic commitment of Péguy, with its emphasis on the Absolute, rebelled against this debasement of a noble ideal. It was a clear case of a "mystique" (an ideal) sinking into a "politique", as he was to put it in 1910.

It was in the midst of the Affair that Péguy founded his *Cahiers de la Quinzaine*. The Socialist Party had refused him the right to publish uncensored material and he reluctantly parted company with them. This did not shake his faith in socialism, which he never lost, but it increased his contempt for the parliamentary Socialist Party. It must be said in his defence that that party was hardly capable of generating genuine enthusiasm in those days and that its obsession with electoral success had almost killed whatever few principles it may have had. It is not too far-fetched to recall that the vices of "parliamentary socialism" were then condemned by none other than Lenin. It would be ridiculous, of course, to compare Péguy with Lenin, but it is a fact that both of them had started by criticizing the activities of European Socialist Parties *from a pure socialist standpoint*. In doing this, they were certainly not behaving as unpractical dreamers! As for the *Cahiers*, Péguy meant them to become a militant platform where free men would tell the truth as they saw it, without fear of offending any party or church. To this ideal, the *Cahiers* remained faithful until he died. An incident which gives a good illustration of the social purpose he had in mind for literature was the so-called *Jean Coste* affair. *Jean Coste* was a novel which described vividly and realistically the miserable life of a village schoolmaster. It had been rejected by Léon Blum, who was then on the Board of Directors of a socialist publishing house, founded in 1896 by Péguy and a few friends, on the grounds that its picture of social misery was exaggerated. "There are no men who are as miserable as that," he is reported to have said. Later, Péguy, in sole control of his own *Cahiers*, published the whole text of the novel as well as an introduction in which he bitterly replied to Léon Blum,

"There are no men who are as miserable as that." I bear no grudge against the rich administrator who, with this simple statement, was quietly killing a book and a man. I am sorry for him. Unless he has genius, a rich man cannot imagine what poverty really is.[12]

Some of Péguy's most important works appeared in the *Cahiers*. They fill many volumes of his Complete Works, and it is of course impossible to mention them all. Attention should, however, be drawn to a few significant ones in his earlier period, such as *De la grippe* (1901) (About Influenza) in which he ridicules the antics of parliamentary politicians; *Pour moi* (1901) (For Me) in which he defends the right of minorities to express themselves, voices his fears about the "contamination" of "revolutionary socialism by its political army, just as the French nation was contaminated by its military army", and defines propaganda as "the communication pure and simple of the truth one knows"; *Personnalités* (1902) in which he refuses to support the anti-clerical laws of Radical Socialists on the grounds that deprivation of freedom is a bourgeois vice; the 1903 *Cahier* in which he criticizes socialist deputies for demanding a state monopoly for alcohol instead of opposing alcoholism as such and showing its links with capitalist profits; the 1904 *Cahier* in which he states his refusal to sacrifice his "socialist ideal" in favour of the "distortions of Radical-Socialism",[a] or "the inalienable rights of personal conscience before the altar of reasons of state"; the 1905 *Cahier* in which he asserts that nothing is more immoral than what is "artificial and against nature"; the *Suppliants parallèles* (1905), written after the Russian Revolution, a *Cahier* in which he compares the Russian peasants with the supplicants of ancient times, saying that both were morally greater than the rulers to whom they addressed their petitions, and in which he defines a revolution, not as a "destructive operation" but as "an act of founding"; *Louis de Gonzague* (December 1905) in which he asserts the importance of culture for a free nation; and the various *Cahiers* (1906–7) in which he published parts of a doctorate thesis which he never completed and in which he goes to battle against intellectualism and the

[a] "Radical Socialism" in this context naturally refers to the "parti radical socialiste", a party which, despite its name, has never been either radical or socialist, but rather a party of the Centre.

modern world.[a] In 1908, he wrote an essay against "historicism" which he called after the Muse of History, *Clio*, but it appeared posthumously.

Péguy's devotion to the *Cahiers* reveals his faith in the power of literature. He seldom envisaged that any other action was possible, except perhaps for street fights when they were needed, as in the days of the Dreyfus Affair. In particular, he rejected the class struggle and pinned his hopes on the written word. This, needless to say, further alienated him from the Socialist Party. Modern socialism, inasmuch as it draws its inspiration from Marx, considers that it is not the logical brilliance of socialist ideas alone which will "convert" the world, but the concrete activity of the working class, for whom a new social system is a vital necessity.

THIRD ENCOUNTER WITH REALITY:
PATRIOTISM

Few works constitute a better illustration of Péguy's poetic reaction to the "shock" of events than his 1905 *Cahier, Notre Patrie* (Our Motherland). It represents an important landmark in his spiritual evolution because it expresses his newly found patriotism. The event itself was the coming of the Spanish king to Paris, with its usual accompaniment of visits to historical monuments and military parades. It produced in Péguy a "startling shock" ("un saisissement")[13] because it made him realize more vividly than ever the powerful national traditions embodied in Parisian monuments, and the function of the Army as an instrument which can safeguard these traditions. He had been aware, like everyone else, of the German threat, but he needed this concrete experience in order to appreciate the value of what was at stake. The poet in him had to visualize "an abstract concept in physical shape and form".[14] He saw the monuments not only as artistic masterpieces but as an expression of the faith and greatness of his people. Such a great and cultured people, he felt, must remain free, and in the face of a possible attack from a powerful neighbour, it had to strengthen its military defences. This led Péguy to praise the Army, an unusual step for an old Dreyfusard, but he was quick to draw a distinction between the Army as an indispensable

[a] Other important works which also appeared in the *Cahiers* are examined separately.

institution and a reactionary General Staff. From then onwards, until his tragic death on the battlefield, he became increasingly convinced of the need to resist Germany by making France militarily powerful. But the whole issue had been suggested to him as a result of a concrete experience, a visual experience: he had seen the monuments, he had seen the parade, and immediately his poetic imagination had gone beyond sensory experience to divine the spiritual truth of patriotism.

In order to appreciate the shock that this discovery represented both for Péguy and for his contemporaries, it is necessary to remember that at the beginning of this century, patriotism (or what passed as such) seemed to be the prerogative of right-wing politicians. Socialists had the reputation of being more concerned with class realities than with national realities, so that the sight of a socialist coming down heavily in favour of "the motherland" and drawing the practical consequence that militarism had its uses was startling and unexpected. For Péguy, however, there was no contradiction. Was not socialism the highest expression of one's love for one's countrymen, and did it not require a land in which it could be built? "Our antipatriots," he wrote a few years later, "will learn the value which a little bit of earth can have as a basis for a Revolution."[15]

Péguy's patriotism, which was a very genuine sentiment, and not a narrow nationalism, did, however, affect his political judgement in a negative way. It led him in the end to support the most chauvinistic and military-minded politicians of his day. He was so obsessed with the thought that 1871 must not happen all over again that he lost his sense of proportion and was prepared to give his unqualified approval to any policy which did not appear to be defeatist. It made him particularly unfair to Jaurès, whose internationalism he interpreted as cowardly pacifism and nothing short of treason. The truth is that Jaurès was not taken in by the patriotic pretence of his own government; he saw war as the way of resolving the economic rivalry between two capitalist states and he counted on the alliance of the working classes in both France and Germany as a means of averting war and of defeating the reactionary rulers of both countries. But Péguy never saw the economic interests behind war. As one of his admirers said, although he could discern the harmful role of money in the internal life of France, he seemed strangely unaware of the part it plays in the preparation of armed conflicts.[16] For his wars were always crusades undertaken to defend Honour and high principles, and it is sad to recall that he fell for the lying propaganda that the 1914 war was a war in defence of civilization. It is equally sad to remember that, a few months before Jaurès was assassinated by a right-wing brute, Péguy had actually demanded that the great leader's voice should be silenced, and had claimed that this was necessary for "national defence". The sincerity of his patriotism cannot excuse this open incitement to murder.

FOURTH ENCOUNTER WITH REALITY:
FAITH

In September 1908, Péguy confided to Joseph Lotte, one of his closest friends, that he had returned to the Catholic faith. It is typical of the man that he spoke of this momentous event in his life almost casually, and right at the end of a conversation. All he said was, "I have not told you everything. I have recovered my faith. I am a Catholic." It is no less typical that he never felt the need to broadcast his conversion to the world. In fact, he refused to speak of a "conversion", and on the few occasions when he later mentioned the event, he described it as "un approfondissement", a deepening of his mind. He insisted that he had always followed "the same straight road" and that faith was the culmination of his spiritual development. With dogged persistence, he repeated that he had nothing to be ashamed of in his past and that if his Complete Works were published tomorrow, he would not disown a single line, nor alter a single comma, with the possible exception, he added, of "seven or eight theological expressions"[17] which might be misleading. As he had refused to be "annexed" by the socialists, he now refused to be annexed by the Catholics, and, what is more, he died an unrepentant anti-clerical. He even found a further theoretical justification for his anti-clericalism when he noted that the politics of the Church represented a distortion of the ideals on which Christianity was founded. He was very unkind to the ecclesiastical hierarchy whom he called "the politicians of spiritual life".

In 1910, when everybody was expecting him to turn against his past and his former friends, Péguy took two steps which are almost unique in the history of converts. He returned to a former work of his and published it again, not with alterations, but with additions, and he wrote an impassioned defence of his youth. The work which he brought back to life and enlarged was *Jeanne d'Arc*. He included a much longer dialogue between Joan and her two friends, Hauviette, the peasant girl, and Madame Gervaise, the nun, and called it *Le Mystère de la charité de Jeanne d'Arc* (The Mystery of Joan of Arc's Charity). The Joan of 1910 does not go back on any of the statements her creator had put in her mouth in 1897, but she speaks of her faith in terms which would have been impossible when Péguy thought he was an atheist. The central problem of the play remains the same. It is the problem of how to fight evil and how to interpret damnation. Thus, the Catholic Péguy does not shirk the issue he had bravely faced in his irreligious youth. What is even more remarkable is that he does not claim to solve it. It is true that this time he allows Madame Gervaise to have a much bigger say, and to put forward the traditional view that Hell is a mystery which belongs to God, but the new Joan remains unconvinced. She repeats the "blasphemy" of the earlier play, and as before offers her own body and her own soul to save the bodies and the souls of the damned. In the second part of the *Mystery* (which was not published in Péguy's life-time), she argues with God as one argues with a friend, and wonders how his saints allow him to behave in this way, how Jesus does not protest! Finally, she asserts that God Himself must be unhappy at the thought of eternal torments. Without probing deeper into the matter, she leaves it at that, realizing the vanity of trying to divine the secrets of eternal life. When Hauviette suddenly returns to tell her the good news that the tide has begun to turn against the invaders of France, she regains all her courage and understands that she must have faith in God's mercy, whilst concentrating upon her earthly duties. It is significant that Péguy's Christian solution to the problem of Hell should be substantially the same as his earlier one—an appeal for greater commitment—but whereas his decision to wage the human battle against evil had previously turned him away from Christianity, he now proclaims that religion provides us with something of infinite importance, hope, "la petite espérance". His next poem, *Le Porche du mystère de la deuxième vertu* (The Mystery of the Second Virtue), is a continuation of the Joan *mystery* and is dedicated to the greatest of all virtues, hope.

The other unusual step which Péguy took in 1910 followed the *Mystère de la charité* by a few months. He proudly defended his youth and published *Notre Jeunesse*. This extraordinary book, which is probably the finest of Péguy's prose works, was an answer to an earlier *Cahier* in which Daniel Halévy, dealing with the same theme, had adopted what Péguy considered to be an unwarranted apologetic tone. It is a difficult book to read because, superficially, it looks like a collection of disjointed remarks and rambling thoughts on a great variety of topics. In fact, it is solidly constructed around a central idea from which everything else stems. This central idea is the poetic vision of the significance of the Dreyfus Case. Everything converges on the Affair. Péguy begins with the background, not the sordid story of forgeries and lies, but the kind of world in which the Affair was born. He calls this world "modern" because it is the first time in history that former cultures have not been given up in favour of a new one, but have been replaced by the universal worship of money and by selfishness. In such a debased world, ideals are bound to lose their purity (this is the famous distinction between "mystique" and "politique" to which we shall return). The condemnation of an innocent man was not only a crime of right-wing military leaders, it was in the logic of "modern" worldly wisdom which puts the temporal interests of the state before the rights of the individual. In this, Péguy remarks, the "modern world" had invented nothing, for it was merely following the wisdom of Ancient Times, a *temporal wisdom*. Those who refused such a shameful theory were animated by a *spiritual* ideal, and Péguy sees the Affair as the meeting-point of three such ideals, that of Israel, which was the continuation of the prophetic thirst for justice and righteousness, that of Christianity, which was the belief that eternal salvation mattered more than temporal salvation, and that of France, which was the tradition of Saint Louis, Joan of Arc and the early Revolutionaries who had all put honour before everything else. And to show how little prepared he was to join with the anti-Semites, among whom most of the Church's supporters were found, Péguy went out of his way to describe in glowing terms the role of his Jewish friend Bernard Lazare, "that atheist who was brimming over with the word of God",[18] and to defend the Jews against the slanders of their enemies. The argument is then taken one

step further in order to show the connection between Drey-
fusism, an essentially French and Christian ideal, and socialism.
Péguy's socialism was neither anti-Christian, because it was
based on charity, nor anti-French, because in his view a
nation which took the socialist road would become stronger
than all the others, economically, politically, militarily and
spiritually. The book concludes with the assertion that the
defence of Dreyfus was a fight for the eternal salvation of France.
"We were great," says Péguy, "we were very great."

The aftermath of the Affair is described by him as a "short-
cut" ("un raccourci") of the way in which a pure ideal becomes
a sordid political manœuvre. This is what he called the degeneration of a "mystique" into a "politique", one of the basic
themes in *Notre Jeunesse*. The actual words he uses are misleading, for they seem to suggest that he favoured a *mystical*
attitude to life and condemned all political movements as
basically corrupt. Even if there was not the example of his
whole life to contradict this view, a careful study of his text
would be sufficient to show that he had something quite
different in mind. What he feared was the permanent danger
that, in the modern world, ideals would become smoke-screens
behind which material interests are pursued. This has happened to so many "isms" in our own day that Péguy's warning
is timely and *realistic* and cannot be dismissed as the dream of
a mystic cut off from life. The origin of his fears and doubts
lay in the exploitation of the Dreyfus Affair by politicians. He
believed this was the age-long fight between committed
devotion to others, the "mystique", and selfishness and greed,
the "politique". He further believed that selfish people never
fight in the open, but need high-sounding moral principles
behind which to hide, and that in modern society, where
money reigns supreme, there was not a single ideal which they
could not in the end distort and exploit. In this, they were
helped by the powerful forces of routine and convention, the
great killers of moral enthusiasm. One of the Bergsonian ideas
which most appealed to Péguy was the denunciation of habit
as a form of passivity. The real meaning of his distinction
between "mystique" and "politique" is that the former is life,
always seeking a new spiritual adventure, and the latter is lack
of ideals, the search for peace and quiet.

This was not so pessimistic as it sounded. There *was* a remedy, and it did not consist in retirement from the world, but in bringing one's ideals into the political arena itself. Péguy made that point abundantly clear when he praised Bernard Lazare for his ability to take part in politics without sacrificing the essentials of his "mystique": "In the field of 'politique' *since one is needed* ... he was in favour of the rule of law" (my italics).[19] We do not read Péguy aright if we fail to appreciate that the fight between "mystique" and "politique" is a fight in which the "mystique" wins, not by ignoring the "politique", but by transforming it. Could this be done in one of the existing parties? After his break with the socialists, Péguy did not think so, but this does not mean that he deemed it impossible to have a party in which ideals would be kept pure and where individuals would be allowed to express their own views without fear of sinning against a "state truth". The first requirement was to reject the worship of Mammon. Péguy's own stand outside all parties did not amount to idle neutrality, nor, in his Catholic days, to communion with spiritual realities alone. Listen to his scathing criticism of the "parti dévôt": "As they lack the courage to belong to one of the parties of men, they think they belong to the party of God!"[20]

The main weakness of *Notre Jeunesse*, in my opinion, even if one accepts the author's philosophy, is that it does not really give an accurate picture of the Dreyfus Case itself, but rather a special interpretation of it which ignores two important aspects. Péguy, in his effort to emphasize the "mystique" of Dreyfusists, simply forgets that many supporters of Dreyfus, no less sincere than he, did not see the Affair as an issue involving the "eternal salvation" of France, but as a straightforward case of a reactionary clique trying to impose its will on the country; and they fought that clique because they considered it highly dangerous as a political force. One can certainly speak of a "mystique" in this context, in the sense that no selfish interests were pursued, but it was a "mystique" which was very much concerned with the temporal. What is more serious is that Péguy, looking back on the event, tends to whitewash the enemies of Dreyfus. When he describes them as being inspired by the "very legitimate" and "highly respectable" ideals of national interest, he really ought to make a distinction between the mass of honest supporters of the General Staff (many of whom may have sincerely held the view that the Army was incapable of a crime and that probing too deeply into the case would be a threat to France's security), and the high-ranking officers who deliberately sent a man to Devil's Island in the full knowledge of his innocence. As Zola exclaimed in *J'accuse*, "For a whole year, General Billot, General Gonse and General Boisdeffre have known that Drefus was innocent, and they have kept this frightening truth to themselves. And these people find it possible to sleep, they have wives and children whom they love!"

Péguy's return to Catholicism cannot be understood without taking into account his special conception of commitment as involving the whole personality of man, his spiritual as well as his temporal needs, and of the fact that the socialist doctrine, *as it existed then and as he himself knew it,* seemed unconcerned with spiritual life. His poetic soul demanded something more, which he found in Christianity. The remarkable thing is that this did not turn him away from commitment, but further convinced him of the need to be actively involved in the struggles of his fellow men. He had gone back, not to a set of dogmas or to a comforting and respectable philosophy, but to the revolutionary spirit of the Gospels. Christianity put an end to his feeling of isolation and taught him the value of *communion* with others. The rationalist would object that the actual ideas which Péguy embraced were illusions, and he may well be right, but illusions which produce such burning concern for the fate of men cannot be entirely negative.

Péguy's active life after his rediscovery of Christianity remained what it had been before—an untiring devotion to the *Cahiers*, which were to him the concrete embodiment of his commitment. His periodic and pathetic appeals to his readers show the almost insuperable difficulties he had to face. He complained bitterly that subscribers were scarce and that in the meantime he had to live and bring up his children. It is in this light that one should judge his wish to enter the French Academy which he confided to some of his friends. (He was unsuccessful in his attempt, as militant commitment is not the best recommendation for joining that august body.) There was an element of pride in this, but there was also the need for material success which the Academy could give him. Yet it is to his lasting credit that he did not change his style nor cease his attacks on hypocrisy, but went on wearing his heart on his sleeve and proclaiming with brutal forthrightness that literature was not an escape from reality but a crusade for Truth. His commitment antagonized, as it was bound to do, all those who prefer the "purity" of the ivory tower to the "dirty hands" of action. The few friends he kept were people who seldom shared his philosophy but who, like himself, "refused to cheat". (This was the only quality he required from contributors to the *Cahiers*.) Péguy's fate illustrates his own statement that different "mystiques" will always have more common ground among themselves than a "mystique" and a "politique" which outwardly belong to the same camp. Is not this due to the fact that genuine devotion to an ideal is the very essence of commitment?

FIFTH ENCOUNTER WITH REALITY:
LOVE

In an article which he wrote for *Temps Modernes* (1960), the Catholic critic Henri Guillemin recalls that around 1908 Péguy fell in love with a young Jewish girl (his marriage was a very unhappy one, as his wife bitterly reproached him with having made a financial mess of the *Cahiers*), and he suggests that his return to Christianity probably coincided with "his first steps in the realm of the human heart". It is almost certain that the girl did not return his affection, and the *Quatrains*, which he wrote a little later but which were published after his death, show that he deeply suffered from her indifference. He realized, however, that a match between them was impossible and he even encouraged her to get married to someone else. When she followed his advice, it took him many an agonizing week to recover, but his genuine wish to see her happy won in the end. The suggestion that Péguy's religious experience was partly helped by his emotional crisis is not irrelevant to the issue of commitment. It should rather be seen as proof that commitment involves a man's whole personality and is not confined to his "public" life alone. In falling in love, Péguy became more vividly aware of the importance of the inner life, and this increased his hatred for the cold intellectualism of the "modern" world. Moreover, if it is true, as Aragon asserts, that genuine love means primarily "getting out of oneself" ("sortir de soi-même"), this was made even more necessary for Péguy, for he had to push aside his own passion and think only of the woman he loved. His victory did not represent a rejection of the "sinful flesh", but rather, as happens in the plays of Corneille (whom he admired so much), a realization that it was demanded by love itself. Committed love, as we shall see in the case of Aragon, is not the selfish satisfaction of individual impulses, but a source of sacrifice for the sake of others. In this victory over the self lies one of the strongest roots of commitment.

Péguy's attitude to the flesh strikingly illustrates the *human* qualities of his commitment. Far from despising the flesh, he glorified it. He thought that the concept of purity would be meaningless for creatures who had no bodies. This is what Madame Gervaise means when she asserts in the *Mystère de la charité de Jeanne d'Arc* that the Virgin Mary was pure, ". . . étant charnelle" (". . . being a creature of the flesh"). Péguy insisted that if the impurity of the flesh was sinful (but so are impure thoughts), the flesh itself was not. He viewed the Incarnation as the culmination of a process *which is going on all the time* and which he called the penetration of spirituality into the material world, the fusion of heavenly and earthly matters.[21] It is impossible to examine here the implications of this original conception, but one is forcibly reminded of a similar approach in the works of Father Teilhard de Chardin, who examined the "phenomenon of man" as a scientist and also stressed the unity of man's physical and spiritual sides. Such an approach, without in the least being reducible to Aragon's materialism or to Sartre's atheism, makes a dialogue between Christians and non-Christians possible and fruitful.

In his article, Guillemin recalls that in one of Péguy's earliest works, *Marcel*, he had described the future "harmonious city", as one in which people would not have to invent new feelings, for "what could they invent that is better or more sorrowful than simple love?"[22] (The idea that love is a source of both joy and sorrow and that all happiness is shot through with suffering, is frequently developed by Aragon, and more particularly in his war-time poem *Il n'y a pas d'amour heureux* and in his recent novel *La Mise à mort*.) Guillemin also shows how the great poems which Péguy wrote between 1910 and 1914 are full of allusions to his ordeal, but that he never felt ashamed of having fallen in love. It would have been a sin for him to have imposed his love, both because of his position as a married man and because of the girl's indifference, but it was certainly not a sin to have loved! In his last work, he rebukes those soulless "dévôts" who, "because they love no one, imagine that they love God".[23]

In the last period of his life, Péguy realized that he could write great poetry. Until then, his commitment had been mainly polemical and had naturally used the medium of prose. Under the influence of Christianity and his great love, he found that he could express his commitment in poetic form. He found the discovery exhilarating, and his friend Challaye saw him one day bristling with enthusiasm at the thought that he was a poet.[24] His poetry was the fruit of his active struggle and it became a tool for continuing the struggle. He published, in quick succession, two *Mystères* (*Le Porche du mystère de la deuxième vertu* and *Le Mystère des saints innocents*—The Holy Innocents), his *Tapisseries* (thus reviving an old mediaeval tradition) and a long poem of over eight thousand alexandrines, *Eve*. The first two poems are dominated by the theme of hope. It is out of despair itself that Péguy builds up his confidence and his faith, and not by denying the tragedy of life. Of the three virtues, faith, hope and charity, hope is the highest, for without it, the other two would be "nothing but a graveyard".[25] Where, the poet asks, does the Fountain of Hope manage to find the "pure waters which flow eternally"? She finds them in the "impure waters" themselves, which she transforms.[26] The secret of her success is that she relies on the renunciation of habit; in a later work, Péguy calls hope a counter habit, "la contre-habitude",[27] for it requires a willingness always to start afresh, a ruthless rejection of what is old and decaying and a bold acceptance of what is new and growing, in other words it demands *commitment*. These two poems are also the finest example of Péguy's blank verse, in which he achieves a remarkable degree of simplicity and colloquialism. Although his themes are the great mysteries of the Christian religion, he feels that

Nothing is so simple as the Word of God.[28]

He refers to the most sacred things in words which may appear almost irreverent. For example the Holy Family becomes a very ordinary human family, and Mary speaks of "her boy" and of the worries he gives her because of his "mission". The Incarnation is simply what happened when Jesus took the trouble to leave His seat at the right hand of God,[29] and Christ's life on earth was just an "errand" for His Father.[30] This colloquialism, the nearest equivalent to spoken language in modern French poetry, is, strangely enough, the result of Péguy's committed interpretation of Bergsonism. He believed with Bergson that words cannot accurately express spiritual realities, but he found that the simple man who had something to say and wanted to communicate it to other people was nearer to primitive, unspoilt "intuition" than the cleverest psychologists. It is not the language of the simple soul, as it springs directly from the heart, which distorts reality, but the intellectualized language of the Sorbonne, cut off from the people, cut off from life.

Péguy's *Tapisseries* are a record of his spiritual experience when he went on a pilgrimage to Chartres. They show the comfort which religion afforded him at the time of his deepest personal anguish and the genuine humility he was able to achieve, for he did not request any favours from Our Lady of Chartres—he simply asked Her to protect "four young heads" —his own children and the newly born daughter of the woman he loved.

His longest poem, *Eve*, was written in 1913. Its purpose was to review mankind's progress from the time of the first woman to the Incarnation of Christ, and show the influence of this cardinal event on future generations. He stressed that nothing in the field of human thought, human activity or human emotions was foreign to Jesus, for at the time of his birth,

He was going to inherit all the endeavours of men.[a]

His disciples, he suggested, must follow in his footsteps, and display the same all-embracing concern for "the endeavours of men". Péguy's own attempt is singularly impressive. One is left with the impression that in becoming a Christian and a poet, his soul had been able to develop in all directions and vibrate in unison with the rest of the world.

The tragedy of mankind, according to *Eve*, is that we have lost the feeling of complete unity within ourselves and of complete communion with God. The poet draws a vivid contrast

[a] "Il allait hériter de tout l'effort humain." (*Œuvres poétiques complètes*, p. 858.)

between the Golden Age, when every moment of life was part of an indissoluble whole and when private property was unknown, and the wretched present, when everything is neatly classified and isolated. Péguy, however, would not be a militant Christian if he thought everything had been lost. Thanks to Christ, we have been made truly aware of our loss, and in this awareness lies our greatest hope. If only we make the effort to be "born again", we can once more reach the state of unity with God. In his own commentary on *Eve*, Péguy states that he has tried to speak with infinite respect, not only of the Christian world, but of the ancient world, and even of the "modern" one. He also repeats that the path which led him back to Christianity was the path of freedom; for him, ". . . it is the complete man, the pagan soul, which is free, and in that freedom, open to grace".[31]

Of Péguy's last prose works, four deserve to be singled out—a 1910 *Cahier* entitled *Victor-Marie Comte Hugo*, in which he clearly shows his predilection for a literature of ideas, *Un Nouveau Théologien* (1911), in which he re-states against the "bien pensants" that his Christianity is not opposed to socialism, and the two *Notes* of 1914, which are largely devoted to Bergson, although one is called *Note sur Monsieur Bergson et la philosophie bergsonienne* whilst the other is *Note conjointe sur Monsieur Descartes et la philosophie cartésienne*. Péguy was an early admirer of Bergson, and in the first of the two *Notes* he hails his philosophy as a spiritual liberation, because it delivers us from habit and routine, and as an inspiration for action, because it emphasizes the importance of the present. Whether Bergson himself fully realized the militant way in which his disciple interpreted his thought is an open question, but what is certain is that few other disciples used the philosophy of the master as a theoretical justification for commitment. Péguy's enthusiastic acceptance of the Bergsonian "present", which he describes, "not as the morrow of yesterday", but as "the eve of tomorrow", i.e. as a challenge to action, serves as a reminder that his denunciation of the "modern" world does not imply a romantic longing for the past. Certainly, he was fond of the ancient virtues of honour and fidelity, but he wanted them to become inspiring ideals for the men of his time. His interest in the past was the interest of the man of action who refuses to give up his responsibility to his contemporaries.

The Note conjointe is Péguy's last work, but he did not have time to complete it before his death. As it stands, it contains nearly all the themes he developed throughout his career. Marjorie Villiers calls it "Péguy's summa"[32] in a chapter fittingly entitled "L'engagé est toujours engagé". His hatred of habit, of intellectualism, of the power of money, of an unjust peace, as well as his committed message that "nothing is ever acquired eternally" and that one must "always start afresh" are stressed once again, and for the last time. It is the moving spiritual testament of a man who, having committed himself to the truth as he saw it, is fighting for this truth with his last breath. This last book shows that commitment is difficult but irresistible, demanding but stimulating. Although written in prose, it is the work of a poet whose imaginative vision and loving heart both led him to take the road of "littérature engagée".

NOTES

1. Quoted in English by Alexander Dru in *Péguy*, p. 89.
2. *L'Argent* in *Œuvres en prose* (1909–1914), p. 1045.
3. Ibid., p. 1054.
4. A. Dru, *Péguy*, p. 4.
5. Cf. N. Jussem-Wilson, *Charles Péguy*, pp. 11–12.
6. Cf. Challaye, *Péguy socialiste*, p. 51.
7. *Œuvres en prose* (1898–1908), p. 3.
8. Ibid., p. 193.
9. *Œuvres poétiques complètes*, p. 949.
10. Ibid., p. 1134.
11. *Œuvres en prose* (1898–1908), p. 1430.
12. *Œuvres complètes*, Tome XI, pp. 231 et passim.
13. *Œuvres en prose* (1898–1908), p. 811.
14. N. Jussem-Wilson, *Charles Péguy*, p. 93.
15. *Œuvres en prose* (1909–1914), p. 43.
16. Jean Roussel, *Mesure de Péguy*, p. 92.
17. *Œuvres en prose* (1909–1914), p. 537.
18. Ibid., p. 572.
19. Ibid., p. 576.
20. Ibid., p. 1388.
21. Ibid., p. 729.
22. Quoted by Guillemin in *Temps modernes*, November 1960, p. 541.
23. Ibid., p. 547.
24. Cf. Challaye, *Péguy socialiste*, p. 157.

25. *Œuvres poétiques complètes*, p. 316.
26. Ibid., p. 278.
27. *Œuvres en prose* (1909–1914), p. 1349.
28. *Œuvres poétiques complètes*, p. 237.
29. Ibid., p. 237.
30. Ibid., p. 237.
31. A. Dru, *Péguy*, p. 52.
32. M. Villiers, *Charles Péguy, a study in integrity*, p. 365.

CHAPTER III

ARAGON

IT IS DIFFICULT to speak of Aragon without passion. He arouses either profound admiration or intense dislike. This is partly due to his temperament, as he is hardly a moderate himself and he generally expresses his own likes and dislikes in rather extreme terms, but the main reason is his political allegiance. French Communists tend to regard his achievement with pride and refer to him as "our great comrade Aragon", whereas anti-Communists are irritated by his enthusiasm as well as by the apparent casualness with which he sometimes tackles serious subjects. The situation is further complicated by the fact that Aragon has managed to stir up considerable opposition among his own friends and to inspire genuine respect among many who do not share his political views. The former sometimes object to the highly personal way in which he speaks and writes, and to his irksome habit of stating what he considers to be the truth in an embarrassingly frank manner. "Ce n'est pas un communiste de tout repos" (he is not the kind of Communist who brings you peace and quiet), one critic wrote recently.[a] His non-Communist admirers point to his superb mastery of the French language, and to the lyrical qualities of his great poems. The foreign critic who approaches Aragon is thus faced with a difficult task. His best plan is to start with a very brief reference to the part played by Communism in modern France, since so much of the passion rests on this, and then to let Aragon speak for himself as much as possible.

The special influence exerted by the French Communist Party is probably due to four important factors: first, to its dynamic philosophy, in which many intellectuals see the culmination of rationalist and humanist trends; secondly, to its political programme which, in addition to Marxism, is based on French republican and revolutionary traditions; thirdly, to its record during the Occupation, which earned it the title of "Parti des Fusillés" (the party of those who were shot); and lastly, to the fact that it has increasingly become the party of

[a] It is fair to add that this was intended as praise, and not as criticism.

the organized working class. When it is remembered that writers like Anatole France, Romain Rolland, André Gide, André Malraux, Paul Eluard, Jean-Paul Sartre, have all, at one time or other, flirted with the Communist Party or actually joined it (even if some, like Gide and Malraux, eventually left and slammed the door behind them), it will be appreciated that Communism is an important intellectual factor in modern France and cannot be easily dismissed. Aragon is certainly its most gifted representative, and he has largely contributed to the destruction of many legends about Communists, both the legend of dogmatic infallibility and that of sheer perversion.

There are two major studies of Aragon, both of which are authoritative in a sense, which no critic can ignore. One is *L'Itinéraire d'Aragon* (1961) (Aragon's itinerary),[a] by the Communist Roger Garaudy, the other is *Aragon, le réalisme de l'amour* (1966) (Aragon—the realism of love), by the Catholic Jean Sur.[1] Garaudy is a personal friend of Aragon and his book was almost certainly written with the latter's approval; as for Jean Sur, his study contains marginal comments by Aragon himself, one of which praises the critic's great understanding of his work.[2] Both authors insist on the importance of realism for Aragon, the former stressing the part played by the objective world, and the latter that of subjective feelings which he has explored through love. There is no contradiction between them. Aragon believes that the task of literature is to explain the whole personality of man, and he feels that both history and love are its constituting factors. It is both symbolic and significant that it was through love that he discovered the existence of others and he never tires of recalling that he owes this discovery to his wife, Elsa Triolet. She has helped him to see the world with new eyes, and Jean Sur's formula is a happy one—his is indeed the "realism of love". His path to commitment is the path of a poet who has constantly sought inspiration from reality. Personal lyricism and social responsibility are happily blended in his art, partly thanks to Elsa who has been for him a source of joy and of self-sacrifice, and partly because he always looked upon reality as being a very wide concept, including, in the words of Ernst Fischer, "all the immense

---

[a] Garaudy's book, although it does not go beyond the early fifties (the second volume promised at the end has not yet appeared), is an invaluable source of information, and I am particularly indebted to it.

variety of interactions in which man . . . can be involved",
"the sum of all relationships between subject and object, . . . not
only events, but also subjective experiences".[3] It may seem
surprising that this great realist started his artistic career with
an assault on reality, i.e. by seeking to turn his back on "the
real world" and looking for truth in the realm of "sur-réalité".
We shall see presently that surrealism, which represents
Aragon's initial faith, grew out of the horrors with which
European youth regarded the world which had been
bequeathed to them by the first world war, and was in a sense
a passionate protest against a disgusting reality, a form of
negative realism.[a] What must be pointed out immediately is
that without this initial negative experience, Aragon could not
have become the conscious realist he now is. He forcefully made
the point himself when he stated in 1959,

> I have not always been the man that I am. All my life, I
> have had to learn in order to become the man that I am,
> but this has not made me forget the man that I was, or
> rather, to be more precise, the various men that I was. And
> if between these men and my present self there is a contra-
> diction, if I think I have learnt a thing or two and made some
> progress, when I turn round and look back upon them, I
> am not ashamed of these past men, for they represent the
> various stages of my evolution; they led to me, as it were, and
> I cannot utter the word "I" without them. . . . Truth was
> not revealed to me at my christening, and I learnt it neither
> from my father nor from the class to which my family
> belonged. All I have learned has cost me dearly, what I
> know has been acquired at my own expense. I did not
> arrive at a single certainty except through doubt, anguish,
> sweat and painful experience. Hence, my respect for those
> who do not know, for the seekers, for those who are feeling
> their way and are getting a few knocks in the process.[4]

We are very far indeed from the traditional picture of the
convert, who having found "the truth", regards his past with

---

[a] Cf. Aragon's own statements, "Surrealists did not, in any way, despise
reality", and ". . . reality, for us, was everywhere, even whenever and wher-
ever we seemed to be denying its existence." (*Entretiens avec Francis Crémieux*,
pp. 16 and 22 respectively.)

bitter shame. Seldom has Aragon better expressed the human quality of commitment than in the above words. It is equally vain to regret his surrealist past, as some Communists, roundly rebuked by Roger Garaudy, have done, or to join company with the few critics who bemoan the fact that he gave up the "purely artistic" principles of surrealism in order to become a "narrow propagandist". It is a matter of pride for Aragon that he never ceased to uphold the values from which surrealism drew its inspiration, and he maintains that the perpetual revolt which the movement required was bound to lead to a rejection of its own dogmas. But he never looked upon it as a complete rejection; it was rather a determination to go forward by retaining the basic aims, whilst at the same time finding new ways of achieving them.

THE ASSAULT ON REALITY:
SURREALIST YEARS (1918–31)

Louis Aragon, who was born in 1897, is a little older than the present century, but it is difficult to think of him as an old man. Youthful passion is still the main feature of his personality, and in everything he writes it is always the young poet whom we see, impatient, impulsive and unpredictable, indelibly marked by what he calls "la couleur des années vingt", "the hue of the twenties".[5] In those days, he was a fiery young man, associated at first with Dadaism, and then with surrealism, eager to express his rebellion against hypocrisy and cynicism. The "Mouvement Dada", founded in 1916 by Tristan Tzara, represented an uncompromising opposition to everything and preached absolute revolt. It found enthusiastic followers among a number of talented young writers who were impatient with their elders' failure to provide them with a sense of purpose. They launched a magazine whose prime object was to "kill" literature, though they defiantly called it *Littérature*. Soon, they went beyond the negative revolt of Dadaism and founded the surrealist school. In their opinion, it was not enough to substitute one set of values for another, or one type of "literature" for a different one; what was needed was the exploration of a new reality which they believed to be endowed with a higher truth than the superficial one hitherto described by conventional art. "Surrealism," Aragon was to write later, "was a desperate attempt to build anew." For this new reality, an entirely different method of writing was required—what came to be known as "l'écriture automatique", automatic writing. It was thought that the only way the poet could avoid being tricked by the ready-made formulae of his age was to commit to paper all the images and ideas suggested by his sub-conscious mind. In their eagerness to give up the rotten world in which they lived, the "angry young men" of those days extended their wrath to the world as a whole. The new poetic medium would no longer describe the world, but free us from it, and the great slogan was "Partir". There was no cowardice in their escapism, but a burning desire to draw upon purer and nobler experiences. As they could not hope to find them in the real world around them, they retreated into a dream world of their own. Aragon's defence, written some thirty years later, is that they had no choice:

> What could we find apart from dreams
> To hurl against Triumphant Falsehood
> We who had nothing to gaze upon
> But Hypocrisy and Treachery[a]

The new magazine *Littérature* published works by André Gide, Paul Valéry and others. It also contained Aragon's first poems, later gathered under the title *Feu de joie* (Bonfire). One line in particular was symptomatic of his desire, even then, to destroy in order to rebuild, and it has remained his life-long purpose throughout numberless vicissitudes and "agonizing reappraisals":

> Down with the world a finer one I build[b]

In an essay which is devoted to Aragon as a committed writer, there is no need to dwell at great length on the other works he produced in his Dadaist and surrealist youth, although it must be stressed once against that an exhaustive study cannot possibly ignore them.[c] Special mention must be made, however, of his novel, *Le Paysan de Paris* (The peasant from Paris) (1926).

[a] *Le Roman inachevé*, p. 46.
> Et qu'opposer sinon nos songes
> Aux pas triomphants du mensonge
> Nous qui n'avions pour horizon
> Qu'hypocrisie et trahison

[b] Le monde à bas je le bâtis plus beau

[c] It is significant that Garaudy devotes two thirds of his book to this period.

Surrealists tended to despise prose and the novel and to condemn descriptions of real places as incompatible with automatic writing. It was therefore a clear sign of Aragon's independence that he decided to shock his friends and publish a second novel (he had already written one in 1921, entitled *Anicet*), based, not on an imaginary city, but on the Paris which he loved so much, and which he never ceased to love. He revealed many unknown aspects of the capital, and although his style is in the best surrealist manner—lyrical, poetic and spontaneous—the source of his inspiration is thoroughly realistic. The distinctive qualities of his future poetry are already there, for he lets his imagination run wild, whilst keeping his feet firmly planted on the ground. The book contains many other indications of the themes which he later developed and which helped him to become a committed writer, such as his passion for "la lumière moderne de l'insolite"[6] ("the modern light of the unusual"), his belief that poetry is a way of life, ("je mène une vie poétique")[7] ("I lead a poetic life"), his conviction, even before meeting Elsa, that love is the highest individual passion, and his awareness of the limitations of philosophical idealism.[a] One can regard the book as the starting-point of Aragon's subsequent evolution.[b]

DEEP INVOLVEMENT IN REALITY: "LE MONDE RÉEL"

Originally, the Surrealist Movement had no definite politics, but it soon gave its support to the newly-formed French Communist Party. The latter seemed to embody the radical departure from convention which surrealists were fighting for, and it led the attack on the hated bourgeoisie. So, in addition to the Marquis de Sade and Freud, Marx and Lenin were frequently invoked in surrealist circles, terms such as "the class struggle" and "revolution" (particularly "permanent revolution") were eagerly seized upon, and the young poets proclaimed themselves the allies of the proletariat. Whether they really understood the mood of the proletariat, its real aims or the full implications of working-class politics is doubtful, but they were willing to learn. They did not always like what

[a] Garaudy describes the book as "an attempt to overcome idealism by using the methods of idealism itself" (p. 138).

[b] Georges Raillard makes the same point in *Aragon*, p. 44.

they learnt. For example, shortly after the "Congress of Tours", [a] Aragon and his friend André Breton visited the offices of the new party, but they were put off by the vulgarity of the official they met. Aragon was so shocked that, in his own words, he "had no desire to stay" and his actual joining was "delayed by six years". [8] The incident is interesting because it illustrates the difficulties an intellectual encounters when he wants to join a working-class movement. If the workers do not immediately come up to expectation, if their attitude or conversation is at first disappointing, the hesitant intellectual is inclined to be repelled by the movement itself. This happens particularly to sensitive poets, with their love for the absolute. In the ninth poem of *Les Yeux et la Mémoire* (Eyes and Memory), Aragon describes how he finally overcame all these obstacles, and although he refers to his progress towards Communism, his account is an accurate description of the path towards commitment in general. The poet stresses that the pressure of "engagement" is irresistible,

> Nothing can prevent . . .
> The march towards the sea . . . [b]

The obstacles, however, are enormous: the old Adam stands in the way—

> All that you carried with you from the depth of ages [c]

so does the passion for absolute revolt—

> This spirit of revolt which nothing can satisfy [d]

and so, above all, does individualism—

> (You) fondly imagined you could break loose by yourself [e]

---

[a] In 1920, the French Socialist Party met at Tours for its 18th Congress, and a majority decided to break away and join the Communist International. The French Communist Party was born.

[b] Rien ne peut arrêter . . .
　　　Cette marche à la mer . . .

[c] Tout ce que tu portais en toi du fond des âges

[d] Cet esprit de révolte à qui rien ne suffit

[e] (Tu) t'imaginais briser toi-même tes amarres

In the end, the path towards commitment is taken in spite of everything—

> You see I did however take to the big road[a]

for it is inescapable—

> Nothing can stop you once the dawn has broken[b]

This description could apply equally to Péguy and Sartre: both have had to fight old ideas and prejudices before they embraced commitment, both succeeded only by transcending their individualism, and both considered their final step as a culmination, an apotheosis, and would have endorsed Aragon's exclamation,

> In the end it is the sea the sea to which we must go[c]

Although Aragon joined the Communist Party in 1927, he did not immediately break with the surrealist group. The poems which he wrote between 1927 and 1929, gathered under the title *La Grande Gaité* (Great Fun), show that his growing awareness of the "real world" had not yet killed his surrealist beliefs. He had, in fact, divided his life into two separate compartments, political and poetic, and he was not yet regarding his commitment as an integral part of his whole self. The *Traité du style* (Treatise on Style), published in 1928, displays the same internal struggle. On the one hand, Aragon seems to delight in shocking the bourgeois by attacking coarsely and recklessly every institution, social and literary, yet, on the other, he is already aware that style is not just an artistic device but is the way of expressing one's philosophy of life. This latter feature leads him to tackle the fundamental problems of human life, and he seems to oscillate between despair and hope. The struggle for complete commitment, which is a struggle about the real meaning of existence, is seen here in its most pathetic and most human form. Twenty years before Camus and Sartre, Aragon denounces the "absurdity" of the world and he even uses the Sartrian term "nausea" in order to describe what an individual feels when he first realizes that he has only one life

[a] Vois-tu j'ai tout de même pris la grande route
[b] Rien ne t'arrête plus quand s'en lève le jour (op. cit., pp. 74–76.)
[c] C'est à la mer enfin la mer qu'il faut qu'on aille

to lead, and no other, and that "life is a fact, and as such unquestionable".[9]

However, just as Sartre, after him, went beyond "nausea" and discovered human solidarity, Aragon, in entirely different circumstances, made the same discovery. In the *Traité du style* he had examined and rejected suicide as a possible solution, but few people knew that he had himself attempted to commit suicide whilst he was staying in Venice. Two months later, he met Elsa Triolet, a Russian girl living in Paris, whose brother-in-law[a] was the poet Mayakovsky. The effect she had on Aragon was considerable, and when he dedicated his first realistic novel to her, he remarked that without Elsa he would have kept quiet, ". . . je me serais tu". Did he mean, as one of his friends hinted, "je me serais tué" (. . . I would have killed myself)? This is not impossible. Perhaps, however, one should not exaggerate Elsa's influence out of all proportion for, as Jean Sur reminds us, when she entered Aragon's life, the latter was not so deeply sunk in despair and ignorance as he sometimes suggests in his verse. The truth is that she came at the right moment, just when Aragon needed a real woman to love, and, what is more, a sensitive and brave woman who could strengthen his resolve to get out of himself and look at the world of other men. It is probably not unfair to point out here that Aragon occasionally forgets that Elsa's remarkable and unique qualities, which he stresses in line after line, hardly entitle him to generalize from his own experience. Be that as it may, it was thanks to Elsa's support and encouragement that the surrealist became a fully-fledged realist, and that the rebel turned into a revolutionary—i.e., to use his own expression, into a man who destroys in order to rebuild. One of the most important steps he took with his wife was a visit to the Soviet Union in 1930. What he saw there filled him with enthusiasm. Until then, his attachment to Communism had been chiefly an emotional impulse, now he was able to watch a whole people at work. In 1930, the "Stalin personality cult" had not yet begun to rear its ugly head, and the country was busily engaged in fulfilling the first Five-Year Plan, courageously accepting many hardships and sacrifices. At least, so it seemed to Aragon, and the poet in him was thrilled. He needed this concrete

[a] Actually, Lili Brik, Elsa's sister, was never legally married to Mayakovsky.

experience in order to make his commitment complete. When he returned to France, he was "no longer the same man".[10] A break with the surrealists, who were still intent on keeping literature and politics apart, became inevitable. It was precipitated by an incident known as "l'Affaire Aragon". In 1932, the poet was found guilty of "anarchist propaganda" and of "demoralizing the army and the nation" in his poem *Front Rouge* (Red Front). André Breton protested against the accusation on the grounds that poetry is outside the law, but Aragon publicly rejected this defence and proudly stated that he was fully aware of the social significance of his poem. What divided him from Breton and his former friends was nothing less than the issue of the committed character of literature, and compromise between them was out of the question. The committed writer had already decided to go beyond the stage of public utterances and manifestoes, and to put his craft ("son métier"), "the inmost part of his craft",[11] at the service of his cause. He threw himself body and soul into the political arena, and as a reaction against his former verse, he wrote little or no poetry until 1939.[a] To many people it looked as if he had become a "soldier of the Revolution", fulfilling his duty "on the cultural front", and as if his "littérature engagée" contained much more "engagement" than literature proper. The fact that he became an ordinary reporter for the Communist daily *L'Humanité*, coupled with his editorship of the monthly magazine *Commune*, reinforced this interpretation. So did the immoderate language which he used when it came to praising everything Soviet, including the famous purges of 1937–38. With his usual passion "for the absolute", he never stopped at half-measures, and although his sincerity was obvious, the same cannot be said for his political judgement. But he was not alone in those days in accepting uncritically all that was done in Russia, the good as well as the bad.[b]

However, journalism and propaganda were only one aspect of his activity, and he probably needed such an apprenticeship in order to stifle in him the ever-powerful temptation to flee from reality. He knew, theoretically, that the greatest poetic

---

[a] A notable exception was *Hourra l'Oural*, dedicated to the "new world" of Communism.

[b] We shall see later how strongly he has condemned this aspect of his own past.

dreams spring from reality, but his own temperament and background were such that theory was not enough to discipline his imagination. The chief result of his new approach was a series of novels to which he gave the general title of "Le Monde réel". In writing them, he combined his personal recollections and his social experience, drawing upon many events of his own childhood and youth, and transposing social and political scenes which he had directly witnessed. Although he intended his novels to have a political significance, his main concern was with private individuals. The clue to his approach is provided by what he says in the third novel of the series, *Les Voyageurs de l'impériale*, translated into English under the title of *Passengers of Destiny*.[a] He breaks through his narrative (a favourite device of his) in order to remark that private life may appear to follow its own course, "without any relation to public affairs, to the history of the world", but that, in fact, it is "inscribed in this history, it derives from it its essential features".[12] Jean Sur was so struck by Aragon's ability to disclose the interconnections between "the secrets of souls and great historical movements" that he called him "the Saint Augustine of Communism".[b]

The first novel, *Les Cloches de Bâle* (The Bells of Basel),[c] deals with the position of women in bourgeois society. In the first part, *Diane*, the central character belongs to Parisian high society. Her husband is a financial crook, and she eventually leaves him to become the mistress of a rich industrialist. The author's obvious intention was to portray the capitalist world as one in which there can be no genuine love. This was necessary before he could show the contrast which, in his view, socialism affords. How he intended to carry out this purpose

[a] This is not a very good title, as it misses Aragon's metaphor. The "impériale" is the upper deck of a bus, and the author's intention was to compare those who remain aloof from public life with those who travel on the upper deck—both miss what goes on in the world below.

[b] op. cit., p. 116. Was it quite fair to add that Saint Augustine was the source of many "heresies"? Surely, the idea of a "correspondence" between history and "private souls" is not heretical to Marxism, though it may have been to those primitive Marxists who once prompted Marx to exclaim, "Personally, I am not a Marxist".

[c] An allusion to the message of peace carried by the bells of Basel, as the Socialist International met in Congress in 1912 and proclaimed that international proletarian unity would be able to prevent the outbreak of war.

when he began his novel is not known because he entirely
revised his plans after reading the first part to his wife. She was
not very impressed with it and asked him the simple question,
"For whom are you writing this? Whom will it help?" ("For
whom do you write?" is, of course, one of the basic questions
which are at the root of commitment. Even before Sartre made
it famous in *What is Literature?*, Aragon's magazine *Commune* had
made it the object of a wide "enquête" among contemporary
writers. It is interesting to note, in passing, that the Dadaist
Littérature had used the other Sartrian question, "Why do you
write?" for the same purpose.) Aragon's answer to Elsa is
embodied in the second part of the book, *Catherine*. Catherine
Simonidzé, a Russian exile living in Paris, was intended to
illustrate the social phenomenon described by Marx when he
spoke of a small fraction of the bourgeoisie "going over" to the
proletariat. She was not an entirely fictitious character, her
model in real life being the Georgian woman Aragon knew as a
child and from whom he received, when he was only twelve, a
book by Gorky. Catherine helps the author to focus attention on
the "woman question". Like Diane before her, she claims the
right to sexual freedom, but for her it is a conscious way of asserting her equality with men. This leads her to hope that a social
revolution will come about and put things right. When she falls
in love with Victor, a socialist taxi-driver, she is almost ready
to commit herself to the revolutionary cause, but her upbringing
stands in the way, and there is no "happy ending" for her.
The final pages of the book take us to the Congress of the
Socialist International at Basel, and we hear the militant
working-class leader Clara Zetkin predict that socialism alone
will bring peace and the emancipation of women. The book
ends on this socialist vision of the future, and Aragon exclaims:

> At this stage, the new romance begins . . . For the first time
> in history, there is now room for true love. Love which is not
> sullied . . . by the sordid stories of dresses and kisses, by the
> financial domination of man over woman, or woman over
> man. The woman of modern times is born, and it is of her
> that I sing.
> It is of her that I shall sing.[13]

Les Cloches de Bâle is badly constructed, as there are no real
connections between its various parts. The pages devoted to

Clara have all the appearance of a contrived moral which is meant to give the novel a socialist message. No attempt is made to describe her own evolution, and, in the main, Aragon's aim (to describe how a few members of the bourgeois class embrace the cause of the workers) is not fulfilled. He was well aware of these faults, and he later admitted that he was just beginning to learn the difficult art of writing realistic fiction. At the end of the book, he addresses the reader and grants that the construction of his novel is poor. His self-defence is hardly satisfactory, for he claims that the world is also badly constructed and that it is necessary to change both!

His next novel, *Les Beaux Quartiers* (Residential Areas), shows a great improvement. It describes the divergent paths of two brothers, Edmond and Armand Barbentane, who both try to give meaning to their lives and rebel against their father, a typical Third Republic politician, and against the stifling atmosphere of their provincial milieu. Edmond is an egotist, and he seeks only personal happiness. He succeeds in making a fortune in the world of Big Business, but the price he has to pay is moral degradation. Armand, on the other hand, is full of youthful idealism. After trying a number of possible solutions, including religion and poetry, he finally gives up his class, and becomes an ordinary worker and a socialist. He also discovers France, his own nation, after hearing a speech by Jaurès in which the socialist leader claims that the workers and peasants are the true patriots, rather than those who exploit the motherland. The real France, Armand realizes, is not in the "beaux quartiers", but among the common people. Aragon made no mystery of the fact that with this "national moral" he was carrying out the Party line as it had just been defined by Maurice Thorez when he stressed the bonds between patriotism and the struggle of the working class. The novel is not a particularly good illustration of this line, as it fails to show convincingly why Armand had to go to work in a factory in order to become a good Frenchman. On the other hand, it depicts fairly well the anti-national character of high finance. As a socialist novel, it is far more successful, particularly in its description of the dual personality of those who have to live in a society torn by class contradictions.[a] The industrialist Quesnel,

---

[a] The idea of "dual personality" reappears in *La mise à mort* (see below, pp. 117–18).

without in the least ceasing to be a "grand bourgeois", con-
fesses that "we live at a historical time which will probably be
characterized as the era of dual personalities".[14]

In *Les Voyageurs de l'impériale*, completed just before the
second world war, the theme is the need for commitment. Once
again, it is with the help of a negative character that the author
makes his point. Pierre Mercadier, one of Aragon's most
tragical figures,[a] refuses commitment in the name of freedom,
thus foreshadowing the stand taken by the Sartrian character
Mathieu Delarue, in the novel *Les Chemins de la liberté*. Both of
them utterly fail in their attempt to become free through their
refusal of commitment, but Mercadier also fails to reconcile
dream and reality in his life. He admires the eighteenth-century
financier John Law because he had not remained content with
watching life from the upper deck of a bus, yet he himself
withdraws from the real world and his only ambition is to write
a biography of Law. Later, he leaves his wife and family in
order to seek adventures in love and travel. Gambling provides
him with temporary relief, and in a few bitter pages, packed
with realism and emotion, Aragon denounces the casinos as
the symbol of a society whose god is Money:

> Money is always based on plunder. Here, at last,
> lies were vanishing in the law of gambling.[15]

In spite of all his efforts, Mercadier ends up alone, ". . . without any friends, without any purpose."[16] It is his son Pascal who,
at the end of the book, draws the obvious moral that refusal to face
facts leads to disaster, both personal and social, and he blames
his father's generation for having made war possible thanks to
"their superb contempt for politics".[17] The novel contains two
other lessons. One, illustrated by the fate of Mercadier, is that
complete selfishness destroys the possibility of love, and the other
is given by the painter Blaise d'Ambérieux when he asserts that
art is one way of contributing to the future happiness of mankind,
provided it aims at a truthful portrayal of reality.

Aurélien, the fourth novel of the series,[b] was entirely written

---

[a] His model in real life was Aragon's grandfather (cf. *Entretiens avec
Francis Crémieux*, p. 95).

[b] For the significance of this novel, cf. Aragon, *J'abats mon jeu*, pp. 144–46,
and *Entretiens avec F. Crémieux*, pp. 48–49 and pp. 96–97; see also pp. 203–5
of this essay.

during the war, but only saw the light of day in 1945. Its central theme is love, and a number of Aragon's friends, including some narrow-minded Soviet critics, were shocked at the thought that he had found nothing better to do in those years. He could have replied, as he said later, that in those years he had "done and written other things as well", but he preferred to despise such attacks. The story of Aurélien Leurtillois begins at the end of the first world war, and finishes in 1940, as the German armies are entering France. He proves himself unable to win the love of Bérénice, a woman who had "a passion for the absolute", because his whole way of life betrays the idleness and selfishness of his class. Aurélien's tragedy is that his "unworthiness before life" made him "unworthy before love".[18]

The last novel belonging to the "Monde réel" series, *Les Communistes*, appeared after the war. It was intended to be the epic of the French people's struggle against the Nazis and was to cover the whole period from 1939 to 1945. Only the first section (in six volumes) has appeared so far, and it ends in June 1940. Why Aragon never completed the work—he even hinted that he probably never would—is a matter of conjecture, and there are no doubt many reasons to account for it. One of them was suggested by the author in his introduction to a book of selected extracts from Elsa Triolet.[19] He recalled the discussion which went on after the 20th Congress of the C.P.S.U. about the real meaning of "socialist realism". Elsa Triolet's contribution to the discussion was a short novel called *Le Monument* in which she described the problems facing an artist in one of the new people's democracies of Eastern Europe. According to Aragon, the reception of the novel confirmed its central thesis, which was that the progressive writer has to contend with the hostility of open foes as well as with the incomprehension of some of his friends. This, he claimed, is why he is reluctant to complete a novel which he intended as a "monument" to his cause:

Why do you think that I cannot, that I find it impossible to write the sequel to *Les Communistes*? Do you think it is because I have changed, because I repudiate *anything whatsoever* (Aragon's italics) of what was my passion and my life?[20]

Another reason for the unfinished character of *Les Communistes* is probably Aragon's awareness of the special difficulties of socialist realism at the present time. In *La Mise à mort* (p. 404), he suggests that so long as certain historical figures are considered "positive heroes" one day and "negative" characters the next, it is very hard to write realistic fiction. If I understand him aright, he is hinting, among others things, at his unwillingness to finish a novel which deals with the war years before the whole truth is known about the period.

As it stands, *Les Communistes* is the climax of "Le Monde réel". Against the background of the German-Soviet pact of 1939, the "phoney war", Dunkirk, the German invasion and the beginnings of the Resistance Movement, Aragon tells the story of a large number of characters, many of whom had appeared in previous novels. Among the new ones, the two who stand out are Cécile Wisner, who is married to a pro-Fascist industrialist, and Jean de Moncey, a young lad whose evolution recalls that of Armand Barbentane. Their love story is one of the main themes of the book. So is their slow, very slow, progress towards what Aragon calls the "light", although neither of them is a Communist or becomes a conscious Marxist at the end of the novel. The title *Les Communistes* is perhaps misleading, for the book is in no way a history of the French Communist Party during the second world war. What it is meant to convey is that the Communists' policy expressed in a systematic way the feelings and interests of France's citizens, workers, peasants, middle classes, and even some big industrialists, who were determined to hold back the invaders. It is true that Aragon takes Communist policy at its face value and never questions its motives, but his account of the situation is historically accurate. It was only the ruling clique, the notorious "deux cents familles" [a] who were responsible for the sell-out to Hitler. They are shown by the novelist as having displayed no interest in fighting the Germans because they were expecting them as "saviours". Yet, even among the rulers, Aragon shows that there were noticeable differences—some were actually working for a German victory, whilst others were merely weak, dreading their own people as much as the enemy at the gate. The workers, on the other hand, wanted to fight. Not all of them

[a] The expression was coined by Daladier and refers to French Big Business, "The two hundred families" which rule France.

were clear about the issues involved, some were even hopelessly confused (in the first volume, the confusion in Communist ranks after the signature of the Hitler-Stalin pact is stressed rather than blurred), but instinctively they wanted France to remain free. French women, in particular, rose to the occasion, and realised that in total war there is no difference between soldiers and civilians, between men and women. Aragon revealed later that he had intended his title, *Les Communistes*, to be read in the feminine, as his prime object was to describe the courage of Frenchwomen, of Communist women in particular, in organising the Resistance Movement.

The book was strongly criticized in some quarters as lacking in objectivity. As it appeared when the cold war was at its height, such a reaction was understandable. If by lack of objectivity, one means that the author does not hide his Communist sympathies, then indeed he must plead guilty. His novel is an obvious "defence and illustration" of the Communist version of what happened in 1939–40. But it is to his credit that his political bias is never forced on the reader, and moreover, that he makes an honest attempt to depict truthfully a large number of people who do not share his views, including some members of the Extreme Right. In an impassioned speech, made a few years later, he reminded his critics of all the non-Communist characters in his novel who are presented objectively and sympathetically, and he stressed that the polemical aspect of a realistic work of art does not derive from the description of one's enemies as "monsters or caricatures", but from "the general interpretation of the times" which is suggested by the artist.[21]

The fact that the book appeared at the height of the cold war, and tended therefore to be regarded as a political rather than a literary event, may also account for the uncritical way in which Communists praised it in France. They hailed it as the most accomplished example to date of the historical novel and were blind to its obvious aesthetic faults, such as lack of organic unity, extreme complexity of some of the situations, and unnecessarily long descriptions of military battles. In England, however, it is interesting to note that the Marxist *Modern Quarterly* published a much more subtle analysis under the pen of Roy Pascal. After praising the ideological content of the book, understandably enough, the author went on to say,

But I finished this six-volume novel with a sense of dissatisfaction ... Valuable as a social picture, the novel is aesthetically faulty. For instance, the last two volumes give an account of the military campaign which is packed full of interest ... But the different situations and personal attitudes are in essence repetitive, and the complex movement of troops very confusing to the reader. . . . The author simplifies like a cartoonist, and however intelligent his point of view is, it appears as a shrewd comment rather than an artistic creation. . . . I feel that Aragon has rushed too quickly to put a mass of experience into his novel, without taking the time to digest it all and reproduce it in a more concentrated form.[22]

With these criticisms, particularly the first one, I find myself in complete agreement. Military battles have always had a special fascination for Aragon, as well as military life in general. In his latest novel, there is a significant allusion to this when the hero's wife expresses her amazement at her husband's incongruous interest in the Army.[23] There is little doubt, in my mind, that we have here an echo of an actual remark made by Elsa to Aragon himself. With regard to the large number of lengthy digressions which Professor Pascal rightly criticizes in *Les Communistes*, they unfortunately occur throughout the whole series of the *Monde réel*. Although they often achieve the author's declared aim of helping us to see events and characters in perspective, they also tend to distract our attention and to irritate us. In *La Mise à mort*, however, Aragon's 1965 novel, the digressions are much more readily accepted by the reader, probably because the novel is itself a series of digressions intended to reveal different aspects of a man's personality. Such a structure is particularly suited to the poetic temperament of Aragon, and one is reminded of his own admission that he finds himself less at home in the novel than his wife Elsa Triolet, because he can seldom resist the temptation of letting his imagination run wild and unchecked.

A CONCRETE REALITY:
THE NATION

It was the second world war which re-kindled Aragon's poetic flame and gave him an opportunity of expressing his militant patriotism. His love for France strikingly recalls Péguy's feelings, for both poets are attached to the soil of their country and to its traditions. The poems which Aragon wrote from 1939 to 1945 had no other ambition than to contribute to the fight of Free France against the Germans. The first book to appear was *Le Crève-Cœur* (Heartbreak), in which the poet expresses his sorrow at being separated from Elsa and his anger at the betrayal of his country. Of this book, he was to say later,

> I believe that if I had not written these poems, if I had not ... refused to give up, in dread of the police, my sense of human dignity, I would not, no indeed, I would not have survived.[24]

One of the finest poems is *Les Lilas et les roses* (The lilacs and the roses) where he contrasts the enthusiasm of May 1940, when French troops entered Belgium and were

> Smothered in lilac by a drunken folk[a]

with the gloom of June in the same year, when the retreating soldiers found "roses all along the way",

> Flowers that gave the lie to soldiers passing
> On wings of fear . . .[b]

Soon after, in *Les Yeux d'Elsa* (Elsa's Eyes), he sang of his two loves, his wife and his country. In his introduction, he took up the famous line of Virgil, "Arma virumque cano" (I sing of arms and man), in order to state the militant character of literature in the new conditions which had been created in France, and he asserted his right to speak of love "in the midst of tragedy" as this was an act of faith and hope. The poem appeared legally, as the Vichy censors failed to detect its

[a] Entourés de lilas par un peuple grisé
[b] Les roses tout le long du chemin parcouru
   Le démenti des fleurs au vent de la panique
   Aux soldats qui passaient sur l'aile de la peur

All the English translations from Aragon's war poems are taken, unless otherwise stated, from *Aragon, poet of Resurgent France* (Pilot Press 1946), where the reader will find interesting articles together with some of Aragon's poems translated by great English poets, such as Louis MacNeice and Stephen Spender.

revolutionary character, but Aragon's subsequent work had to be published by the underground press or in neutral Switzerland.

In *Le Musée Grévin* (the "Musée Grévin" is the French equivalent to our Madam Tussaud's), he used satire to attack the Pétain regime, and he also dedicated a moving poem to the Auschwitz martyrs. This is how he greeted them:

> I salute you Marys of France of a hundred faces[a]

giving a new meaning to the old Catholic invocation "Hail Mary" (in French "Je vous salue, Marie"). He concluded with a salute to the whole of France,

> I salute you my France snatched from the ghosts
>
> . . . .
>
> I salute you my France with eyes of the turtle-dove[b]

In many other poems, *Brocéliande* (1942) and *En français dans le texte* (1943),[c] Aragon continued his powerful attack on the occupiers and their French lackeys. He was now eagerly read by underground fighters of all parties, and when Gilbert Dru, a Catholic, was arrested by the Gestapo, a copy of *Brocéliande* was found in his pocket. This enthusiasm on the part of a Christian was not due to the fact that Aragon had played down his irreligious philosophy, but rather to the special kind of brotherhood which existed among the underground fighters. There was no unsavoury ideological compromise among them, for the bonds which united them were those of patriotism.

---

[a] Je vous salue Maries de France aux cent visages
[b] Je vous salue ma France arrachée aux fantômes

. . . .

Je vous salue ma France aux yeux de tourterelle

Aragon's own comment on this line is that it was a sign of great hope on his part to endow France's eyes with the changing colour of a turtle-dove's eyes, as it implied his belief that the look of humiliation would soon make way for the look of victory—an interesting illustration of the significance of poetic metaphors in committed poetry.

[c] The title literally means "In French in the text", the implication being that Aragon was writing real French because he was defending the motherland's independence, whereas official Vichy propaganda was using the French language against the real interests of France.

People who can easily sacrifice their own principles are opportunists of the worst kind; what was established in the ranks of the Resistance Movement was something far greater—it was the acceptance by all sides of the humanity of their partners, and it carried with it the will not to allow differences to stand in the way of co-operation for a common cause.

Lastly, Aragon published *La Diane française* (French Reveille), in which he sang of the patriots' coming victory. It contains some of his best known poems, such as *La Rose et le réséda* (The rose and the mignonette), dedicated to Catholics and Communists, and already quoted; *Il n'y a pas d'amour heureux* (There is no such thing as a happy love), in which he recalls all the suffering that must be endured in order to enjoy a few moments' happiness,

All the sobs which are needed for the tune of a guitar [a]

ending with the following words, addressed to Elsa,

> There is no such thing as a happy love
> Yet such is our mutual love [b]

Ballade de celui qui chanta dans les supplices (Ballad of one who sang at the stake), written in memory of his comrade Politzer, shot by the Nazis for refusing to betray his friends,

> "If it had to be done all over
> I would take this road again"
> The voice that sang tomorrow's song
> Rose from the iron chains [c]

Paris, a hymn celebrating the liberation of the capital by its own children,

[a] Ce qu'il faut de sanglots pour un air de guitare
[b] Il n'y a pas d'amour heureux
Mais c'est notre amour à tous deux (My translation.)
[c] Et s'il était à refaire
Je referais ce chemin
Une voix monte des fers
Et parle des lendemains

This is an allusion to Politzer's last words, "Je vais préparer des lendemains qui chantent." (I am going to prepare singing tomorrows.)

Paris Paris of herself liberated[a]

and finally, the poem *Du poète à son parti* (From the poet to his party), where he claims that it was Communism which gave him back "le sens de l'épopée" (the sense of the epic) and "les couleurs de la France" (the colours of France).

Aragon does not separate his Communism from his patriotism, and in 1958 he stated that he could never have written his novel *La Semaine sainte* (Holy Week), a book filled throughout with love for France, if he had not been a Communist. He also stressed that, although the background of his story was the national tragedy of 1815, he had drawn upon his 1940 experience. What he describes are the feelings of Louis XVIII's officers during the fateful Easter week when the king had to leave France because of Napoleon's sudden return. In particular, the artist Théodore Géricault finds his whole conception of painting affected by the few days he spends as a musketeer in the royal household. He accidentally overhears popular leaders, as they are secretly assembled at Poix to decide whether they should support Napoleon or the king. As he himself had no time for either, and had joined "the gouty monarch" for purely private reasons, he is amazed to find that the people on whom he is eavesdropping tackle the issue very seriously; they come to the conclusion that they must choose the lesser of two evils and side with the emperor, for he is, after all, the heir of the French Revolution, whereas the monarchy is willing to accept the help of foreign bayonets in orders to reinstate its dominion in France. If Aragon had presented Géricault after that meeting as one suddenly visited by grace and eager to become a democrat, we might justifiably dismiss him as a talented propagandist who oversimplifies reality. But there is nothing so crude as that in the novel: Géricault remains a king's officer, with less conviction than ever, but he has discovered the existence of *others*. This forces him to reassess his approach to art and to reflect on the need to portray real human beings. Théodore, however, is only one of the characters. The general message of the novel is that each historical period compels men to make a choice. If they are moved by a high conception of honour (patriotism, for example), their choice is likely to be "à la hauteur de l'histoire", 'worthy of history'. It

[a] Paris Paris soi-même libéré.

has been truly said of *La Semaine sainte* that, in dealing with the
past it is basically directed towards the future. [a] It is the work of
a committed writer who has himself taken sides in the issues of his
age, and is working, according to his lights, for the future.
French critics were almost unanimous in their praise of the
novel, and Emile Henriot, a member of the French Academy,
unlikely to be biased in favour of Aragon, hailed it as the finest
one to have been written in the last twenty years. To those who
thought they could make political capital out of the fact that
the characters were all Royalist officers, and who believed that
the author was giving up socialist realism because he was
dealing with the past, Aragon replied in the following terms:

> The critics who have drawn attention to those aspects of the
> book which they consider *surprising* on the part of a Com-
> munist have, in nearly every case, drawn attention to an
> aspect which constitutes in fact an issue of principle for
> Communists, and which contradicts, in a *surprising* way
> their own erroneous ideas of Communism. (Aragon's
> emphasis.) [25]

He went on to say that he had not thrown socialist realism
overboard, but had developed the method and extended it.
In his view, it is by no means compulsory to confine oneself to
contemporary subjects—Marxism is a philosophy of history,
and it claims that it is able to explain the past as well as the
present. [b]

TAKING STOCK:
LOOKING BACK ON REALITY

In the last few years, Aragon's work has tended to become
increasingly autobiographical and personal. The public man
has gradually made way for the private individual, with his
sorrows and his hopes. The explanation that this approach is to
be expected from an old man may be partly true, but the poet's
main purpose seems to be an anticipated repudiation of the
edifying picture that well-meaning friends might be tempted
to draw of him, particularly after his death. Commitment, he

[a] "C'est une œuvre où l'avenir a plus de place que le passé" (François
Nourissier, quoted in *J'abats mon jeu*, p. 46).
[b] Cf. p. 203 for a further discussion of this point.

protests, has not reduced him to being the impersonal spokes-
man of a cause; although he feels himself part of

> . . . That majestic and sad herd of men[a]

he is not a colourless actor in the drama of life; there is something else behind his mask,

> Something without which I would be but a stone amidst the
> stones[b]

there is Elsa, his "tragedy", and his "inner theatre".

(i) *A political autobiography: 'Les Yeux et la mémoire'*

The circumstances which gave birth to *Les Yeux et la mémoire*
in 1954 have already been mentioned in Chapter I.[c] This is the
first book published by Aragon which consists of a series of
poems around a central theme—in this case, the author's
political philosophy and his committed struggles. Significantly,
it is with an assertion that life is worth living that he starts,
and after listing all "the miseries that flesh is heir to", he concludes an early poem with the following line,

> In spite of everything I shall say that this life was beautiful[d]

Aragon's optimism, like Péguy's, is not achieved by denying
tragedy but by transcending it, and although in subsequent
books the accent is definitely on tragedy, the difference is only
one of emphasis. If *Les Yeux et la mémoire* strikes a more confident
note than the poems and novels which followed it, it is probably
because it was written before the 20th Congress of the C.P.S.U.,
an event which came as a painful shock to all Communists,
and to Aragon in particular. Yet, already in 1954, he was
waging the fight against narrow-mindedness in his own ranks.
To the rigid Marxists who asked contemptuously whether
poetry should sing of love and the beauty of landscapes instead
of glorifying social struggles, the poet replied that his dreams
were not an escape from action, but a preparation for action:

[a] *Elsa*, p. 53. . . . Ce troupeau grandiose et triste des hommes
[b] *Ibid*, p. 54. Autre chose sans quoi je ne serais que pierre parmi les pierres
[c] See above, p. 23.
[d] *Elsa*, p. 21. Je dirai malgré tout que cette vie fut belle

Is it really a crime

To dream of happiness whilst in the lion's mouth
And to say at midnight that the lark is near
My friends my friends to think that it should be you
Who make such an accusation[a]

He felt particularly entitled to demand the "right to dream" as he had never tried to run away from the "hell" where his fellow men toil and suffer. The sixth poem is in fact called *L'enfer* (Hell), and in lines which are reminiscent of Péguy, he rejects Pushkin's idea that habit is a gift from heaven, a substitute for happiness:

Alexander Sergueievich oh pessimist
Let me never find happiness at that price
Happiness born from habit is too sad a happiness
I prefer the hell where man burns and screams[b]

It is this profound feeling of sympathy for the suffering of others which turned Aragon into a committed writer. He embraced Communism because it seemed to him to be the modern embodiment of human brotherhood:

Hail to thee my Party which denied misery
And showed man as a brother to his brothers in arms[c]

Although joining the Party meant a break with his Surrealist friends, all he wishes to remember of them now is their youthful idealism:

[a] op. cit., p. 30.
Est-ce vraiment un crime
De rêver au bonheur dans la gueule du loup
Et de dire à minuit que l'alouette est proche
Mes amis mes amis que cela soit de vous
Pourtant qu'en vienne le reproche
[b] op. cit., p. 52.
Alexandre Serguéievitch ô pessimiste
Rien ne me tienne lieu de bonheur à ce prix
Le bonheur d'habitude est un bonheur trop triste
Je préfère l'enfer où l'homme brûle et crie
[c] op. cit., p. 84.
Salut à toi Parti qui nias la misère
Et montras l'homme frère à ses frères armés

Oh do not think too harshly of them
Pathetic children so soon fallen from the skies
Some broke their glass when they saw spring approaching
Others had a light shining in their eyes[a]

After describing the way in which he, Aragon, made the journey which led to commitment,[b] he devotes his last few poems to the future:

I sing of the future as of a natural Heaven[c]

Faith in the future and working for the future, this is what enables him to overcome the fear of death. In lines of great poetic beauty, reflecting his humanistic philosophy, he refuses to let the shadow of death overcome him with grief and despair. For him, dying is a universal process in nature, "Mourir et mûrir sont la même chanson"—'To die and to ripen are part of the same song' (a translation which unfortunately misses the close likeness of the two verbs in French). Everything around us dies, including our own childhood, our own youth, in order to give birth to the new. The individual's death, absurd if it is seen in isolation, loses part of its tragedy when one thinks of those who will continue him. Elsa Triolet calls this the only immortality man can achieve, "To be continued, this alters everything."[26] And Aragon returns to the same idea in *La Semaine sainte* where he speaks of ". . . that great spring made up of graveyards, which we call the future,"[27] and writes,

One cannot die since there are others. What one has thought, believed, loved so strongly, so passionately, turns green again with those who are growing up, with those children whose bodies and souls develop . . .[28]

Both Aragon and Péguy see in the child of today the man of tomorrow. The author of the Mysteries on the "Second Virtue"

[a] op. cit., p. 67.
     Ah ne les jugez pas de façon trop sévère
     Pathétiques enfants si tôt déchus des cieux
     Il en fut au printemps qui brisèrent leur verre
     Certains avaient de la lumière au fond des yeux
[b] See above pp. 87–88.
[c] op. cit., p. 136. Je chante l'avenir comme un ciel naturel

and on "The Holy Innocents" might well have written the poem *L'Enfant* (The child) in *Les Yeux et la mémoire*, and in particular the following line,

People look for the future in far away lands yet it is close at hand[a]

The last two poems of the book are dedicated to the modern couple, a union of two equal partners, and to peace, without which no future can be imagined. Inspired by the end of the Indo-China war, Aragon pleads for a general cease-fire, so that lovers may love without fear and anguish, so that children may go on learning and playing, so that science, constructive labour, art and beauty may continue to flourish, so that all differences should be settled in a spirit of friendship.

(ii) *A personal autobiography: 'Le Roman inachevé'*

The political autobiography was followed in 1956 by a more personal one, *Le Roman inachevé* (The Unfinished Novel). The title deserves some explanation. On the back cover of his poem, Aragon points out that the word "roman" is used in two senses, in the mediaeval one, which describes long narrative poems, and in the modern sense, to indicate that out of his personal recollections, the author has created a work of fiction. The word "inachevé" also serves a double purpose; it is meant to remind us that aspects of Aragon's life which he described elsewhere have been left out, and probably to stress that the story is by no means over since the central character is still alive. The poem lacks the central theme of its predecessor; instead, what unfolds before us is a succession of events viewed and experienced subjectively. The poet speaks of his childhood and his school days; he discreetly evokes his mother's unhappiness; he relates the death of a relative in hospital as well as the death of soldiers in the trenches; he recalls his Surrealist illusions and sentimental disappointments; he writes about the martyrs of the last war, and in particular of his friend Pierre Unik, the poet who escaped from a German concentration camp and died of cold in the mountains of Slovakia; he tells of his walks through Paris and through Moscow (where he so often "dreamt of the future"); he sings of nature, of the sun, flowers, happiness, and,

[a] op cit., p. 117. On va bien loin chercher l'avenir il est là

above all, of Elsa. This list does not claim to represent a digest
of the book, but simply to give some idea of the wealth of
topics it deals with, and of Aragon's attempt to approach reality
in its totality.

It is not only because of its subject matter that *Le Roman
inachevé* represents a break from Aragon's previous poems, but
because it illustrates his skill in handling the widest variety of
metres. These correspond to his various moods and they are a
magnificent proof both of the deeply human content of commitment and of the fact that in "littérature engagée" technical
achievement is far from despised. The traditional metre of
French poetry, the alexandrine, still keeps a privileged place,
as if to stress Aragon's rejection of the surrealist dogma that
it was a "decadent" metre, but many others find their way into
the poem, including blank verse, free verse and the prose poem.
The sixteen-syllable line is probably the greatest novelty introduced. He selected it because it corresponds to a "respiration
profonde" (a deep breathing), as he explains in the poem which
bears that title,

> Now I shall use a different metre in order to dispel the
> bitterness in my soul[a]

It is also used when the poet wants to show the contrast between
the two feelings we experience about time,

> Young people how long and how short is time ahead of you[b]

This idea haunts him, and he returns to it on more than one
occasion, as for example, when he exclaims at the end of the
book,

> Oh how long and how brief this endless night seems to my
> heart[c]

Lastly, Aragon often uses the sixteen-syllable line in order to

[a] op cit., p. 21. Je change ici de mètre pour dissiper en moi l'amertume
[b] op cit., p. 12. Que le temps devant vous jeunes gens est immense et
qu'il est court
[c] op cit., p. 198. Que cette interminable nuit paraît à mon cœur longue et
brève

speak of Elsa, for it helps to convey the feeling that his vision
was widened after he met her,

> Without you how could I have broken loose from the bonds
>   of my folly
> People might tell me there is no miracle in this field
> And that those men towards whom I was going had other
>   fish to fry
> And were looking down upon me from the height of their
>   wisdom
> Yes I wept but in your arms from this inhuman indifference[a]

Sometimes, the poet's agony becomes uncontrollable by any
metre, and it is only in a disorderly prose, "helter-skelter", that
he can speak of it. At other times, he wants to forget everything
and takes shelter in nonsense poems:

> Voulez-vous parlons d'autre chose
> Il y a des esprits moroses
> Des esquimaux des ecchymoses
>
> Desnos disait des mots exquis
> Il neige sur les mots en ski
> Chez qui chez qui   (p. 152)

(In this case, translation is impossible, as the whole effect would
be lost.)

The last two poems deserve to be singled out, *La Nuit de
Moscou* (Moscow Night) and *Prose du bonheur et d'Elsa* (The
prosody of happiness and of Elsa). In the former, the contrast
between dreams about the future and the reality of the present
is vividly brought out:

> I expected a happiness as wide as the ocean
> · · · · · · · · · · · · · · · ·
> But reality works in a different manner
> And it is in its own way that it achieves miracles

---

[a] op cit., p. 183.
> Comment aurais-je pu sans toi rompre les liens de ma folie
> On me dira qu'il n'y a pas de miracle dans ce domaine
> Et que ceux-là vers qui j'allais avaient d'autres chats à fouetter
> Et qu'ils me regardaient du haut de leur supériorité
> Oui j'ai pleuré mais dans tes bras cette indifférence inhumaine

So much the worse for dreamers so much the worse for utopia [a]

and also:

I shall not reach the end of the night
. . . .
What does it matter so long as the night is finally broken
. . . .
I carry the sun within my darkness [b]

Such indomitable faith in happiness would have been impossible without Elsa, and it is to her that the final poem is dedicated:

All the things which I know I have learnt from you
That there is daylight at noon that a sky can be blue [c]
. . . .
But this wisdom of which you write and which you teach
    whence does it come to you
To you thanks to whom I understand all that throbs and
    all that bleeds [d]
. . . .
Tear up my flesh break up my body
What will you find but Paradise
    Elsa my whole light [e]

[a] op. cit., p. 232.
            J'attendais un bonheur aussi grand que la mer
            . . . .
            Mais la réalité l'entend d'une autre oreille
            Et c'est à sa façon qu'elle fait des merveilles
            Tant pis pour les rêveurs tant pis pour l'utopie
[b] op cit., pp. 232-33.
            Je n'arriverai pas jusqu'au bout de la nuit
            . . . .
            Qu'importe si la nuit à la fin se déchire
            . . . .
            Je porte le soleil dans mon obscurité
[c] op. cit., p. 238.
            J'ai tout appris de toi pour ce qui me concerne
            Qu'il fait jour à midi qu'un ciel peut être bleu
            . . . .
[d] op. cit., p. 242.
    Mais d'où te vient cette science à toi qui l'écris et l'enseignes
    Toi par qui je comprends tout ce qui palpite et tout ce qui saigne
    . . . .
[e] op. cit., p. 244.
            Déchirez ma chair partagez mon corps
            Qu'y verrez-vous sinon le paradis
            Elsa ma lumière

(iii) *What is poetry? What is commitment?*

For Aragon, taking stock of reality does not only involve reviewing his past life, but also reflecting on the meaning of his art and on the purpose of his commitment. In a remarkable poem published in 1960, *Les Poètes* (Poets), he tries to divine the secret of poetic creation, drawing upon the experience of other poets, past and present, as well as his own. Once more, it is a new and unexpected aspect of Aragon which is revealed. This is particularly the case when we hear him say that his chief passion "in this age of adventures, of downfalls, of crashes, in this age of tragedies," has been the magic of language, the fascination of translating poetic images into words and vice-versa. After the initial moment of surprise, of shock even, the meaning becomes clear: what has always appealed to him is the reflection of reality embodied in language and in the images of poetry. For example, he recalls how Mayakovsky once used the word "hare" in one of his poems in order to describe, as is common in Russian ". . . the reflection of the sun which one can move up and down on a wall or in a room with the help of a pocket mirror", and he adds that when Mayakovsky was in prison,

> that hare was all that entered his cell from outside life
> and for that hare that hare on the wall that yellow hare
> I would give all the poems of Mayakovsky . . .[a]

This attachment to language is the poet's only way of exploring reality. But Aragon's art, as well as his dreams, are his gift to other people, for he has nothing but contempt for the man who thinks of himself alone:

> Woe unto him who dreams of himself who dreams of nothing
> but himself[b]

The whole purpose of *Les Poètes* is to claim for poetry its

[a] op. cit., p. 160.
> ce lièvre était tout ce qui pénétrait de la vie au-dehors
> et pour ce lièvre ce lièvre de mur ce lièvre jaune
> je donnerais tous les poèmes de Maiakovski

[b] op. cit., p. 173.
> Malheur à qui rêve de lui-même à qui ne rêve rien
> Que de lui-même

rightful place in the new world of technological and scientific changes. Poetry, together with science, increases human knowledge and enriches human experience, and many of Aragon's metaphors are borrowed from the latest scientific discoveries. In his last poem, he introduces a new metre, the 20-syllable line, so as to give his imagination "the size of reality":

I chose to spread my verses and give them that look of crucifixion

. . . .

To provide the mantle of my fiction with the size of reality[a]

Although the confident optimism of *Les Yeux et la mémoire* has gone, the message is still one of hope: struggles and disappointments will never end, but it is up to the future to contradict the poet's pessimism. Aragon effaces himself because "others will sing", and he concludes,

Men of tomorrow breathe on the burning coals
It is for you to say what I see[b]

After the success of *La Semaine sainte*, Aragon gathered a number of essays and articles in a book which he called *J'abats mon jeu* (I lay my cards on the table.) This is how he explains the meaning of his title, which in French implies that his activity is just a "game":

I am playing a game. Yes. . . . I am on the side of those who always lose and are fed up with losing. My game is theirs. I am playing in order to give them weapons. From my early youth, I chose the game of writing . . . I want to win, not with the help of surprise, but with the help of evidence. I am laying my cards on the table . . . I gathered these texts to convince myself that I am not alone. In the hope that

[a] op. cit., p. 209.
 J'ai choisi de donner à mes vers cette envergure de crucifixion
 Pour à la taille de la réalité faire un manteau de mes fictions
[b] op. cit., p. 213.
 Hommes de demain soufflez sur les charbons
 A vous de dire ce que je vois

others, seeing what my game is, will join me. For them, I
lay my cards on the table. For I am against secret
diplomacy.[29]

The book contains most of the texts which explain Aragon's
purpose and method in *La Semaine sainte*, as well as a number of
others dealing with the issue of socialist realism. We shall have
occasion to return to them in a later chapter devoted to the
relationship between realism and commitment. At this stage,
suffice it to mention the spirit of the book, which is one of
open-mindedness towards all genuine artistic and literary
efforts. Aragon approaches the work of other writers without
any dogmatic preconceptions, and says he asks nothing from a
work of art but the power to make him "feel dizzy". Roger
Garaudy accurately described his attitude when he wrote that
for him, literary criticism is a "school of enthusiasm".[30] This
outlook, which strikingly recalls Péguy's, is sharply opposed to
the all-too-often negative stand taken by most professional
critics. It leads Aragon to rebuke those of his own friends who
are incapable of appreciating artistic masterpieces which either
contradict or ignore their political beliefs:

I am not like that. I take an interest in the diverse paths
followed by all men, in the gradual steps of the most hesitant
thought as it is groping towards the light, and what is more, I
am convinced that my own light would grow dim if it were
mine alone. Far from being proud of my ability to see among
the blind, I deem this ability to be of little value unless it
is shared. That is why I listen with some anxiety to those
voices which are yet unknown, and I follow with passionate
attention all that is being done in the field of literature, which
happens to be my job. I am convinced that in each man, there
is, in varying degrees no doubt, a small part of the truth, a
part which I cannot reach. Each man advances towards
truth at a pace which is his own, and if I notice a weakness
in his approach, I remember the blunders which were mine
vividly enough to believe myself still capable of them.[31]

It is because of his commitment, not in spite of it, that Aragon
can write in this vein. For him, "socialist realism" is but one

way—the best one, naturally!—of depicting 'the real world';
yet it can afford not to be an exclusive club because the battle
it is waging is not confined to the field of literature:

> There is a fundamental difference between the development
> of socialist realism and that of previous literary schools. The
> latter could not thrive unless they set themselves against
> their opponents, unless they condemned all trends different
> from their own. The struggle waged by socialist realism is of
> a different kind, it takes place *elsewhere*, and for this very
> reason, socialist realism can benefit from all works which
> emerge outside its own ranks, it can always interpret, and
> direct, even those elements which are opposed to it, because
> its aim is not the triumph of a *style*, but of a conception of the
> world. I am not quite sure that all those who proclaim their
> attachment to socialist realism would agree with me, but
> what can I do about it?[32]

(iv) *The realist in the dock: 'La Mise à mort'*

In 1965, Aragon made a critical reassessment of his past in a
novel which he called *La Mise à mort*—a title which literally
means 'putting to death', as if he meant to convey that he was
striking a death blow at his own illusions, his own mistakes and
his own limitations. He achieved his effect by a remarkable
blending of humour and tragedy. The best introduction to the
book is provided by the blurb on the inside cover, written by
the author himself. The story, we are informed, concerns a
man "who has lost his reflection in the mirror", and with a
touch of mischief Aragon asks himself whether this allegory is
"compatible with realism". Without bothering to answer the
question, he proceeds to tell us that the main character,
Anthoine, became a realistic writer under the influence of his
wife, "Ingeborg d'Usher, whom he secretly calls Fougère" (an
obvious allusion to Elsa Triolet's impact on Aragon). Fougère
is a great singer, and one day, as he sat listening to her, Anthoine
became aware, for the first time, that other people existed
beside himself. This discovery, made possible because his wife's
song was an echo of reality, had a profound effect on him—he
was radically "modified, transformed, bowled over". However,
as we learn in the next paragraph, Anthoine has no real
existence, he is but the public image of another character,

Alfred, and it is this public image alone which Fougère loves,
much to Alfred's annoyance, for he is madly jealous of his other
self. We begin to realize that there is more than one theme in the
novel, and at this stage the author intervenes in order to ask
aloud, "What is the real subject of my book, a man who has
lost his reflection in the mirror, the life of Anthoine Célèbre
and Ingeborg d'Usher, song, realism or jealousy? It might
also be a novel about the plurality of the human self, about
fictional creation, or a novel about a novelist. Choose for your-
selves." All these themes are actually dealt with, but against
the background of "life in the twentieth century, two world
wars, the Popular Front, Gorky's death, and the present time,
for one can turn the real world in all directions, it still remains
the real world." Above all, we are asked to believe Alfred
when he says that everything he writes is "a long, an endless
love letter" addressed to Fougère. As for the title of the novel,
Aragon tells an imaginary interviewer that it was suggested
to him by the following lines in one of Pasternak's poems,
translated by Elsa Triolet:

> When one gets old, one is like Rome,
> Rejecting chariots and stilts,
> And demanding, not comedy,
> But that the execution should take place.
> (Or être vieux c'est Rome qui,
> Au lieu des chars et des échasses,
> Exige, non la comédie,
> Mais que la mise à mort se fasse.)

"Perhaps," Aragon concludes, "this is, after all, the subject of
the novel. 'What? Old age, death?' Lord, how you tire me!
Whilst you're at it, why don't you also ask me *who* Fougère is?"

La Mise à mort is the sequel to *Les Yeux et la mémoire* and *Le
Roman inachevé*, as it continues Aragon's exploration of his past.
The first few chapters, in particular, are a kind of *Notre Jeunesse*,
but unlike Péguy, who felt he had nothing to disown, the novelist subjects his youth to merciless self-criticism, and the pages in
which he condemns his blind acceptance of Soviet propaganda
in the thirties are among the most bitter he ever wrote. Yet
this is not the work of a renegade. Its tragic and moving
character is rather due to the undying loyalty which Aragon

displays—he remains attached to his cause, despite the monstrous distortions which it suffered, and one does not have to be a Communist in order to respect his grief as well as his constancy. His disillusioned exclamation about "ideas, and what they become!"[33] has a true ring of Péguy about it, reminding one of the degeneration of "mystique" into "politique".[a] In fact, later in the book, Communist politicians are strongly rebuked for their unwarranted pressures on writers and artists, and for their dogmatic insistence on "positive heroes":

> . . . it is not the novelist's brain which needs changing, but the world. Yet, the strange thing is that the very men who wanted to change the world should have thought they could begin by changing the novelist's brain . . . And it would be only fair if writers sharply upbraided politicians for not having done enough to produce those positive men whom they need as models for their novels . . . Instead, it is the politicians who condemn writers when they do not supply the people with positive heroes they can follow. Isn't this the world upside down?[34]

Aragon's attack is well in keeping with the spirit of Marxism, as it forcefully reminds Stalinist and post-Stalinist rulers that they have "put the cart before the horse" and, in so doing, have been guilty of philosophical idealism. The materialist view, expressed by Lenin, that literature is a "reflection" of reality, carries with it the corollary that its purpose is not to embellish the present, but to depict it as it is, with its contradictions and its limitations. Short of this truthful disclosure, the vision of the future suggested by art would necessarily become utopian.

It is impossible to summarize *La Mise à mort*, or even to mention all its themes. At times, it is a straightforward novel, at others a lyrical poem, yet at others a critical reflection on life, on literature, on love, and lastly, as if to complicate matters still further, it contains three short stories, said to have been written by Anthoine, but without any immediate link with the

---

[a] Cf. also what Albérès writes about Sartre, ". . . (he) attacks those moral values which debase themselves into routine conventions, this is what Péguy meant by a 'mystique' sinking into 'politique' " (*J. P. Sartre*, p. 53).

main "plot". All one can do is to single out a few salient points, without claiming to have exhausted the subject. In addition to realism, an idea which recurs time and again in the book is the dissociation of personality, the fact that a man is split up into two or more different parts. "I want to write about a fellow who was two fellows," R. L. Stevenson said when he explained the meaning of *Dr. Jekyll and Mr. Hyde*. The phrase is often quoted by Aragon whose ambition goes further—he wants to write about a fellow who is many fellows, and he remarks in passing that in addition to the good side and the bad side in a man's nature, there is at least a third character, the Indifferent. His hero has more than one "image", and I am inclined to agree with Jean Sur that Alfred's tragedy, which drives him mad in the end, is not the plurality of his self, but his failure to recognize in it his fundamental unity.[35] "I is someone else," Rimbaud used to say, a quotation which Aragon puts at the beginning of one of his chapters. It reminds us of what he had said in a speech already quoted about the various men who co-exist within him, and without whom he could not utter the word "I".[36] There is an interesting passage in the novel where he stresses this dialectical unity of opposites: the occasion is the report of a speech attacking the Chinese leaders' thesis that, according to dialectics, 'one splits up into two'. The Peking dogmatists, the speech goes on, forget that, in addition to the struggle of opposites, there is also the unity of opposites, and Aragon remarks,

. . . perhaps it is also this business about 'one into two' and 'two into one' which disturbs me. For reasons of my own, different from the speaker's. And yet not so different, after all. Suppose one went to the bottom of the matter, as one says, *to the bottom*.[37]

Clearly linked with this theme of the plurality of the self is the misadventure of the character who has lost his reflection in the mirror. This allegory can have different meanings. On one level, it represents the end of Anthoine's individualism, the fact that he has begun to think of others instead of himself. Fougère is responsible for this, because she is a woman who always puts other people first, even when some of them behave unfairly towards her.ᵃ On a different level, Anthoine's loss suggests the gulf between dreams and reality, the inability of modern man to recognize his hopes and his ideals in the "real world" around him:

What a mess, my God, what a mess! I am not the only one to have lost my reflection. A whole generation can no longer find any likeness between its soul and what it sees. There are millions of us who are the stray children of this huge divorce.[38]

The mirror itself plays an important part in the novel. We see the author's past through it, as it reflects its various images. In the end, Alfred breaks it because he cannot bear to go on looking at one particular image, that of Anthoine, the "man" loved by Fougère. This is the climax of his jealousy, a feeling which torments him all the time. Never has Aragon spoken so poignantly of jealousy, which he describes not as a morbid passion, or as a form of selfishness, but as an emotion which springs from the extent of a man's love and from his sense of the absolute. Because no amount of scientific knowledge can ever give him "the certainty that he is loved",[39] art and imagination must come to his rescue. They are both a form of "lying", yet not in the sense that they falsify the truth; they rather represent the imaginative hypothesis by which man transcends himself and his experience. (Aragon gave one of his latest short stories the significant title of *Le Mentir vrai*, "Truthful lying.") "The highest form of lying," he writes, "is the novel, where lying helps to reach the truth."[40] In the end, however, jealousy becomes self-destroying because it is no longer kept in check. By "killing" Anthoine, Alfred loses his sanity, and the doctor summoned by Fougère delivers the following verdict, "Madam, understand me well, he has loved you *to distraction*."[41] Thus the novel ends, but the actual word "end" has been deliberately left out, in order to suggest that there is no final solution to the problems raised—the quest must go on.

ᵃ After Fougère has quoted, with great emotion, an extract from the nineteenth-century French actress La Malibran which says that 'others are my own self', an anonymous caller vulgarly insults her over the telephone, but she rebukes Alfred for saying, with a touch of bitterness, "What do you think now about others being my own self?" (pp. 312–13).

THE "REAL WORLD" OF HISTORY:
THE PARALLEL HISTORY OF THE U.S.A. AND THE
U.S.S.R.

In 1959, an enterprising publisher suggested that André Maurois, a liberal, and Aragon, a Communist, should write a parallel history of the U.S.A. and the U.S.S.R. Aragon eagerly agreed. To write a truthful account of Soviet developments was one way of making up for his responsibility in echoing Stalinist propaganda. The work appeared in 1962. It consists of four volumes, one devoted to America, written by Maurois, two to Russia, written by Aragon, and a fourth one being the record of conversations between the writers and representative American and Soviet citizens.

From the start, Aragon was well aware of the difficulties of the new type of work he had undertaken. He wrote in an article,

> The worst of a historian's task is that he has to believe in the history he is writing. As for the novelist, no sooner has he related events in a certain way than he is allowed to view them in an entirely different way through the eyes of another one of his characters. There is not, strictly speaking, any fictional truth. But there is such a thing as historical truth. There's the rub![42]

In order to do justice to historical truth, he decided to keep his feelings and his imagination in check. Gone are the poet's flights of fancy or the novelist's personal interventions. They are replaced by an approach which is exclusively factual, almost dry, a most unusual feature for Aragon. However, on two occasions at least, one is reminded that he is not a "pure historian"—whatever the phrase might mean. In the opening chapter he reveals his skill in selecting the significant detail and presenting it in an arresting manner. His *History* does not start with an account of Tsarist Russia's economic condition, as one might expect from a Marxist, but with the statement that "on the 1st of January, 1917, at dawn, a policeman . . . discovers the body of Rasputin". The killing of Rasputin is the first visible crack in the fabric. It reveals the corruption of Tsarism and its rottenness. From now on, one feels, things cannot go on as before, and the stage is set for the revolutions which will follow. The atmosphere of Soviet history is immediately conveyed to the reader. At the end, the poet breaks loose from his bonds and speaks with visible enthusiasm about the prospects opened up by the building of Communism. Even if one does not share Aragon's confident belief that in twenty years' time the basis will have been laid in the Soviet Union for general prosperity and abundance, one will be impressed by his emphasis on the peaceful character of Russia's new course. "The twenty-year plan," he writes, "the perspective of Communism is a wager for peace, it is tantamount to the certainty that war can be averted." No attempt is made to present Soviet achievements as having been smooth and easy:

> All this did not happen in an imaginary world, but in the heart of a moving reality, amidst all the obstacles stemming from the refusal of the dying past to yield to the growing future, . . . and even those who had, at first, been the heralds of the new, fall by the wayside, . . . or become ossified at a speed which is as staggering as the age, and already with them, what was only a seed has become a dogma.

On the subject of Stalin, Aragon avoids both excessive praise and excessive denigration. The late Soviet ruler is shown as a mixture of good and bad, of energy, drive, and political understanding, on the one hand, and contempt for people's initiative, inordinate vanity, and ruthlessness on the other. His cruel reprisals against mistaken, but honest foes, and his arbitrary condemnation of thousands of innocent people had the most disastrous consequences for the Soviet Union. These consequences are not blurred by Aragon, although one feels he could have been much more vigorous in his exposure. It would be idle to claim that the book is free from ideological bias, any more than Maurois's companion volume on the U.S.A. Neither author hides his own sympathies, and their interpretation of events can often be challenged. On the whole, however, both have tried to be fair in sifting the evidence before them and in presenting a balanced account of the events they relate.

THE "REAL WORLD" OF THE SOUL:
LOVE

If Aragon is to be believed literally, he is nothing but a 'shadow' of Elsa Triolet. He has protested so often and so vehemently that whenever he says this, he means it absolutely, and is not resorting to "I know not what elegance"[43] of style, that his claim must be examined seriously. He provided a clue to his meaning in one of the ten radio interviews which took place in 1964 between Francis Crémieux and himself.[44] Referring to what he had written in his 1963 poem, *Le Fou d'Elsa*, "I am created by the one who loves me", he explained that his intention was to do for mysticism what Marx had done for Hegel's idealist dialectics, viz. "to put it back on its feet". He was trying to reverse the proposition put forward by one of the greatest Arab mystics, Ibn Arabi, that "a man can only love the Being who created him": instead of communion with a spiritual God, he offers the concrete love of a woman as the highest form of overcoming individualism and self-centredness. Love is placed on such a high pedestal by Aragon because he feels he would never have become the man he is without Elsa —it is her love which "created" him, in the sense that it opened his eyes, inspired him and encouraged him. Moreover, in genuine love as he conceives it, *the couple* is more important than either partner taken singly, and this implies mutual respect. On his part, it goes hand in hand with an attitude of profound admiration for women in general. He has always refused to endorse the prevalent masculine idea that women are either mysterious or inferior creatures. In his poems and in his novels, they are endowed with a personality of their own, and they stand revealed as human beings who are different from men in many respects, but not in some unfathomable way. One can look in vain for any traces of the familiar clichés about "l'éternel féminin" in his writings. His favourite saying concerning Elsa in particular is that she "is not a myth", but a real woman of flesh and blood, who is socially and professionally situated. He loves her beauty and her charm as well as her mind, and he is fond of reminding us that she is a great novelist and a born realist. When he writes about her, he gives at least as much attention to her feelings and to her ideas as he does to his own. For this woman is not a temporary visitor in the poet's life— she is his wife, his everyday companion. It is a striking fact that married love has seldom tempted the poet, the novelist or the playwright; the French critic Denis de Rougemont once remarked ironically that if one were to judge the men of Western Europe on their literature, adultery would seem to be their favourite occupation. If such adulterous preoccupations are totally absent from Aragon's poetry, it is not because he has undertaken to uphold the sanctity of marriage as an institution, but because his love for Elsa is based on companionship. He shares with her his joys and his sorrows, his triumphs and his doubts, his whole activity, his complete being. We cannot think of him without thinking of her. There are few examples of such complete devotion in any literature, and the couple Elsa Triolet—Louis Aragon is in many ways an *exemplary* couple.

Such a couple does not selfishly seek happiness away from the world. "There can be no happy love in the midst of general misfortune,"[45] Aragon told Francis Crémieux, and that is what he meant when he wrote the famous line, "There is no such thing as a happy love":

> You will find this idea in all the poems I wrote in the last forty years . . . But the way in which misfortune is presented in my novels, the way in which it is presented in *Le Roman inachevé* or in *Elsa* does not in the least imply that I do not believe in the possibility of happiness, provided a solution is found to general misfortune. It means that, in this respect, there is a kind of priority in the duties of man . . .[46]

"A priority in the duties of man . . ." It is because Aragon strives for the absolute in love, as in other things, that he goes beyond it and embraces commitment. It is his burning desire for *absolute* happiness which makes him work for the happiness of others. He knows and he feels that in a society where there is misery, fear and the threat of nuclear death, the fate of a couple will always be precarious. Commitment for the sake of love, commitment in order to ensure that love will one day be a happy love, such is the significance of Aragon's whole life. The future for which he is working and of which he dreams will make the highest form of union between man and woman, the couple, fully possible. This is what he expressed in *Le Fou d'Elsa* when he wrote that "Woman is the future of Man"—another conscious echo of Marx who had said that "Man is the future of man" in order to stress the humanistic character of his philosophy.

Although Aragon's work is filled with his love for Elsa, three of his poems are specifically devoted to her. In 1940, *Les Yeux d'Elsa* expressed the cruelty of separation and the hope of early reunion. In 1959, he published *Elsa*, the first of his books, according to him, to have a "positive hero". He gave voice to his love, his gratitude, his admiration for Elsa's genius, his jealousy when she is creating fictional characters of whom he knows nothing, and his belief that one day, his love verse will be understood as a Song of the Future:

One day Elsa my verse people will grasp it better

Then under my raving accents
My words full of darkness my senseless cries
They will find thanks to this love of thee
The great human briars which will blossom tomorrow
. . . .
They will know that my night was preparing the dawn[a]

Le Fou d'Elsa (Elsa's fool[b]), which appeared in 1963, is Aragon's longest poem to date. Roger Garaudy hailed it as "a modern epic". This is a fair description, for it is not a conventional love poem; it is rather a poem inspired by love which grapples with the basic issues of human destiny. The action takes place in 1492 when Granada fell to the Spaniards, and one of the characters is the vanquished King, Boadbil. Granada is here a symbol for human life, and Aragon writes,

Each man has the misfortune of Granada for his destiny[c]

If the poet wants to rehabilitate Boadbil, it is not only for the sake of historical accuracy, but also in order to suggest that under the impact of defeat and of war, we are all placed in what

[a] op. cit., pp. 124–125.
Un jour Elsa mes vers on les comprendra mieux

Alors on entendra sous l'accent du délire
Dans les aveugles mots les cris de déraison
Par cet amour de toi sourdre la floraison
Des grands rosiers humains promis à l'avenir
. . . .
On saura que ma nuit préparait le matin
[b] The word 'Fool' designates a fifteenth-century "Medjnun" who is "possessed" with love for Elsa four and a half centuries before her birth.
[c] op. cit., p. 197. Tout être a pour destin le malheur de Grenade

Sartre calls an "extreme situation", compelling us to reflect on the meaning of existence. Then, we are introduced to the "Medjnun", a man accused of idolatry because he worships Elsa, a woman yet unborn, instead of Allah. He sings the "zadjal"[a] of the future which foretells what lies in store for man—happiness through love, provided he *commits* himself to the cause of general happiness:

> I tell you that man was born for
> Woman and born for love
> Everything in the old world will change
> First life and then death
> All things will be shared
> White bread and bleeding kisses
> People will see the couple and its kingdom
> Snowing down like orange trees[b]

Occasionally, the poet talks to the "Medjnun" and to his modern readers. He protests that his journey into the past is not a dream divorced from action,

> I never separate doing from dreaming[c]

but an effort to understand the meaning of progress,

> He who accuses me of looking back towards the past does not know what he is saying or doing. If you want me to understand what will come, and not only the *horror* of what will come, let me cast a glance at what was. It is the primary condition for a certain kind of optimism.[47]

[a] In his Glossary, Aragon explains this word as "the specifically Andalusian form of Arabic poetry" (p. 451).
[b] op. cit., pp. 166–167.
> Je vous dis que l'homme est né pour
> La femme et né pour l'amour
> Tout du monde ancien va changer
> D'abord la vie et puis la mort
> Et toutes choses partagées
> Le pain blanc les baisers qui saignent
> On verra le couple et son règne
> Neiger comme les orangers

[c] (op. cit., p. 184.) Je n'ai jamais séparé le faire du rêver

"Optimism" would not be a bad word with which to conclude this brief account of Aragon's evolution, provided it were qualified. Aragon's optimism could almost be called "deferred optimism", in the sense that it is a belief in the *future* happiness of mankind, "that great posthumous happiness", as he called it in *Le Roman inachevé*,[48] which will blossom out of tragedy itself and will be the fruit of the sacrifices made by the present generation. For him, as for Sartre, "human life begins the other side of despair",[49] but it is not very fair to suggest, as Jean Sur does, that "his work is even more discouraging than Sartre's".[50] Fighting for the future is the antithesis of despair, and perhaps the last word had better be left to Aragon himself:

"Happiness exists and I believe in it."[a] I am not going back on that. Notice, however, that this line, written in 1956, is first and foremost a protest, a cry of sorrow against all the forces which are threatening and destroying happiness . . . the happiness in which I believe is not, I would say, that petty selfishness of two people which one often meets, and which I refuse to look upon as love, or as the attitude of a genuine couple.[51]

NOTES

1. For other studies of Aragon, see Bibliography.
2. Jean Sur, op. cit., p. 188.
3. *The Necessity of Art*, pp. 105–6.
4. *J'abats mon jeu*, pp. 134–35.
5. *Le Roman inachevé*, p. 84.
6. op. cit., 18.
7. Ibid., p. 249.
8. *Les Yeux et la Mémoire*, p. 181.
9. op. cit., pp. 78 and 92.
10. *Pour un réalisme socialiste*, p. 53.
11. Ibid., p. 55.
12. op. cit., p. 617.
13. op. cit., p. 441.
14. op. cit., p. 268.
15. op. cit., p. 334.
16. Ibid., p. 310.
17. Ibid., p. 626.
18. op. cit., p. 427.

[a] "Le bonheur existe et j'y crois" (*Le Roman inachevé*, p. 239).

19. *Elsa Triolet, choisie par Aragon* (Gallimard).
20. op. cit., Introduction, p. 53.
21. *J'abats mon jeu*, pp. 154–55.
22. *The Modern Quarterly*, Summer 1952, pp. 176–78.
23. *La Mise à mort*, pp. 334–35.
24. *L'Homme communiste* (I), p. 84.
25. *J'abats mon jeu*, p. 142.
26. *Le Cheval roux*, p. 417.
27. op. cit., p. 580.
28. Ibid., pp. 578–79.
29. op. cit., pp. 8–10.
30. *L'Itinéraire d'Aragon*, p. 279.
31. op. cit., pp. 135–36.
32. Ibid., pp. 139–40.
33. op. cit., p. 174.
34. Ibid., p. 405.
35. Jean Sur, op. cit., p. 17.
36. *J'abats mon jeu*, p. 135.
37. op. cit., p. 175.
38. Ibid., p. 58.
39. Ibid., p. 125.
40. Ibid., p. 125.
41. Ibid., p. 421.
42. *France Nouvelle*, December 1959.
43. *Elsa*, p. 16.
44. Cf. *Entretiens avec Francis Crémieux*, Gallimard (1964).
45. op. cit., p. 102.
46. Ibid., p. 103.
47. op. cit., p. 409.
48. op. cit., p. 21.
49. Sartre, *Les Mouches* in *Théâtre*, p. 102.
50. Jean Sur, op. cit., p. 166.
51. *Entretiens avec Francis Crémieux*, p. 116.

CHAPTER IV

SARTRE

Unlike Péguy and Aragon, Jean-Paul Sartre is not a poet, and his commitment is not the outcome of poetic imagination or temperament. It would be tempting, and partly correct, to sum him up by saying that he is a philosopher, but this is perhaps to do an injustice to his artistic achievement (which, incidentally, cannot be properly appreciated without some reference to his philosophy), and it would obscure the important fact that commitment has affected him as a man, as a philosopher, as a critic, as a novelist and as a playwright. Although it is very artificial to divide him into separate compartments, it may, however, be useful to do so in order to become aware of the many-sided facets of his contribution. At the same time, it must be stressed that this division is merely a useful device and that, in fact, the various aspects of Sartre's activity are fused into his personality, which remains one of the most versatile and most controversial of our time. Many studies of his work have already appeared on both sides of the Channel,[a] and the following pages are not an attempt to replace any of them. They simply aim at re-examining his achievement in the light of his committed approach.

THE MAN:
COMMITMENT AS A REQUIREMENT AND AS THE CULMINATION OF AN EXPERIENCE OF LIFE

"Everything is decided before the age of twelve," wrote Péguy about himself. Sartre might have said the same thing: his decision to write was made when he was still a little boy. His latest book, *Les Mots*, describes his experiences as a child, and shows that the two great events of his early life were "Reading" and "Writing". The book throws a very interesting light on his personality because it is is not the usual kind of autobiography which simply relates events—it is a work of analysis and of

---

[a] In English the best studies to date are Philip Thody's *Jean-Paul Sartre* and Maurice Cranston's shorter essay, *Sartre*. A recent study by A. Manser (*Sartre—a philosophic study*) is mainly concerned with Sartre as a philosopher.

explanation, and could be called "the story of Jean-Paul's childhood" by Sartre, for the author is looking at the boy he was with intended detachment and obvious dislike. "Ce Sartre qui n'aime pas Jean-Paul," wrote one of the critics. (A Sartre who does not like Jean-Paul.)

Jean-Paul Sartre was born in 1905 in a petty-bourgeois milieu, puritanical and reactionary. The amused irony with which he describes the foibles of his grandfather and his entourage can hardly hide the bitterness with which he regards the class into which he was born. The seeds of rebellion were implanted in him at an early age, though at first his revolt was confined to day-dreaming about a world of which he was the hero. His father died when he was only two, and as his mother returned to live with her own parents, the young lad was soon aware of being "different": his mother he treated more as an elder sister, and the lord and master of the household was too distant a figure and too much the incarnation of authority to replace the father he had lost. Later, Sartre described the orphan as a "false bastard" and saw in his own situation the explanation of his feeling of sympathy for illegitimate children. His friend and biographer Francis Jeanson suggests that the theme of "the bastard" plays an important part in his work, and it is possible to see in this one of the many manifestations of Sartre's concern for the under-dog, be he a victim of society or of family circumstances.

The most important feature of his character which is revealed by his autobiography is his fear of being an outsider and his almost organic need to be accepted by others. The phrase "a man among men" which so often recurs in his writings corresponds to this basic requirement in his nature. There were many things which made it difficult for young Jean-Paul to feel at ease with his fellows, among which were his ugliness, which was for a long time his "negative principle",[1] and the way in which he was treated at home. His grandfather admired his inquisitive and imaginative mind and encouraged him in the belief that he would grow up to do "wondrous" things. At first, he was being educated at home, but eventually it was decided to send him to school. For the first time in his life, he mixed with other boys, he felt "integrated",[a] and he began to lose some of his shyness. To this day, he has retained the feeling of intense joy

[a] "At last I had some friends! . . . I had been adopted from the start."[2]

which comes from losing oneself in a crowd. Yet he was also, and has remained, a lonely man.[a] This contradiction within his nature accounts for the difficulties of Sartre's path towards commitment and for many pathetic pages in his writings. In this respect, the central character of his greatest play, *Le Diable et le bon Dieu* (Lucifer and the Lord), is a reflection of himself. Goetz is a bastard, who is feared by men, and longs for their companionship. In his final decision to join the Peasants' Army which is fighting the sixteenth-century German barons, there are traces of Sartre's own view about his mission as a writer: both men remain alone at the very time of their deepest involvement in the struggles of their fellows—Goetz, because his qualities of leadership naturally suit him for the post of general, where he is not only cut off from the ranks, but is compelled to issue harsh commands in order to maintain revolutionary discipline, and Sartre, one feels, because his literary ability makes him different from other mortals. Yet the same limitation was not felt by either Péguy or Aragon, and I would suggest that Sartre's inability to become part of a wider group is largely due to his nature, and cannot be properly understood in the sole light of the various explanations he himself has put forward, from time to time, in order to rationalize his position. I am not suggesting that his arguments are unconvincing, but that whatever their general validity, his own personality played no small part in shaping his attitude. The logic and the purpose of commitment are both intended to make of each individual "a man among men", yet this is an aim which Sartre has always found it difficult to achieve for himself.

There were other aspects of his childhood and personality which had a decisive influence on his development, such as his early realization that most adults around him were "play-acting", (perhaps his first glimmer of "mauvaise foi"), his highly critical attitude towards himself[b] which has made him perpetually dissatisfied with his achievement and eager to reach the next stage which would contradict and overcome the present, and, above all, what he calls his "religious atti-tude" to life. By this last phrase, he does not mean actual

[a] We shall see that, in his philosophy, loneliness is the first thing which confronts the individual when he faces an unfriendly world.

[b] "For self-criticism, I am well gifted, provided no one tries to impose it on me."[3]

attachment to Christian dogma, but the strictly moral approach, that "humanisme de prélat"[4] which had such a hold on him that, for years, he looked upon literature as a "mandate". The worst part of this attitude was the tyranny of words, for it was through words that the world was progressively revealing itself to him, both the words of his voracious reading and of his first attempts at writing, and for a long time he proved unable to distinguish between the label and the contents.

> "I was a Churchman," he writes bitterly, ". . . I confused things with their names: this is believing . . ."[5]

We have already seen that his savage self-criticism did not lead to the rejection of commitment, but to its assertion in a new form, free from all illusions. The value of his retrospective glance at his past is made clear at the end of the book where he writes,

> What remains? A whole man, made up of all men, and worth all and any of them.[6]

This recalls the way in which Jean-Jacques Rousseau apostrophizes God in his *Confessions* and exclaims, "Let any man say before Thee, if he dare, 'I was better than this man.'" Neither Rousseau nor Sartre is guilty of vanity, in my opinion, for what they are both trying to say is that each one of us should make an honest self-appraisal in order to discover his own humanity, i.e. that he is neither better nor worse than the rest of mankind.

Les Mots does not take us beyond the first few years of Sartre's life. For details about his youth, pending further volumes of his autobiography, the most reliable document is the Memoirs of Simone de Beauvoir.[7] Sartre met her when they were both students, and they have remained together ever since, although they did not consider it necessary to conform to bourgeois prejudice and get married. Their attitude in pre-war days was essentially intellectual, both of them feeling a moral aversion for the bourgeois, but being unwilling to worry unduly about public affairs:

> "Man was going to be remoulded, and this would be partly our doing. We did not imagine any other way of contributing to the change except by writing books; public affairs

bored us. We counted on events turning out according to our wishes without any need for us to intervene personally." [8]

It was the war and the Occupation which brought about a deep change in his outlook. After spending a few months in the Meteorological Service, Sartre became a prisoner of war and was sent to a German concentration camp. There, he discovered something he had not dreamt of in his philosophy—human solidarity. It was an experience as important for him as Aragon's discovery of *other people*. Simone de Beauvoir stresses that he was profoundly affected by it and that it was the starting-point of his reflections on the meaning of responsibility and commitment in modern times. Traces of this experience can be found in *La Mort dans l'âme*—the third volume of *Les Chemins de la liberté*—in which he describes how Brunet, a French prisoner-of-war, managed to bolster up the morale of his companions and endeavoured to make them lead a human life in spite of their inhuman environment. The concentration camps are presented both as an example of the depths of cruelty to which human beings can stoop in their treatment of defeated foes and as a school of daily heroism and comradeship. The same comradeship existed among the members of the Resistance Movement, which Sartre joined soon after he was released by the Germans because of his defective eyesight. What he learned from his involvement in the struggle was that human solidarity was not a "value" imposed from outside, but a *fact*. His first play, performed in a Nazi-dominated Paris, emphasized that working for others is the only way in which an individual can manifest his liberty. The hero of *Les Mouches* kills a tyrant in order to save the people, and that is the fulfilment of his mission. [a] At the end of the war, Sartre was thus able to deliver the message that commitment, and more particularly political commitment, was both a requirement of human nature and a duty. He had arrived at this conclusion because he had found that political involvement satisfied *his basic need of feeling "integrated" and was the culmination of his experience*. It was a concept drawn from life—his life and that of his generation.

An account of Sartre's political evolution is largely an account of his relations with the Communists. From the start,

[a] "Oh, my people, I love you, and it is for your sake that I killed." [9]

his hatred of the bourgeoisie had drawn him towards socialism and the Left. In his book on *The Writer and Commitment*, John Mander argues that commitment is not necessarily a left-wing concept. In theory, he is right, for there is nothing in the idea of linking literature with life which leads necessarily to socialism. In practice, however, this is what tends to happen, and it is not really surprising: interest in social problems usually springs from the wish to change the present system, and one can hardly associate the crusading spirit of committed literature with attachment to the status quo. Although there are vast differences between Péguy's moral and "utopian" socialism and its Marxist variety, as adopted by Aragon, and very gradually by Sartre, they both rest on the assumption that a classless society and a co-operative economy are the conditions for any real social advance. As far as the writer is concerned, this involves the belief that in order to speak to the majority of the people, and not to an exploiting minority, he must give up the bourgeoisie and embrace the workers' cause. In one of his first pronouncements on the subject, Sartre stated that "the fate of literature (was) linked with that of the working class",[10] and that socialism was its "only chance".[11] Whilst admitting that the Communist Party was the organized expression of the working class, and even that it was impossible to reach the proletariat except through the Party,[12] his early attitude was far from friendly. In *What is Literature?*, he accused it of displaying the same weaknesses which Péguy thought he had found in the Socialist Party of Jaurès and Guesde, viz. attachment to a materialist philosophy[13] and betrayal of revolutionary principles. The Communists retaliated by calling his existentialist preoccupations with subjectivity "petty-bourgeois", and the whole of his work "literature for grave-diggers". Sartre in turn replied that a "petty-bourgeois" could have something to teach the present generation, and that "grave-diggers" were honourable people, most of whom, no doubt, belonged to a Trade Union! But the verbal battles could not do away with his dilemma, which was a very real and very acute one: if a committed writer remains outside the only existing working-class party, he is not only cut off from "the masses", but he lays himself open to the accusation that his commitment is merely "an intellectual's pastime".[14] *What is Literature?* does not solve the problem, but offers as the only possible remedy the use of "mass media" (Sartre uses the English phrase)—the press, the radio and the cinema. It was in this spirit that he founded the monthly periodical *Temps modernes*, of which he is still the editor. In the first issue, he claimed that his magazine would be political, but outside all parties, and that its aim was the total liberation of man, a liberation affecting biology as well as economics, sexuality as well as politics. He criticized middle-class parties for their inability to comprehend social reality, and Marxists for stressing social determinism and forgetting the individual. His solution was that man, although totally conditioned, is unpredictable because he is free, not free to stand aloof, for ". . . abstention is itself a choice",[15] but free to give meaning to his situation.

A few months later, Sartre thought he had found an even better way out of his dilemma when he agreed to become one of the foundation members of the "Rassemblement Démocratique Révolutionnaire" (Revolutionary Democratic Rally). He looked upon it as a special political organization, which would replace neither the Socialist nor the Communist Party, but would give individual supporters of both a chance of finding a meeting ground. It was a shortlived experiment, mainly because members were not forthcoming, and once more Sartre found himself in a self-imposed political wilderness.

In the early fifties, his attitude towards the Communist Party became particularly friendly. Undeterred by the revelations about Soviet Labour camps and by the sectarianism which was prevalent in the Communist movement in those days, Sartre was taking the view that the Soviet Union's policy was in favour of peace, and that French Communists were the only ones to defend the workers' interests. He broke with a number of his friends, particularly Camus, and later Merleau-Ponty, because of his stand, and in a series of articles in *Temps modernes*, he came closer to the Communists' position than he had ever been. The most important of these articles was *Les Communistes et la paix*, in which he asserted that the class struggle had not disappeared in modern society and that it was not likely to do so until the workers had become the collective owners of the means of production. Of the Communist Party, he wrote that it displayed exceptional historical understanding of the situation and that, guided by Marxism, it was unlikely to go wrong. It almost looked as if it was only a matter of days before he decided to join its ranks. After the changes brought about by the 20th Congress of the C.P.S.U., the door was practically open for his final "conversion", but the Hungarian crisis ushered in another period of cooling off and of hostility. Sartre was horrified at Soviet intervention, not so much because he was against all forms of violence, but because he felt that, in those specific circumstances, it was not necessary. He regarded the Hungarian uprising as a spontaneous revolt of "the masses", which was being drowned in blood by a Great Power. A bitter controversy ensued, and in a special interview with the correspondent of *L'Express*, he announced that he was reluctantly compelled to "break" with the Party leadership, although he was still on the same side as the Communist rank and file. He went as far as to say that "after having deserved the admirable title of 'party of those who were shot', the C.P. could now be called the 'party of those who do the shooting'."[16] He positively refused, however, to become an anti-Communist, believing that all anti-Communists were "swine". He later expressed his new dilemma by saying that nothing could be done "with the Communists or without them".

Meanwhile, another form of injustice, the extent and real nature of which he had hitherto not suspected,[a] was being discovered by Sartre—colonial exploitation. The Algerian war brought him face to face with the problem, and he began to pin most of his hopes on the struggles of subject nations against imperialism. He endorsed the thesis, put forward by Fanon in *Les Damnés de la terre*, according to which the truly revolutionary forces of today were the peasant masses of the under-developed countries, and in 1958 he wrote a preface to Henri Alleg's book *La Question*, which denounced the French Army's use of torture in Algeria. Although Alleg was a Communist, Sartre found himself at variance with French Communists on the Algerian issue. They argued that their duty was to oppose the war, but that they had to work in France, among the

[a] One must not confuse his life-long interest in the colour problem (see in particular his preface to an anthology compiled by Senghor, the Negro poet) with his approach to the National Liberation movement in recent years. The latter is not only an extension of the former, but an attempt to remould the revolutionary strategy of Western Socialists in the light of the anti-imperialist struggles taking place in the "third world".

French people, and that their tasks could not possibly be the same as the Algerian patriots' in the F.L.N. (the National Liberation Front). Sartre, on the other hand, felt it his duty to devote himself entirely to the Algerian cause, a view which he expressed by saying that he was ready "to carry suitcases" for the F.L.N. More than once, *Temps modernes* found itself in hot water with the authorities for its uncompromising stand, and Sartre himself was a victim of a nearly successful terrorist attack by the right-wing O.A.S.

In recent years, his attitude towards the Communists has been that of the friendly, but critical, outsider. He agreed to take part in philosophical debates with them, and he wrote a friendly letter to Roger Garaudy, for inclusion in the latter's book, *Perspectives de l'homme*, a study of modern philosophical trends in France. He stressed, however, that "contemporary Marxists" were not paying sufficient attention to human beings as such, and he further developed this idea in his 1960 book, *Critique de la raison dialectique*. French Communists, for their part, have become less critical of his work, and whilst still stressing ideological differences, most of them now regard him as a troublesome but faithful ally.

After de Gaulle's return to power in 1958, Sartre seems to have become increasingly disillusioned about the prospects for left-wing parties in France, and he has tended to voice his disappointment in rather tragical and extreme terms. For example, in a preface to a new edition of a book by Paul Nizan,[a] he spoke of the Left as a "carcass which stinks", and remarked bitterly on the "radical impotence" of his generation. He complained of being completely cut off from the youth of his country, and the same mood of despair can be found in Simone de Beauvoir's Memoirs, where the word "exile" recurs with persistent monotony. When the parties of the Left came closer to co-operation than they had ever done since the days of the Resistance, and jointly supported François Mitterand in the presidential election, Sartre refused at first to recognize that any real change had taken place and he was not far from dismissing the whole thing as an unprincipled electoral

[a] Paul Nizan was a life-long friend of Sartre's. A Communist, he broke with the Party in 1939, after the Soviet-German pact, and was killed during one of the early battles of the second world war. The book which Sartre agreed to preface was *Aden-Arabie*.

manœuvre. At the last minute, however, he grudgingly agreed
to throw his weight and that of *Temps modernes* on Mitterand's
side. It is easy to accuse him of lack of political realism, and
some Communists have even suggested that he is displaying at
times the same kind of "romanticism" as that of Hugo Barine,
the young dreamer whom he castigates so well in *Les Mains
sales*. What can hardly be denied is that, on the individual level,
he expresses a thoroughly genuine attitude. It may well be that
he fails to understand the political world, which is even
"dirtier" than he had imagined, but like Péguy before him,
he insists on voicing his disgust every time he fears that his
"mystique" is waging a losing battle. His anxiety and his feeling
of confusion are shared by so many people today that they
should command sympathy and understanding.[a]

Sartre's political commitment has enabled him to take a
stand on a great number of topical issues. One of the most
interesting examples was his approach to the Jewish question, a
problem which Péguy had already tackled in *Notre Jeunesse*.
The Christian writer had stressed that "antisemites do not
know the Jews"[17] and that he felt bound to speak up on behalf
of all the poor ones he had known, adding that he had found
them hard-working, devoted to their friends and faithful to
their "mystique". He admitted, however, that his was only a
personal testimony, and that the historical analysis of antisemitism had yet to be written. Sartre's ambition was to fill
that gap with *Réflexions sur la question juive* (Thoughts on the
Jewish question). He began with a portrait of the antisemite
who, according to him, is a coward;

> He is afraid. Not of the Jews, of course, but of himself, . . . of
> society and the world.[18]

Antisemitism is an easy way of explaining the evils of society
and of justifying the failure of the individual in a hostile world.
In addition to the conscious antisemites, there are those who are
drawn to the movement because of its "snob" appeal, and there
are also the false friends of the Jews. These false friends are
the lukewarm democrats who extend their tolerance to the
antisemites as well as to the Jews, and who claim that they

[a] Cf. Jean Rony's article in *Nouvelle Critique*, No. 173–74 (March 1966), for
a Communist assessment of Sartre's political activity.

only know men as such, thus denying the Jew's concreteness
as a Jew. But what is a Jew? Sartre's reply was that "A Jew
is a man who is thought of as a Jew by other men",[19] a definition which is well in keeping with existentialism,[a] but which
has been resented by modern Jews.[b] Sartre's advice to them
was that they should assert their Jewishness, not in order to
perpetuate their differences with the Gentiles, but in order to
become aware of their position as an exploited minority and
swell the ranks of the revolutionaries. For only the social
revolution would put an end to antisemitism, argued the
author, as a classless society has no need of scapegoats. His
distinction between "authentic" and "inauthentic" Jews
strikingly recalls Péguy's contrast between "those who are
consumed with Jewish anxiety, and who resort to all sorts of
pitiful play-acting in order to deny it, . . . and those who are
consumed with Jewish anxiety, and do not even think of denying it".[20] (Péguy incidentally draws the same contrast between
genuine and false Christians.)

THE PHILOSOPHER:
COMMITMENT AS A LOGICAL NECESSITY

A full account of Sartre's philosophy is outside the scope of
this essay, except in so far as it concerns the logical and
theoretical justification of commitment. It must be stated, from
the outset, that there are contradictory features in his philosophy, and that some of its early theses can hardly be recon-
ciled with the author's subsequent crusade in favour of
commitment. He is well aware of these contradictions, and in a
special interview with Olivier Todd in 1957, he admitted
having changed his views in some respects.[21] As a philosopher,
Sartre is known as an existentialist, and his latest book, the
Critique de la raison dialectique, is, in his own words, an attempt
to reconcile existentialism and Marxism. It is therefore necessary to begin with a few words about the meaning of existentialism. Its basic principle is the simple proposition that
"existence precedes essence", or, in other words, that to begin
with, man *is*, and defines himself afterwards. Sartre explained

[a] See below, p. 141.
[b] Writing in the Catholic periodical *Esprit*, a Jewish critic, who calls
himself "Rabi", says that he prefers Péguy's approach because it does not
dehumanize the Jews, as Sartre tends to do.

the difference between "existence" and "essence" by showing
that when a workman creates an object, a paper-knife for
instance, he starts by imagining it in his head, and eventually
produces it according to his conception: the object owes its
existence to the artisan's mental idea of it, so that its essence
or function came before its actual existence. This is not the
the case for man, because what he becomes is not predetermined
in advance by a God or by some forces outside his control, it is
the result of his conscious choice. *Man is free.*

From this basic principle, Sartre draws a number of important conclusions. In the first place, he interprets it as a
necessary implication of atheism: man was not created in
God's image, in which case essence would have preceded
existence, he creates himself. Religion is at the same time a
consequence and a denial of freedom—as long as man is free,
he is free to reject his liberty and invent another Being who
can be relied upon to dictate his essence to him. This is so
much easier and more comfortable than having to create one's
own values, but such cowardice is encouraged by society when
it feels the need to strengthen social commands by giving them
a religious origin. In *Les Mouches*, the king of Argos illustrates
this view, for in order to establish his authority, he artificially
engineers among the people a cult of remorse and fear of the
gods—an obvious allusion to the way in which Marshal Pétain
exploited France's defeat by preaching repentance and a
return to the Church. But why should man be afraid of his
liberty? The answer is that freedom is not a gift or a blessing;
it is first experienced as loneliness in a hostile world, and the
experience is accompanied by a feeling of "anguish". "We are
anguish,"[22] states *L'Être et le Néant* uncompromisingly. Freedom
puts man's responsibility squarely on his shoulders and shows
him that no one will help him but himself. "Liberty," writes
Sartre, "could pass for a curse; it *is* a curse, but it is also the
only source of human greatness."[23] Because liberty is absolute,
so is man's responsibility. He is not fixed once and for all, but
is continuously compelled to choose and decide courses of
action for himself. He is "condemned" to be free and to define
himself by his deeds. "Each man is nothing else but that which
he makes of himself."[24] The concrete manifestation of his
liberty is a "project", i.e. the choice of a deed, and the fulfilment of that deed. In making decisions, he is accountable to

no one but man, and in this respect Sartrian existentialism is an emphatic assertion of humanism. It is again in *Les Mouches* that we find an illustration of this conception, when the hero is accused of rebelling against his Maker by taking the law into his own hands; he brushes the accusation aside with the proud statement that "justice is a business which concerns men, and I do not need a god to teach me it".[25] The criterion which enables us to decide whether a deed is good or bad is not the will of God, but the degree to which it can help to assert and manifest our liberty. Does this mean that "total" freedom gives us the right to do what we like? Existentialism has sometimes been interpreted in this way, but Sartre's view is that it is only in theory that we can say with Dostoevsky that "if God did not exist, everything would be permitted". In practice, we are *situated*, we encounter conditions which are not of our making or choosing, and liberty consists in giving meaning to each particular situation; for example, a political prisoner who refuses to betray his principles is more free than his jailers, for he has transcended his situation—he has said "no" to outside commands and found his justification in his own conscience. On the other hand, those who passively accept their situation, who use their liberty in order to deny liberty, are guilty of "mauvaise foi"—a phrase which I prefer to translate by "self-deception" because it is primarily an attempt to "kid" oneself that one is not free. Sartre calls such people "salauds", a very strong term which might be rendered by the English word "swine".

If existentialism were confined to the above principles, its integration into Marxism would be a comparatively simple matter. The Marxist might frown a little at the special emphasis placed on Liberty as an Absolute, but he would not find it difficult to endorse the atheism, the humanism and the appeal to action. Things, however, are not so simple, because Sartre's philosophy is also an "ontology", i.e. a metaphysical explanation of Being. In his first major philosophical treatise, *L'Être et le Néant* (Being and Nothingness), he develops a number of interesting ideas, of which the most important for our purpose are the distinction between consciousness and objects and the theory of human relations. On the first point, he opposes matter to human consciousness by saying that the former exists "in-itself" ("en-soi")—it has objective existence and can be perceived—whereas the latter exists "for-itself" ("pour-soi"), because, in the act of perceiving objects, it isolates them from their surroundings, and at the same time it asserts itself as different from them. When I perceive a chair, for example, I abstract the chair from the rest of reality, but I also prove to myself that I am different from the chair. Broadly speaking, Sartre gives "Things" the name of "Being" and "Consciousness" the name of "Nothingness". Man is the one creature by which "Nothingness comes into the world".[26] The use of these abstract philosophical terms should not obscure the significance of Sartre's assertion, which, according to Albérès, merely consists in saying that ". . . man is a consciousness which detaches itself from things and gives them meaning". Albérès adds the comment that ". . . this view is clear, straightforward, honest and commonplace".[27] I am not so sure that the theory of Nothingness means little more than a "commonplace" idea, for it is accompanied in *L'Être et le Néant* by elaborate descriptions of the "void" which separates the self from objects, and by reflections on the meaning of "absence", "negativity" and many other issues, all of which require full philosophical treatment which would take us well beyond the strict limits assigned to this essay. I do agree, however, that the basic theory is comparatively simple, and that it is part of Sartre's permanent belief that the world has no significance apart from the one which we choose to give it. It is easy to see the links between such a belief and commitment. The idea that the world awaits our undertakings, our "projects", leads to the view that commitment is not just desirable, but inescapable, because in everything we do, we assert our personality and create our own essence:

> Man is a totality, and not a collection . . . He expresses himself in full in the most insignificant and superficial of his deeds.[28]

What does, however, constitute a stumbling block is the theory of human relationships elaborated in *L'Être et le Néant*. Very briefly, it amounts to saying that human relations can only be based on conflict:

> One must either transcend the Other, or let oneself be

transcended by him. The essence of relations among different consciousnesses is not the "Mitsein" [the feeling of fellowship, M.A.]; it is conflict.[29]

The reason for such a gloomy pronouncement is that, according to Sartre, I discover myself under the impact of other people's "gaze", a term which describes moral judgement rather than mere physical look. Consequently, I generally try to conform to the views which others have of me, and most of my actions become a form of "play-acting": I "play" at being what I am expected to be. This means that other people deny my freedom (how then can it be absolute?!), and we get the negation of "being for-itself" inasmuch as we are now dealing with "being for-others". It is not necessary, of course, to accept other people's views—I may refuse to do so, and in my turn deny the Other's freedom. Human relations therefore continuously oscillate between imposing one's look on others and being looked at by them. They are in a state of perpetual conflict. Mr Maurice Cranston, in a brilliant essay on Sartre, draws attention to the fact that this theory not only contradicts in a dramatic fashion the views subsequently put forward by Sartre, but that it involves a contradiction within L'Être et le Néant itself. He quotes a footnote in the book to the effect that an "ethics of deliverance and salvation" is possible, but only after "a radical conversion", and adds the comment ". . . if this theory is true, there is no room for a conversion, 'radical' or otherwise."[30] This is why, according to Mr Cranston, Sartre has been unable to keep the promise he made at the end of his book and produce a coherent ethical system. This, incidentally, is not the view of another critic, Marc Beigbeder, who feels that the delay is in keeping with the existentialist principle that "existence precedes essence", and that Sartre has decided to approach moral problems in a concrete way in his novels and his plays before evolving his ethics of "deliverance and salvation".[31] But Beigbeder was writing in 1947, and to this day, twenty years later, the famous Ethics has still not appeared. The reason seems, quite simply, as Mr Cranston suggests, that such an ethics cannot be deduced from L'Être et le Néant. It is only to the extent that Sartre has discarded some of its theses and has adopted Marxist philosophy that he has been able to get out of his dilemma. This was already suggested by Francis

Jeanson, himself a Marxist, though not a member of the Communist Party. In *Le Problème moral et la pensée de Sartre*, a book which first appeared in 1947 (with a preface by Sartre himself, endorsing its interpretations) and has just been re-published and revised in 1966, Jeanson put forward the view that human relations are based on conflict when we remain on the level of individualism, but that the "radical conversion" involves a socialist revolution.[a] I am inclined to agree once again with Mr Cranston that "Jeanson's talk about 'levels' is hardly satisfactory as serious philosophy".[32]

There is a further contradiction between *L'Être et le Néant* and the rest of Sartre's work. It concerns the sombre conclusion that "man is a useless passion". I cannot see how it fits in either with the need for commitment or with Sartre's description of himself as an "unrepentant optimist". His friend Simone de Beauvoir, however, thinks differently, and I should like to quote at some length from a book she wrote in 1946, not because I agree with her, but because I feel that she unwittingly reveals Sartre's *wish* to transcend his own limitations:

> It is claimed that existentialism is a philosophy of anguish and despair, . . . Indeed, does not Sartre say that man is a useless passion, that he tries in vain to achieve a synthesis between the "for-itself" and the "in-itself", to become God? This is true. But it is equally true that the most optimistic ethics always start by stressing the element of failure in man's condition; without failure, there can be no ethics . . . The failure described in "Being and Nothingness" is final, but it is also ambiguous. Man, says Sartre, is "a being who *makes himself* lack of being *so that* there should be being". This means that passion is not imposed on him from outside. He has chosen it . . . The phrase "so that" clearly indicates intentionality . . . And here we have, not failure, but success; the aim which man sets himself by accepting to be lack of being is finally achieved by him.[33]

[a] Other Marxist critics suggest that what Sartre mistakes for the ontological roots of conflict are in fact historical roots, in other words, that conflict is inevitable in class societies. I am inclined to agree, but I believe that the messianic idea that socialism will automatically put an end to all human conflicts is foreign to Marx: he simply asserted that the classless society would do away with *social* conflicts, with the clash of economically antagonistic interests.

Those who find the above passage difficult to grasp may draw some comfort from the fact that it comes from a book entitled *For an ethics of ambiguity*! In an article published much later, the same author remarked that in his subsequent evolution, "Sartre has stressed more and more the committed character of liberty."[34] This is perfectly true, but it hardly proves that the "committed character" was initially implied in *L'Être et le Néant* taken *as a whole*.

The fate of Sartre's lecture on *Existentialism and Humanism* (1945), later reproduced in book form, further illustrates the contradiction. For in "popularizing" the themes of existentialism, Sartre was led to emphasize its optimistic character, but he later regretted his talk and called it "premature". Does not this imply that the humanism was not *yet* apparent in the first book of the master? And is not this confirmed by his admission to Olivier Todd, already quoted, that "some elements have altered"?

Be that as it may, *Existentialism and Humanism* served a useful purpose in clarifying some of the concepts of Sartrian philosophy. In particular, it stressed its dynamic character and showed that man's only salvation lay in his activity; it brought out vividly the compelling need to "invent man" "at every instant",[35] and it gave a human content to the concepts of "anguish" and "abandonment": the first one was assimilated to the "sense of complete and profound responsibility"[36] which any man must experience when he is going to act and when he knows the potential value of his actions, and the second one was interpreted as a philosophical way of saying that we are accountable to ourselves alone and cannot push on to others the burden of responsibility. The essay also provided a different interpretation of human relations by insisting that I cannot will my liberty without willing that of others (although the theoretical justification for such a humanistic view was feeble or almost non-existent), and that man, "in choosing for himself, . . . chooses for all men".[37] In his book on *Existentialist Philosophies*, Emmanuel Mounier drew an interesting parallel between Bergsonism and Existentialism. Other philosophies, he said, "are bent on ridding the world of man's presence",[38] but in doing so, they serve only one purpose, to secure peace and quiet. They are, according to Péguy, "systems of tranquillity which are liked because under them we can take it easy".[39]

Until he published an essay on "dialectical reason" in 1960, Sartre illustrated his philosophical tenets chiefly through the medium of novels and plays. They will be examined in due course, but it is necessary to point out that, with the exception of *La Nausée*, which is a pre-war novel, written in 1938, and which deals with the "anguish" produced by the "feeling of existence", and the short stories of *Le Mur*, which also date back to the pre-war period, the characters of Sartre's fictional world emphasize his "ethics of deliverance" rather than his ontology. This is even true of *Huis clos* (In Camera), a play where the "damnation" of three criminals is described in sole terms of their having to put up with the hostile "gaze" of one another. For them, "hell is other people", but this is because they are dead and cannot act. It is by no means certain that Sartre's intention was to suggest that the same applies to the land of the living, a point to which I intend to return.

When Sartre published *Critique de la raison dialectique*, and stated that he considered himself a Marxist, the announcement did not come as a real surprise. Apart from his "rapprochement" with the Communists on political issues, there had been many pointers suggesting that he was finding in Marxism the answer to his philosophical problems. Not that he felt that this would dispense him from further research. From the outset, he saw Marxism as a method rather than as a finished system, and in his letter to Roger Garaudy he stated categorically that Marxist philosophy had yet to be elaborated ("Le marxisme est à faire") and that his own existentialism, provided it acknowledged its links with historical reality, was "the only Marxist research to be both legitimate and concrete".[40] His reasons for accepting Marxism were given to Olivier Todd, as early as 1957:

> I take it [he said], that one cannot go beyond Marxism today because the really important questions of contemporary philosophy are still within a Marxist framework ... Marxism is an all-inclusive whole reflecting our age. No one can go beyond it. If one thinks one does, one either falls back on to a pre-Marxist concept, or one works with a concept implicit in Marxism.[41]

In the same interview, he complained that present-day

Marxists lacked ". . . what one might describe as the point of insertion between the individual and the social . . . what one might call mediations".[41]

These ideas are developed at greater length in the *Critique*. On the subject of "mediations", in particular, Sartre suggests three ways of achieving concrete studies of individuals— psycho-analysis, sociology and phenomenology. The merit of the first is that it discloses the links between a man and his class in the specific setting of family relationships; Sartre illustrates his point with a few brilliant remarks on Flaubert who "lived privately his petty-bourgeois generality". In addition to the family, there are other social groups which influence the individual and shape his character; sociological analyses can help us to understand these connections. Lastly, phenomenology is the study of intentionality: it explains the deed by relating it to the aim of the doer.

The basic aim of the *Critique* is to lay the foundations for a Marxist anthropology. Man, according to Sartre, is a dialectical being, and one must start with a "critique", in the Kantian sense, of dialectical reason. Modern Marxists, he feels, are content to deduce dialectics empirically, but there can be no such thing, Engels notwithstanding, as a "dialectics of nature", because it is essentially a human characteristic. The philosopher's task is therefore to establish dialectics "a priori", and to recognize that its source is the concrete human agent, the individual and his activity:

The driving force is individual activity.[42]

He is careful to point out that "a priori" must not be interpreted as meaning "preceding experience", but as "the universality and the necessity which are contained in every experience, and which go beyond each individual experience".[43]

French Marxists' reactions to the *Critique* were, on the whole, frankly hostile. Whilst welcoming the author's "conversion" to Marxism, they accused him of "idealism" (probably the worst sin in the Marxist philosophical calendar) for failing to see that nature, no less than man, behaves dialectically, and they claimed that the "individual" was an abstraction, and not really the concrete and living reality Sartre fondly imagined. Naturally, they also bitterly resented his attacks on their lack of achievements, and among the many names they hurled at him, to prove him wrong, it was interesting to find Aragon's. Outside France, criticism was less virulent. For example, the Polish philosopher Adam Schaff, in his book *Philosophy of Man*, maintained that existentialism was not Marxism and could not be integrated into it, but he admitted that it raised certain human problems which have not yet been satisfactorily solved by Marxists. Sartre himself does not claim that his present position is entirely satisfactory, and with great honesty he acknowledges its contradictions; writing in *Temps modernes* at the end of 1957, he stated his belief that ". . . historical materialism provides the only valid interpretation of history, and that existentialism remains the only method of approaching reality in a concrete way." And he added,

> I do not intend to deny the contradictions in this attitude . . . Many people's lives are still dominated by the tension which this double demand produces.[44]

In philosophy, as in politics, Sartre does not offer comfort but "tension". I do not agree with many of his views, but I would be prepared to endorse Professor Thody's opinion that

> Those who hold that any worthwhile philosophy must be the expression of personal anguish will find in Sartre a disturbing but stimulating ally.[45]

THE CRITIC:
COMMITMENT IN LITERATURE AND IN LIFE

Sartre has written a considerable number of articles and essays. Many of them are included in the seven volumes of *Situations* which have appeared so far. They deal with various literary and general topics and are a lively proof of the author's keen interest in his time. It is of course impossible to summarize them or even to mention them all here. Let us note in passing the attack on Mauriac in *Situations I*, in which the Catholic novelist is accused of determining his characters' fate in advance and behaving like a God towards them, which prompts Sartre to exclaim that "God is not an artist; neither is M. Mauriac";[46] the article on *Nationalisation de la littérature* in *Situations II* (most of the volume is taken up by *What is Literature?*), in which Sartre warns that literature is threatened with becoming impersonal propaganda, whereas true commitment requires that the writer's individuality be reflected in his work; the essay on the Occupation in *Situations III*, in which we are told that Frenchmen were never more free than under Nazi rule, because the choice facing each one of them "... was made in the presence of death" and compelled every man to examine "...the limits of his own freedom";[47] and in the same volume the long article on *Matérialisme et Révolution* which describes Communist materialism as "bourgeois"; the essays on aesthetics in *Situations IV*, and in particular the study in which he reverses his earlier stand about prose being the only form of committed art, and praises the painter Lapoujade for achieving commitment through his refusal to be granted special "privileges" as an artist (the article is called *The Painter without Privileges*), and the essay on Tintoretto (*Le Séquestré de Venise*) in which he shows the relationship between the painter and the rise of the bourgeoisie in the Venetian Republic; the essays dealing with colonialism and the National Liberation Movement in *Situations V*; and the numerous articles on Marxism in *Situations VI* and *VII* which describe his political and philosophical evolution, already referred to.

Of Sartre's longer essays, one of the most interesting is his study of Baudelaire, in which he claims that the author of *Les Fleurs du Mal* was a typical example of anti-commitment. He contests the prevailing notion that Baudelaire's unhappy life was undeserved, and asks,

> Suppose he had deserved his life, though? Suppose that, contrary to generally accepted ideas, men never had but the life they deserved? The matter requires closer examination.[48]

His own conclusion is that Baudelaire *wanted* to be unhappy because he was terrified by the prospect of having to acknowledge his responsibility as a free man. His life illustrates the truth that

> ... the free choice which man makes of himself is completely identified with what people call his destiny.[49]

When Baudelaire's father died, two things happened to him —on the one hand, he came to look upon his mother as an idol, and on the other he discovered "in shame" that he was alone in the world. The trouble was that he retained these two attitudes throughout his life: for fear of making personal decisions, he allowed his family to make them for him, and he embraced his loneliness "with frenzy" in order to delude himself that it came from within himself. He was the man who, having discovered his true condition, passionately endeavoured to hide it from himself. His attitude during his trial was particularly revealing, because not once did he challenge the moral values of his judges. He accepted those values, as in his view liberty merely consisted in sinning against them. He ate of the forbidden fruit, not *"in spite* of its being forbidden, but *because* it was forbidden"[50] (Sartre's italics). Being exclusively interested in himself, he sought refuge in art, and not content with standing aloof from the struggles of his time, he devoted pages and pages of his personal diaries to attacks on the Republicans. Sartre's merciless verdict is that Baudelaire suffered because he chose to suffer. And it served him right!

Mr Cranston makes much of the fact that Baudelaire's original "choice" was made when he was only seven, and he writes,

> Freud, and others like him, have made us more compassionate, . . . less ready to blame and punish the young. . . . But Sartre's psycho-analysis is directly opposed to Freud on this question. His absolute libertarianism makes children morally responsible agents . . . it can only be described as harshly reactionary.[51]

There is some truth in the accusation, but I am not quite sure the author is fair to Sartre. What the latter objects to in Baudelaire is not so much his reaction as a child when his father died, but the attitude of servility and dependence on others which he displayed *as a man*, in other words, his inability to grow up, and this is not quite the same as making children "morally responsible agents". Certainly, Sartre is very hard on Baudelaire the man, and his unkindness is not always justified, but his criticism is levelled at the adult, and not at the child. I think we can exonerate him from the charge of being "harshly reactionary".

With regard to Sartre's complaint that Baudelaire ran away from commitment, Professor Thody comments that he

... is implying that it is better for literature to concern itself
with moral rather than with aesthetic values ... he would
have preferred Baudelaire to have been a third-rate early
Socialist pamphleteer rather than a first-rate lyrical poet.[52]

Is this quite the point Sartre is making? I rather think that
his view is that artistic genius cannot excuse moral weakness,
and I must confess I agree with him. It is not the quality of
Baudelaire's poetry which he is assessing, but his decision to
seek in art a substitute for "the good". If this is the price one
must pay for great art, I would not hesitate in saying that we
are better without it, but I hasten to add that, fortunately,
there are other ways of achieving "first-rate" lyrical poetry.
What, in my opinion, is a very serious fault in Sartre's study is
precisely that it does not discuss the qualities of Baudelaire's
art. The poetic beauty of *Les Fleurs du Mal* is superbly ignored,
instead of being honestly admitted. Surely, the case for commitment is by no means weakened when one grants that masterpieces can be written by unworthy men? My own view is that,
in writing great poetry, Baudelaire partly made up for his
unworthiness, inasmuch as he expressed, perhaps in spite of
himself, the mood of his generation. I would also add that I
am naïve enough to believe that his art would have gained
immensely in human greatness if it had not been marred by the
personality it reveals. All the perfumes of *Les Fleurs du Mal*
cannot sweeten his reputation!

Another grave defect of Sartre's analysis is that it does not
attempt to discover *why* Baudelaire, after flirting for a while
with the Revolutionaries, glorified his lack of commitment. It is
not enough to speak of his cowardice without examining the
historical conditions of his age. Aragon's judgement seems
much more balanced. He explains Baudelaire's wavering stand
and his fear of revolutionary changes by the weakness of popular
forces at the time, and by the poet's dejection at their successive
defeats. But, says Aragon,

one must be fair: all the horrors and contemptible feelings
which are expressed in Baudelaire's diaries and articles
cannot prevent his having been a very great poet. ... One
must be fair: ... the contradictory features in Baudelaire's
work are a reflection of working-class defeats. ... One must

be fair, and learn to sort out, in Baudelaire, the poetic jewel from the foulness of his class.[53]

"One must be fair." This is just what Sartre failed to be.

On the other hand, when he dealt with Jean Genêt, he went to the other extreme, and praised him for rejecting middle-class morality and living according to his nature, i.e. as a homosexual and a thief. It is difficult to share Sartre's admiration. Admittedly, Genêt is brutally frank and he tells the bourgeois a few home truths, but to call him a saint, and a martyr to boot,[54] is a trifle excessive. One can refuse to join the hypocritical chorus of Genêt's respectable critics without going to these lengths.

THE NOVELIST:
FROM THE INTUITION OF LIBERTY ("NAUSEA") TO LIBERTY IN ACTION (COMMITMENT)

Sartre began his literary career in 1938 with a novel called *La Nausée*,[a] which is also a philosophical manifesto containing in embryo the future themes of existentialism—the gratuitousness of existence, the sham character of ready-made values, and the need for man to assert his freedom by giving life a meaning. The book is supposed to be the diary of Antoine Roquentin, a thirty-year-old bachelor to whom nothing spectacular happens until he discovers the "contingency" of objects and people around him, i.e. the fact that the world exists but could very well not have existed, and that everything, including himself, is superfluous, "de trop". This discovery, accompanied by profound disgust for the smug complacency of his provincial milieu[b] and for his own flesh, fills him with "nausea": he is overwhelmed by the thought of his immense responsibility when he realizes that, although he has to face a "situation" which is not of his own making, he is

---

[a] The American translation of the book is called *Nausea*, but the English version is entitled *The Diary of Antoine Roquentin*. It seems a pity to emphasize the diary-form of the novel rather than its actual content. Note, however, the recent Penguin edn., correctly entitled *Nausea*.

[b] There is little doubt that the town of Bouville, where Roquentin lives, stands for Le Havre, where Sartre taught in his youth, and probably for La Rochelle, where, at the age of eleven, he followed his mother after her second marriage. He grew to dislike provincial life intensely, and Roquentin's feelings on the subject are an echo of his own.

absolutely free to decide how he should act. *La Nausée* is not a committed book, as neither character nor author is yet in a position to suggest positive steps, apart from the vague idea that salvation lies in the deed and in finding a purpose in life. However, the negation of traditional values and the vigorous search for authenticity constitute the first step towards commitment. In the same way as Aragon before him, Sartre begins his journey with absolute revolt.

La Nausée brought its author great fame in literary circles. A year later, a collection of five short stories, gathered under the title of *Le Mur*,[a] was favourably reviewed by the critics. What was particularly noticeable was that the attack on hypocrisy and self-deception continued unrelentlessly, and also that middle-class sensibilities were given quite a jolt by the frank treatment of sexual topics. But the book is still far removed from commitment. A possible exception is the last story in the collection, *L'Enfance d'un chef* (A Leader's Childhood), which represents Sartre's first incursion into the social field. With powerful irony, he describes the bourgeois upbringing of Lucien Fleurier, a member of the upper classes, who finally proves his fitness for leadership by utterly despising the Jews and by joining Fascist gangs. The tone is already that of *Réflexions sur la question juive*, where antisemitism is revealed as a bourgeois evasion of the real issues, and of *La Putain respectueuse*, a play which denounces the American racialists' belief that Negro-baiting is the "virile" prerogative of a social élite.

Sartre's great committed novel, *Les Chemins de la liberté* (The Roads to Freedom),[b] appeared after the war. It bears the imprint of his recent political experience and of his discovery of human solidarity, although its central character is just as negative in his approach to life as was Antoine Roquentin. The essential difference is that the author himself has gone beyond that stage, a fact which is illustrated by the construction of the novel, which allows the hero's stand to be judged by others (we are free to identify ourselves with any of them, as Sartre carefully avoids a direct intervention which would be contrary to

[a] *Le Mur* (The Wall) is the title of the first story. The English version, *Intimacy and Other Stories*, took its title from the fourth story.

[b] The French title does not clearly indicate whether the novel deals with the roads *of* freedom, or with roads *to* freedom. My own view is that its real subject is the latter.

his conception of the novelist's function), and by his own inability to achieve real liberty.

The novel is divided into three parts. In the first one, *L'Age de raison* (The Age of Reason),[a] Mathieu Delarue is a teacher of philosophy in pre-war France, and like Sartre in those days, he has left-wing sympathies, but is unwilling to commit himself to any party, or even to vote, for fear of giving up his freedom. He is surrounded by admiring young disciples, but is attacked as a fraud by his brother Jacques, a "grand bourgeois" who prides himself on living as a "grand bourgeois", and, at the other pole, by his Communist friend Brunet. The latter ridicules his obsession with freedom, and asks him pointedly,

> "But what is the use of your freedom if you do not commit yourself?"[55]

Mathieu is impressed in spite of himself, and he cannot help thinking that his friend is "freer than" himself—he has given up everything, but

> . . . everything has been given back to him, including his freedom.[56]

However, Brunet's commitment has its negative side—it carries with it uncritical acceptance of the Party line and is as much a form of "mauvaise foi" as Mathieu's fruitless neutrality. Sartre's depiction of Brunet reflects his attitude to the Communist Party at the time: he accepts the idea of joining a working-class movement, but he cannot stomach authoritarianism and regimentation. Mathieu's personal life is as unsatisfactory as his political one, because it is dominated by his fear of losing his liberty by tying himself too closely to his mistress, Marcelle. Most of the novel is taken up by his attempts to find a large sum of money in order to pay for an abortion when he learns that Marcelle is pregnant. He finally succeeds in stealing the money from a wealthy acquaintance, but finds that Marcelle has changed her mind and has decided to marry his homosexual friend, Daniel Sereno.

---

[a] The title is intended to describe the hero's progress: he reaches "the age of reason" when he begins to suspect the futility of his uncommitted freedom; but at the end of Volume I, it is only a faint suspicion.

Book II, *Le Sursis* (Reprieve) describes the reactions of the characters to the Munich crisis in 1938: Mathieu passively accepts developments, as he feels unable to do anything about them, Brunet is actively engaged in anti-war propaganda, Daniel looks forward to the war as an escape from reality, and Jacques only thinks of his own safety. In addition, we see many others, and among them Gomez, a Spanish Republican who loves war and hopes it will shake bourgeois intellectuals out of their complacency, Philippe, a pacifist who lacks the courage of his convictions, Gros-Louis, an illiterate peasant who is conscripted without knowing what the fuss is all about, Milan and his wife, two Czech anti-Fascists, anxious to resist their country's being sold out to Hitler, and Charles and Catherine, two cripples who fall in love with each other as they are being evacuated in the same railway carriage. The fate of all these characters is dominated by a historical event few of them understand—the Munich conversations between Chamberlain, Daladier, Mussolini and Hitler. An interesting literary device, borrowed from John Dos Passos, helps to stress the links between individual destinies and politics; it is the device of simultaneity, whereby the author mentions in the same sentence the most diverse people, some in France, some in Czechoslovakia, some in New York and some in Germany, thus emphasizing how their fate is affected by the one central event.

Book III, *La Mort dans l'âme* (Iron in the Soul), is divided into two parts. The climax of the first one comes when Mathieu at last manifests his freedom in a positive, and somewhat melodramatic, way: he refuses to allow himself to be captured by advancing German soldiers, and desperately fires at them, giving each of his shots the value of a symbol:

It was an enormous revenge; each shot avenged him for an old scruple. . . . He fired: he was pure, he was all-powerful, he was free.[57]

The second part deals with Brunet's experience in a German concentration camp and has already been briefly discussed above.

Les Chemins de la liberté is unfinished. There was going to be a fourth part, called *La Dernière Chance* (The Last Chance), but only extracts have so far appeared in *Temps modernes* under the title of *Drôle d'amitié* (Strange Friendship). They describe

the semi-homosexual affection between Brunet and another
Communist internee who is opposed to the Hitler-Stalin non-
aggression pact. They both try to escape, but are denounced
by Communist prisoners, and Brunet's friend is shot, complain-
ing that he has been killed by the Party.

Various explanations have been put forward to account for
the unfinished character of the novel. My personal view is that
Sartre's inability to complete it expresses his own political
dilemma. So long as he feels unable to provide a more satisfactory solution than his empirical approach to political life,
and to the Communist Party in particular, he is naturally
reluctant to indicate "the last chance" available to his generation. Whether one agrees with him or not, it must be seen as a
measure of his intellectual honesty. Professor Thody thinks
that "it is tempting to seek for other reasons than the most
evident political and philosophical ones to account for Sartre's
failure to complete *The Roads to Freedom*", and he suggests that
the most important one of these ". . . is that, as Iris Murdoch
said, he has not the sympathy with the ordinary stuff of human
life which characterizes the true novelist".[58] I cannot altogether
share this view. I believe that Sartre's deliberate purpose is to
show the limitations of social misfits and negative characters,
and that is why he peoples his novels with such pathetic
figures. They help him to focus attention on the collapse of
values in modern society and to sound the alarm. "Existentialism," says Henri Peyre, "does not ignore despair. But it
attempts to lead away from it after having drunk from its cups
to the dregs."[59]

There are two aspects of *Les Chemins de la liberté* which deserve
closer examination. One is the unmistakably socialist character
of the novel. Sartre is no longer content to speak of man in
general terms, but is concerned to show that the bourgeois has
only one way of committing himself—he should give up the
values of his class and its whole way of life. The tragedy of
Mathieu is that he fails to do that. It is ironic that it should be
his bourgeois brother who reminds him of his inconsistency:

"You despise the bourgeois class, and yet . . . you lead the
life of a bourgeois."[60]

It is also Jacques who first tells him that he ought to know better, because he has reached "the age of reason". But Jacques is a "swine", he accepts himself as a bourgeois, whereas at the end of Book I, when Mathieu repeats to himself his brother's remark about "the age of reason", he interprets it in an entirely different way, as meaning that he is old enough to realize the futility of freedom when it is not committed and asserted through action. Earlier in the book, Sartre shows how the reality of Mathieu's class filters through the most insignificant details of his life:

> He got up. An official[a] got up, an official who had money worries....[61]

It could be objected that in giving his novel a socialist message, Sartre is allowing himself to interfere, as a novelist, with his characters' freedom, and is guilty of the fault he denounced in Mauriac and in others. We shall see later that committed realism claims that a novelist's "impartiality" is neither possible nor desirable,[62] but at this stage the objection can be countered by showing that it is never the novelist who judges his heroes, but the logic of their situation. In an interview published in *Les Lettres françaises* in 1945, Sartre explained that each of his characters was free because,

> ... after having done anything (he) can still do anything,

and he added,

> I consider the situation and a freedom chained in a situation ("une liberté enchaînée en situation"). What I am concerned with is the development of the situation.[63]

The accusation that Sartre does not apply his own principles, which has been made by a number of critics, fails to take into account that, in his system, it is impossible to separate freedom from the specific situation which faces the free man.

The other interesting aspect of *Les Chemins de la liberté* is its "Jansenist"[b] character. The word was used by Sartre himself

---

[a] The French word 'fonctionnaire' is here applied to a schoolmaster, as he is paid by the state.

[b] Jansenism is the seventeenth-century heresy which stressed man's utter dependence on God and the sinful character of all his passions.

when he wrote in *What is Literature?* that

> We are Jansenists because the age has made us so. . . .[64]

What he meant was that the tragic circumstances of the war had compelled literature to deal with "extreme situations" and to concern itself with the ultimate questions of human life, just as the seventeenth-century Jansenists had reacted against the Jesuits' compromise with the world and its prosaic values by emphasizing the tragic character of human destiny. Such an approach is particularly evident in Books II and III of *Les Chemins de la liberté*, as their central theme is war—first, the short "reprieve" afforded by the Munich surrender, and then the war itself with its train of unhappiness and suffering. Gone is the casualness displayed by most characters in the first volume; now, each of their decisions brings them face to face with their destiny. But the philosophy of Jansenism also implies a gloomy attitude towards man, and more particularly towards the flesh. I am quite sure that in *What is Literature?* Sartre was not thinking of that aspect at all, but there are obvious traces of it in all his works, and certainly in his novels. Sexual relations are generally shown as dirty, women as basically impure, and love as sullied by its associations with sex. There are elements of puritanism in Sartre, and in this respect he stands in sharp contrast, not only to Aragon, the poet of Elsa and of Love, but also to Péguy, the Catholic who did not despise the flesh. There is even a clear contradiction between his presentation of the subject in some parts of *Les Chemins de la liberté* and his own statement justifying his interest in bodily functions on the grounds that nothing human should be foreign to the realistic writer:

> In my opinion [he told Gabriel d'Aubarède], a writer should take hold of a man in all aspects of his being.[65]

It is one thing to "take hold of man in all aspects of his being", and quite another to describe "the body and its lowest functions" in such a way as to inspire revulsion. Personally, I find Sartre's motives, as expressed above, entirely admirable, but his practice less satisfactory. I am disturbed, as any reader must be, by the fact that his characters never experience genuine love.

THE PLAYWRIGHT:
HUMANISM AND COMMITMENT

The plays of Jean-Paul Sartre illustrate the various stages of his path towards commitment. They can be examined from three different angles—one can study how the concept of action is progressively enriched, as we pass from the deed *for* others to the deed *with* others; one can follow the way in which Sartre tackles the basic ethical question facing committed humanism—the problem of ends and means; and lastly, one can show how some of his plays enable him to intervene in the topical debates of his time. Naturally, all these aspects overlap, but for the sake of clarity they can be discussed separately.

Les Mouches (The Flies) is Sartre's first play, and although it is contemporaneous with *L'Être et le Néant* (1943), it already represents a remarkable advance on the latter. Whereas the philosopher elaborated his system mainly on the basis of his pre-war research,[a] the playwright draws upon his experience as a member of the Resistance Movement and strikes a powerful blow at the forces which are enslaving his country. The action takes place in Argos, fifteen years after Agamemnon has been murdered by Aegisthus, who has now replaced him as king and as Clytemnestra's husband. Agamemnon and Clytemnestra had two children, Electra, who is ill-treated by her stepfather, and Orestes who, at the beginning of the play, returns incognito to his native city, accompanied by his teacher. Orestes is a very modern character, whose "mal du siècle" is embodied in his yearning for companionship and for a sense of purpose. He learns with horror that the people of Argos, although they had no part in the killing of their former king, are made to believe that only collective atonement would appease the wrath of the gods. His teacher advises him to forget the whole sordid business and leave the wretched city to its fate. He appeals to him in the name of liberty, suggesting that he knows better than to commit himself—and therein lies his strength. We recognize the approach which Mathieu Delarue was going to illustrate a few years later. But Orestes's reply foreshadows the assertion made in *Existentialism and Humanism* that "I cannot make my liberty my aim unless I make that of others equally my aim'.[66] He tells his teacher that nothing short of a

[a] According to Sartre, *L'Être et le Néant* is the culmination of his philosophical research since 1930.

practical deed can make him free, and that, if he wants to earn his fellows' love, he must act for them. Genuine freedom is inseparable from commitment and responsibility, and Orestes's duty is to save his countrymen by killing their two tyrants, the usurper and his queen. Before he can perform this deed, he has to vanquish political, spiritual and personal forces. The former are represented by Aegisthus, who is by no means a conventional villain, but a man who, like Anouilh's Créon (in the play *Antigone*), puts forward the view that in order to rule men one must resort to lies and deceptions. Unlike Créon, however, he is weary of his role and hardly offers any resistance to his assassin. Spiritual tyranny is represented by Zeus. His powerful argument is that the path of obedience to the gods is easier than having to "invent" one's own way; but Orestes passionately claims the human privilege of deciding things for himself. Zeus is powerless against him, because man is free, and He is forced to admit that

> Once the idea of freedom has exploded in the soul of a man, the gods can do nothing against him.[67]

Orestes's personal obstacles are the most difficult to overcome, as he has to stifle his love for his sister, who deserts him at the last minute, and his filial affection. Abandoned by everyone, he chooses to act all the same, because he *is* what his deed makes him. At the end of the play, he finds himself more lonely than ever, for although he has delivered Argos, he has not earned its love: the people fear him even more that the despicable Aegisthus he has just killed. Such is the noble, but uncomfortable, lot of the free man.

The next play, *Huis clos* (In Camera), represents a slight advance on this somewhat aristocratic conception of freedom and commitment. It concerns three people who are in hell because of the selfishness they displayed throughout their lives, and who are therefore unworthy of enjoying the same kind of solitude as Orestes after his deed. Their punishment consists in the eternal gaze of the other two, and as one of them puts it, for them "hell is other people". This allegorical formula soon acquired considerable notoriety and was immediately linked with the theory of human relationships expounded in *L'Être et le Néant*. There is no doubt that the illustration of this theory is one of the basic themes of the play, but it is not the only one, nor, in my opinion, the main one. *Huis clos* is primarily concerned with showing that life and action are inseparable. The effect is achieved because the characters are placed in an absolutely "extreme" situation—immediately after death. They realize then that what they have lost is the power to act. Not the power to feel, or to think, or to talk, which is theirs, literally, for ever—but only the power to act. That is their tragedy. Incidentally, Sartre returned to the theme in a later work, a film-script called *Les Jeux sont faits* (The Chips are Down), in which two of the characters continue to "live" after death, but find out that they are denied the privilege of action. Viewed in this light, *Huis clos* acquires a special significance: the penalty which egotists have to pay is the hostile judgement of others, a judgement they can never avoid or destroy by new deeds. This carries an urgent message for the living, for they, at least, are still free to act. To forget that the action of the play takes place in hell, and consequently that the events it depicts are not to be taken literally, is to run the risk of misunderstanding Sartre's purpose. It would be more correct to view *Huis clos* as a landmark in his evolution, which represents the stage when he was still obsessed with the idea that conflict is the essence of human relations, but was, at the same time, beginning to visualize the shape of an "ethics of deliverance and salvation".

That such an ethics should be based on the principle of co-operation becomes increasingly clear in the play which succeeded *Huis clos*. *Morts sans sépulture* (Men without Shadows) is a dramatic description of the last thoughts which assail a number of French patriots who have been captured by the Vichy police and are awaiting death. Most of them give way to despair, but a notable exception is the veteran fighter Canoris who thinks that his death will not be meaningless as there are others to continue the struggle. He advises his companions to forget their pride and pretend to yield to torture by giving their captors false information. He wants them all to live so that they can still be of service. The play appeared in 1946, and in subsequent editions Sartre revised the last scenes in order to give more prominence to Canoris's positive message.

By 1948, when he wrote *Les Mains sales*, he was already convinced that real commitment implies taking part in collective action. His hero is a working-class "militant", but as he is

also a leader who has to work in illegal conditions imposed by
Fascist dictatorship, he is compelled to make individual
decisions. The main object of the play, as we shall see, is to
oppose political realism to the illusion that abstract principles
matter more than compromises. The theme of "working with
others" is intentionally left in the background. This is not the
case in Sartre's greatest play to date, *Le Diable et le bon Dieu*
(Lucifer and the Lord). The central character is Goetz, a
mercenary general who fights on the barons' side during the
Peasants' War in sixteenth-century Germany. He delights in
cruelty, believing that doing nothing but evil is the best way
of asserting his independence. One day, for the sake of a wager,
he goes to the other extreme, and decides he will do nothing
but good. He sets up a model community in which property is
outlawed, and urges his newly-freed peasants to keep aloof
from the revolt, for all violence is a form of evil. Basically, however, he has not changed, because he still believes in himself
rather than in others. He has not really espoused the cause of
the exploited, but has merely tried to thrust happiness on them
and to foist his own ideas on his so-called brethren. His is a false
paradise, as he soon discovers. His individual gesture does not
put an end to the war, and the barons, bent on destroying him,
manage to rouse other peasants against him. It is then that he
really alters. With genuine humility, he seeks the advice of
Nasty, the popular leader, and agrees to join the revolutionary
army as "a man among men". He is still alone, for he cannot
share his great discovery that "God is dead" with his men for
fear of undermining their morale, but it is a new kind of loneliness. Unlike Orestes, who had to leave Argos after his deed,
Goetz remains with the peasants and fights with them.

The play also deals with the problem of ends and means, but
in order to understand Sartre's stand on this issue, it is now
necessary to return to *Les Mains sales*, where two different
approaches to politics are contrasted. A young intellectual
represents what might be termed the romantic approach, and
a hardened Communist leader the realistic one. The action
takes place in Illyria, an imaginary country of which we are
simply told that it has a common border with both Russia
and Germany, during the second world war. The tide is beginning to turn against the Nazis, and when the play opens, the
idea of forming a National Government, including Royalists,

middle-class patriots and Communists, is eagerly discussed. A number of Communists are opposed to what they consider an unnecessary and premature deal, and they want to remove the general secretary, Hoederer, who favours such a solution. They entrust Hugo, a former bourgeois intellectual, with the job of killing Hoederer, and manage to introduce him into his home as private secretary. Hugo agrees, not because he looks upon the murder as politically expedient, but because he feels a revolutionary party must keep its hands pure and refuse to co-operate with the class enemy under any circumstances. However, when he is face to face with the great man, he finds it very difficult to kill him, and he allows himself to be drawn into a heated political argument with him. [a] Hoederer contemptuously dismisses his self-made scruples, and tells him bluntly that ". . . purity is the idea of a fakir or a monk".[68] His vision of the future is no less bright than Hugo's, but he knows that the road which lies ahead is long and tortuous, that it is full of mud, dirt and blood. To take this road is inevitably to get one's hands dirty. An ethical system which lays down in advance that certain courses of action are always right whilst others are always wrong may appear to keep its hands pure, but it does so at the cost of giving up the struggle altogether, and Hoederer bitterly criticizes his young comrade's "purity" as an excuse for doing nothing. Moreover, "dirty hands" does not necessarily mean heroic acts of violence. (These Hugo would not spurn; in fact, he is thrilled at having been selected as Hoederer's murderer, because it makes him feel important.) Often, it simply means the acceptance of a compromise or the discarding of obsolete slogans.

In a comment on his own play, Sartre stated that he considered Hoederer's attitude as "the only sound one".[69] Hugo, on the other hand, although he is drawn with a touch of sympathy because his hesitations typify the initial pitfalls of many young bourgeois when they first indulge in working-class politics, is shown as being guilty of intellectual pride: he persists in the selfish delusion that what goes on in his mind matters more than the requirements of reality itself. The playwright

[a] He does kill him in the end, but only because he finds him kissing his wife. This accounts for the English title of the play, *Crime Passionel*—an unfortunate title because it places the emphasis on Hugo's motives rather than on the political significance of the play.

believes that such an attitude leads to contempt for other men, and he makes Hugo admit that it is only what people might become which interests him, not what they are. Hoederer's reply that men must be taken, and even loved, as they are, is meant to represent the humanist viewpoint and to carry with it the conclusion that no action should be rejected out of hand if it is likely to achieve greater happiness for mankind.

> All means are good [says Hoederer], so long as they are effective.[70]

I do not think Sartre would be satisfied with this formulation today. The concept of "effectiveness" is too vague and does not take into account that certain means which degrade men are incompatible with the aim of building a highly civilized society. They may appear, for a time, to be a necessary evil, but in the long run they have to be cast aside as they hamper the end which is pursued. But *Les Mains sales* is not the playwright's last word on the subject. It is rather the initial step of his humanist ethics and does not yet go beyond the assertion that means must be judged in relation to the ends they achieve, as any other criterion would be outside the realm of human experience. It would be misleading to sum this up by saying that the end justifies the means. Not that it would be bad logic or bad ethics, according to Sartre, but because of the unfortunate historical connotations of the phrase, which, in the past, has often been used by people who preached laxity in morals and were prepared to excuse any crime, provided some pretence could be made about the purity of the intention. Sartre's solution, on the other hand, is neither an easy escape from responsibility, nor a comfortable one. It assumes that study, analysis and a thorough appraisal of the situation must precede action, and it rejects as irresponsible the suggestion that one can rely on a hypothetical "innate" moral sense. His approach seems to be far removed from Péguy's stand, and there are indeed basic differences between the existentialist philosopher and the Catholic poet. All the same, one can detect striking similarities between them. For example, in one of his *Cahiers*, Péguy attacked Kant's "categorical imperative" in terms which might have been used by Sartre himself,

> Kantism has pure hands, but this is because it has no hands.[71]

Moreover, Péguy did not believe that evil could be fought by moral exhortations alone. His attitude to war is instructive in this respect: he always held the view that "in order to kill war, one must make war."[72] One may disagree with his assessment of the 1914 conflict as a "war to end all wars", which merely echoed official propaganda, but I feel that his rejection of uncompromising pacifism was sound and realistic. Lastly, Péguy thought that the "mystique" sinks into "politique", not when "dirty" *means* are used, but rather when "dirty" *ends* are pursued. He never regretted having taken part in street fights at the time of the Dreyfus Affair, and one of his criticisms of the "politicians" was that they were too cowardly to do so. I think both Péguy and Sartre would agree that when we pass from the realm of thought to the realm of practice, every positive action is "dirty" in the sense that it is affected by the very faults it is trying to remove. Sartre would probably add that concrete evils are not sucessfully fought by an abstract good, but by a lesser evil. A humanist takes into account the fact that man is still trying to emerge from the animal kingdom, and that, in the process, the means he uses are nearly always coloured by his animal nature. He believes that the "natural goodness" of man, preached by Rousseau, is a myth, and that the problem is to make social man, the only real man, increasingly more human.

Les Mains sales has often been interpreted, particularly when it first appeared, as an attack on Communist moral relativism. It is true that most of the Communist characters, apart from Hoederer, seem brutal and inhuman, but nowhere does the playwright suggest that it is wrong to adapt one's policy to changing circumstances. Even in 1948, at a time when he had bitter disagreements with the Communist Party, which he accused of not being revolutionary enough, he shared with Marxists the belief that morality must be flexible. Later, in 1952, he refused to allow a performance of his play during the Communist-sponsored Peace Congress which was then being held in Vienna, and which he attended. He was afraid that it might be misunderstood and that people would notice only the callousness of some of the Communist characters. This incident is significant because it shows that Sartre was aware of the ambiguity of his play, and felt that the issue of ends and means required clearer and fuller treatment.

He tackled it once more in *Le Diable et le bon Dieu*. First of all, he improved Hoederer's statement about judging means by their "effectiveness' and made one of the peasants' leaders say,

> Nothing is forbidden when it is a question of saving men.[73]

Here, means are clearly related to the end, instead of being pragmatically assessed as "effective". But it is mainly in Goetz's development that one can trace Sartre's own progress. Goetz's mistake throughout the play is his acceptance of absolute principles—either absolute evil or absolute good. He passes from one to the other with comparative ease. What is far more difficult for him to realize is that good and evil are relative concepts, and that man's hard task consists in choosing, in each specific case, the kind of action which involves the least possible evil and is conducive to the greatest good. When Goetz finally looks at the matter in that simple way, he is in a position to see where his duty lies:

> I wanted pure love: nonsense! To love one another is to hate the same enemy. I am therefore ready to embrace your hatred. I wanted to do good: foolishness! On this earth, and at this time, good and evil are inseparable. I am willing to be evil in order to become good.[74]

It is little wonder that, on hearing this, Nasty exlaims, "You have changed." Goetz is indeed a changed man, because he has recently found out that "God is dead". God was the symbol of Absolute Good, and His "death" is also the death of Lucifer, who embodies Absolute Evil.

> God does not exist. . . . No more heaven! No more hell! The earth alone remains. . . . Away with monsters! Away with saints! Away with pride! There are nothing but men.[75]

Goetz's atheism, far from being a form of "sinful pride", implies genuine humility, because human beings, *other* human beings, are his only judges. He joins with them in seeking to deduce principles from reality, and is prepared to alter his principles when reality alters.

It is again with ends and means that Sartre is concerned in

Les Séquestrés d'Altona, a play written in 1959.[a] Most of the
characters belong to the von Gerlach family, which is dominated by "The Father". The latter is a powerful shipowner
who, together with other industrial magnates, helped to bring
Hitler to power in order to fight the workers at home and
Communism abroad. Now, after the defeat of Nazism, he
continues to make huge profits in West Germany and he
dismisses his responsibility for the recent past with the comforting story that he and his likes were not the real criminals.
Significantly, he is always called "The Father" because he
behaves as if he were Authority Incarnate. His eldest son, Franz,
soon grew impatient with his oppressive rule and with the strict
Lutheran atmosphere surrounding his upbringing. In order to
find freedom, he became an officer in Hitler's army in which he
thought he was making decisions for himself. During the war,
he tortured Russian prisoners in the belief that anything was
permissible to prevent Germany's enslavement by the Allies.
As he has not left his room since his return home in 1946, he
now believes that this is in fact the fate which is meted out to
the German people. He does not want to be disillusioned and
refuses to see anyone, except his sister Leni who has an inces-
tuous love for him. Alone in his room, he addresses an imaginary
crowd of Crabs, who symbolize the thirtieth century, before
which he vainly attempts to justify himself. It is of no avail.
All he manages to do is to torture himself with the reminder
that he was a torturer. The Father, who knows he is going to
die soon from a cancer in the throat, asks his second son
Werner and his wife Johanna to live in the old family house in
order to look after Franz, but Johanna, the only sane character
in the play, is horrified. She succeeds in entering her brother-
in-law's voluntary prison in order to tell him a few home
truths. For a short while, she falls in love with him, but when
she learns how he behaved during the war, she is utterly
disgusted. In the meantime, Franz has learned that Germany
is a prosperous country, so that all his crimes turn out to have
been useless. At this stage, he agrees to talk to his father, and
both of them, conscious of their guilt, decide to do away

[a] There are two English versions, one called *The Condemned of Altona*, and
the other, *Altona*. Neither title conveys Sartre's message, for he wanted to
show that all the von Gerlachs were "prisoners" of their past and of their
prejudices.

with their lives. The play ends with this double suicide.

Sartre wrote *Les Séquestrés d'Altona* at the time of the Algerian war in order to show his countrymen that torture degrades those who use it. By calling his hero Franz (an obvious symbol for France) and by making him a Nazi, he intended to remind Frenchmen that they were behaving towards the Algerians exactly as the Germans had behaved towards them and other nations during the second world war. The similarity of methods was inevitable because rotten political régimes have no other way of keeping themselves alive. Cruelty is their one and only weapon. Their inhuman means are the direct result of their inhuman ends. In the play, Franz becomes a torturer because he fails to understand the relationship between ethics and society. There is something pathetic in the fact that like all Sartrian heroes he desperately wanted to be free, yet he ended as a tool of the Nazis. His mind had been conditioned to acknowledge only absolute values. Having rejected his father's brand of authoritarian Christianity, he proved incapable of creating his own moral code. Instead, he sought another ready-made philosophy which would not make any demands on him apart from blind obedience. He found such a philosophy in Fascism. His tragedy shows that man cannot do anything he likes and then try to justify it by saying that the end he pursues is good. He must start by proving objectively to himself that the end is indeed good, and this cannot be done with the help of emotional appeals or irrational prejudices. Franz's uncritical acceptance of the Nazi lie that Germany had to enslave other nations in order to avoid being enslaved herself made it inevitable that he would resort to torture and murder. *For this type of end, there can be no other means.* Herein lies the new contribution which the play makes to the problem. It reveals that *the end determines the means*.

Shortly after he wrote *Les Séquestrés d'Altona*, Sartre explained in an interview that in raising the problem of torture, he wanted his twentieth-century audience to realize that the danger of becoming a torturer is inherent in each one of us. Rigid morality is no safeguard, for once its basic assumptions are rejected or shown to be disproved in practice, the whole building crumbles down and makes way for an orgy of cruelty and crimes. That was the fate of Franz. Reliance on one's family is no safeguard either, for children whose problems are always solved by their parents grow up to be irresponsible tyrants like Franz or contemptible wrecks like Werner. What is the answer then? All that Sartre suggests in his play is that man must create his own values. Personally, I do not think this is enough. The only solid basis for morality is either God or the social group. Sartre does not believe in the former, but in *Les Séquestrés d'Altona* he says very little about the latter. In this respect, the play is a step backward from *Le Diable et le bon Dieu*, where Goetz finds a solution in the collective struggle of the revolutionary army. For Franz, there is no way out apart from suicide. It is a gloomy end to a very gloomy play, and it probably reflects Sartre's mood of despair at the time. The warning which he intended to issue is unfortunately obscured as a result.

There are other weaknesses in the play. It tries to deal with too many themes, it is at times heavily symbolic, it leaves one wondering whether the failure of the von Gerlachs was the failure of a social system or of life itself, and it does not suggest, even by implication, what positive action was available to a young German who wanted to be really free. Sartre's reply to the last criticism would be that it is up to the spectator to try to solve the problems raised by the dramatist. But the latter should at least suggest avenues for him to explore.

Perhaps one should mention another Sartrian work in which the issue of ends and means in politics is also treated, although it is not, strictly speaking, a play, but the scenario of a film. In *L'Engrenage* (In the Mesh), written two years before *Les Mains sales*, the dilemma which faces the hero is roughly the same as Hoederer's. As president of a small Communist republic, he has to choose between immediate nationalization and a temporary postponement of his socialist programme in order to avoid being crushed by a hostile capitalist power. He chooses the latter, but has to lie to his followers and to resort to dictatorial methods which he dislikes. He is put on trial by his party and executed, but his successors have no option but to continue his policies.

Two more plays must be mentioned, as they illustrate Sartre's committed stand on topical issues. *La Putain respectueuse* (The Respectful Whore) is an attack on racialism in the U.S.A. Lizzie, the main character, is a prostitute who nevertheless respects the moral values of her society. Hence, the ironic

title.ᵃ The story is quite simple: A senator's nephew kills a
Negro in cold blood, and Lizzie, who has witnessed the incident,
is asked to testify that the white man was trying to save her
from being raped by the Negro's friend. At first, she refuses,
but when the senator himself appeals to her patriotism and
uses big words in order to confuse her, she reluctantly gives in.
The accused Negro, however, seeks shelter in her flat, as a
lynching mob is after him, and Lizzie's natural pity wins. The
whore proves to be more humane than the respectable pillars
of society. I cannot agree with Geoffrey Brereton's view
that *La Putain respectueuse* is a "crude little anti-American
pamphlet".⁷⁶ Admittedly, the senator and his son have no
redeeming features, but that was intentional: they are merely
symbols, over-simplified to the point of caricature, of the crafty
politician and the ruthless upper-class youth, whom Sartre
loathes, whether they are American or of any other nationality.
On the other hand, Lizzie's character is very complex. She is
torn between respect for her betters and her innate moral sense
which her social status has not quite stifled. She is full of
conflicting prejudices, and when she finally turns against the
senator, it is partly out of pity for the Negro, and partly out of
her bitterness at having been "rewarded" with one hundred
dollars instead of the friendly letter the senator had promised
her. To the extent that the play denounces a specific evil in
American society, it is 'anti-American', but one does not have
to be an enemy of the U.S.A., or a socialist, in order to be on
the same side as Sartre on this issue. Lastly, *La Putain repectueuse*
has real dramatic qualities and can hardly be called a "pamphlet": its construction is faultless and the action proceeds at a
lively pace. It is not Sartre's greatest work, but neither is it mere
propaganda.

The same can be said of Sartre's only comedy, *Nekrassov*,
which ridicules cold-war prejudices in the West. The play is
very obviously dated, as the excesses denounced belong to the
past, but it is salutary to remember that it is, alas, a very recent

ᵃ Unfortunately, the title gives the false impression that the play deals
with sex or with prostitution, whereas it is, in fact, political and social, and
has not the faintest suggestion of pornography. I must add that the English
translation is inadequately entitled "The Respectable Prostitute", whereas
the American one rightly uses the adjective "respectful", but seems afraid
to render the coarse word "putain" by its English equivalent "whore".

past. The central character is a clever crook, Georges de Valera, who hits upon a brilliant idea for making money. He claims he is the Russian minister Nekrassov. As the latter has not been seen in public for about ten days, speculation concerning his fate is rife, and it is easy to pretend that he has escaped from the Bolshevik inferno and has "chosen freedom". He is immediately believed by the editor and administrators of a popular Parisian newspaper. After many hilarious scenes and farcical encounters, the truth is finally revealed. The play has no deep philosophical, or even political significance. It is an amusing farce, aimed at discrediting the gutter press and anti-Communist hysteria. The critics' reactions were predictably hostile among the right-wing, and friendly among the left.

Sartre is one of the leading writers and thinkers of our time. Shortly after the war, much of his fame rested on the fact that existentialism was then a "fashion"—his own expression—but with the passage of time his work stands out as a passionate effort to reach the truth and as a triumph for the committed approach; he is often irritating, but he makes you think. He has frequently been compared with Voltaire, with whom he shares a remarkable versatility in nearly all literary genres and a militant conception of his function as a writer; but I think his work bears an even closer resemblance to that of another eighteenth-century "philosophe", Denis Diderot, who once summed up his purpose by writing at the beginning of a book,

Young man, take this, and read. . . . As my aim is not so much to instruct you as to make you think, it matters little to me whether you accept my views or reject them, provided they retain the whole of your attention.

NOTES

1. *Les Mots*, p. 210.
2. Ibid., p. 184.
3. Ibid., p. 199.
4. Ibid., p. 54.
5. Ibid., p. 209.
6. Ibid., p. 213.
7. *Mémoires d'une jeune fille rangée* (Memoirs of a Dutiful Daughter),

La force de l'âge (The Prime of Life), *La force des choses* (Force of Circumstance) (all Gallimard).

8. *La force de l'âge*, p. 19.
9. *Les Mouches* in *Théâtre*, p. 108.
10. *Situations II*, p. 277.
11. Ibid., p. 316.
12. Ibid., p. 287.
13. Cf. *Matérialisme et Révolution* in *Situations III*, pp. 135–225.
14. *Situations II*, p. 287.
15. *Présentation des Temps modernes* in *Situations II*, p. 28.
16. *L'Express*, Supplement to No. 281, 9.11.1956.
17. Péguy, *Œuvres en prose* (1909–14), p. 628.
18. *Réflexions sur la question juive*, p. 67.
19. Ibid., p. 88.
20. Péguy, *Œuvres en prose* (1909–14), p. 1313.
21. The interview was reproduced in *The Listener*, 6.6.1957.
22. *L'Etre et le Néant*, p. 81.
23. *Sartre par lui-même*, p. 157.
24. *Existentialism and Humanism*, p. 28.
25. *Les Mouches* in *Théâtre*, p. 80.
26. *L'Être et le Néant*, p. 58.
27. Albérès, *Jean-Paul Sartre*, p. 60.
28. op. cit., p. 656.
29. Ibid., p. 502.
30. M. Cranston, *Sartre*, p. 83.
31. Marc Beigbeder, *L'Homme Sartre*, p. 114.
32. M. Cranston, op. cit., p. 86.
33. *Pour une morale de l'ambiguité* (Introduction).
34. *Merleau-Ponty et le pseudo-sartrisme*, in *Temps modernes*.
35. op. cit., p. 34.
36. Ibid., p. 30.
37. Ibid., p. 29.
38. op. cit., p. 8.
39. Ibid., p. 10.
40. *Perspectives de l'homme*, letter by Sartre, p. 113.
41. *The Listener*, 6.6.1957.
42. op. cit., p. 361.
43. Ibid., p. 130.
44. *Temps modernes*, No. 139, p. 351.
45. Philip Thody, *Jean-Paul Sartre*, p. 237.
46. op. cit., p. 59.
47. op. cit., p. 11.
48. *Baudelaire*, p. 18.
49. Ibid., p. 223.

50. Ibid., p. 80.

51. M. Cranston, op. cit., pp. 97–98.

52. P. Thody, op. cit., p. 148.

53. Aragon, *L'Exemple de Courbet*, p. 31.

54. Sartre's book is entitled *Saint Genêt—comedien et martyr*.

55. op. cit., p. 125.

56. Ibid., p. 127.

57. op. cit., p. 193.

58. op. cit., pp. 62 and 67.

59. Henri Peyre, *The Contemporary French Novel*, p. 236.

60. *L'Age de raison*, p. 114.

61. Ibid., p. 56.

62. See pp. 182–87 of the present essay.

63. *Les Lettres françaises*, 24.11.1945.

64. op. cit., p. 251.

65. Interview with Gabriel d'Aubarède in *Le Figaro littéraire*, 1.2.1951, quoted by P. Thody in op. cit., p. 29.

66. op. cit., p. 52.

67. op. cit., p. 79.

68. op. cit., p. 209.

69. *Sartre par lui-même*, 49.

70. op. cit., p. 208.

71. *Œuvres en prose* (1909–14), p. 825.

72. *Œuvres poétiques complètes*, p. 31.

73. op. cit., p. 88.

74. Ibid., p. 228.

75. Ibid., pp. 221–22.

76. G. Brereton, *A Short History of French Literature*, p. 341

PART II

LITERARY PROBLEMS

REALISM AND POETRY IN THE LIGHT OF COMMITMENT

CHAPTER V

REALISM AND COMMITMENT

The real problem is not . . . that 'littérature engagée' should deal with all issues in the social world; what is required is that the man of whom it speaks, who is both the Other and ourselves, should be immersed in that world. . . .[1]

THE ABOVE EXTRACT from a recent talk by Sartre spotlights the importance of realism for commitment. If he wants to fill his readers with the will to act, a committed writer must provide an adequate description of the living process of reality. The kind of action demanded by "engagement" is based on lucid awareness of the facts and not on distortion.

WHAT IS REALISM?

In order to view the works of Péguy, Aragon and Sartre as examples of "realism", one must begin by interpreting the word in the most obvious way, and forget, for the time being, the various literary and philosophical meanings it has been given. The *Oxford Dictionary* defines "realism" as "Fidelity of representation, truth to nature. . . ." This definition should suffice for our present purpose, as it helps to disclose the basic approach of "littérature engagée". It raises, however, a number of issues. The first one might be called a question of fact rather than value; in other words, before discussing whether literature *ought to* achieve "fidelity of representation", it is necessary to ask whether it *is* representation at all. Is art a *reflection of reality*, and if so, what does committed literature understand by that? Péguy did not discuss the problem, and Sartre touches only indirectly upon it. Aragon, on the other hand, has devoted a life-long interest to it. "The great debate in my life," he once said, "has been concerned with the expression of that which exists independently of myself."[2] The idea that art, like all mental processes for that matter, is a reflection of an objective reality, preceding man and existing independently of his mind, is basic to philosophical materialism and is a self-evident axiom for Marxists. It is interesting to see how Aragon interprets it, not because his views are necessarily valid for all committed literature, but because he has always fought against a narrow, mechanistic interpretation of the "reflection" theory, which he claims is a caricature of Marxism. The comparison between the human mind and a passive mirror is misleading, he would say, because our angle of vision is neither arbitrary nor all-embracing, but selective. To believe that an artist provides us with a "slice of life" pure and simple is to be a naturalist, not a realist, says Aragon in numerous essays. Although the realistic writer does not create his material out of his imagination alone, he does arrange it, he gives it a certain structure. Herein lies the difference between impersonal documents and art. Moreover, art is a special form of knowledge, and in recent years Marxists have increasingly stressed the active side of knowledge. Roger Garaudy, for example, states that human knowledge is a "reflection" when we consider its *nature*, but a creative construction of concepts if we examine its *method*.

In his study of Stendhal, Aragon pointed out that *Le Rouge et le Noir* was politically committed, despite the author's assurance that the novel was merely a "mirror" reflecting facts objectively without taking sides. Such an assurance, Aragon claimed, was never meant seriously, but was an oratorical precaution taken by Stendhal as a safeguard against the police and the prevailing "cant" of his time. In *La Mise à mort*, the "mirror theory" becomes one of the main themes of the book, and the plot, if there is one, consists in a succession of highly selective images, sometimes distorted, sometimes conflicting, which are reflected in a revolving mirror which is nothing but the novelist's mind, and is therefore never neutral and never perfect. In order to deal a further blow at the mechanistic interpretation, Aragon mentions some images which cannot be seen in the mirror at all. This is the case for Anthoine who has no real existence, as we know, but whose presence is allegorical. Aragon does not only believe that allegories have their place in realistic art, a view which readers of Bunyan and Swift will readily endorse, but he uses the allegory of the man who has lost his image in order to focus attention on the problems of realism and its limitations. With a touch of irony, he remarks at one stage that

This book is the novel of realism. Of contemporary realism. With its difficulties, its contradictions, its problems. Had you not noticed it? Yes, of course, it is a book about jealousy. As well. About the plurality of the human self. Granted. But above all, above all. At any rate, on this page. A book about realism, I tell you.[3]

It is fair to conclude the examination of this issue by saying that committed realism necessarily implies that literature does more than simply mirror the world, it actively intervenes in order to change it. If that were not so, the whole concept of commitment would lose its "raison d'être". Aragon's work, although it is, I repeat, based on Marxist conclusions which other committed writers need not share, constitutes a remarkable illustration of this vital point.

The second issue which is worth examining is the difference between realism, as defined by the *Oxford Dictionary*, and other literary theories. I think it is possible to think of four main trends which are opposed to it—naturalism, "objectivism", surrealism and abstract art. None of these can achieve "fidelity of representation", the first two because they aim to do the impossible and present facts without shape or structure, whereas it is a characteristic of human observation that it *gives* shape and structure to the objects perceived, and, what is more, does so *at the time* of perception and not as an afterthought; the third one, because it rejects a wide area of reality—the outside world and consciousness—and rests on the belief that the source of all art is the unconscious, "the all-powerful character of dreams", as André Breton said; and the last one, because it does not even aim at representation at all, but concentrates on the formal elements of art. It may seem strange that romanticism is not included among the opponents of realism, but I believe that there is no real conflict between them. Historically, in European literature, realism arose as a reaction against the subjective character of romanticism: a school which had over-stressed the importance of the poet and had put him at the centre of the world was succeeded by another one which claimed that the artist had to efface himself behind his material. But self-effacement is by no means indispensable for achieving "fidelity of representation" and "truth to nature". As Aragon once said, the "moi" is not necessarily "haïssable",[a] because it all depends

[a] An allusion to Pascal's belief, shared by the whole Classical school, that "le moi est haïssable"—the self is hateful, and should not be the subject of literature.

what kind of self one is dealing with. The "moi" of a committed artist, who looks upon himself as a "man among men", reflects the feelings of more than one individual and can legitimately claim to be the "écho sonore" (the resounding echo) of reality that Victor Hugo thought he was by virtue of being a poet. Moreover, if romanticism involves dreams which are based on reality, yet are not immediately and automatically suggested to average mortals, it is a valuable complement to realism, and more particularly to committed realism. For "littérature engagée", the truthful depiction of the world is not an end in itself—it is but the means by which the artist instils in his reader the will to act. To the images which embody the essence of reality, he adds an imaginative vision of what reality could be.

Thirdly, the question arises whether realism, as defined above, is an attitude or a method. I think it is both. It is the former inasmuch as it involves the aim of giving a faithful and truthful portrayal of life, but it also implies the latter because the *conscious* realization that reality is the source of all art carries with it a special way of approaching artistic creation, viz. an endeavour to make observation the starting-point and the basis of a work of art. It is necessary to add that realism, like commitment, is not a single method, but includes a great variety of methods. As reality is perceived differently by different people, the widest diversity of methods is not a concession to some vague "democratic" ideal, but a fundamental requirement of realism itself. For it is through the diversity of approaches that an increasing number of aspects of the world can be explored, revealed and clarified, and that our knowledge of reality becomes richer, and consequently truer.

Lastly, one must examine whether the lumping together of Péguy, Aragon and Sartre under the label of realism does not tend to obscure the great differences among them. No one can claim that the "spiritual realism"[4] of the Catholic poet is the same as Aragon's materialism or as Sartre's atheistic interpretation of existentialism. All the same, there is a remarkable similarity in their orientations, first because they all interpret "fidelity of representation" as being inseparable from a special viewpoint—they all think that their own commitment equips them for the great adventure of seeking the truth—and secondly because none of them mutilates man and the world: the author of *Eve* does not think that spirituality is something that floats

about in mid-air, but feels it is "deeply rooted" in the temporal
world, so much so that the "tree of grace" and the "tree of
nature" are of the "same essence";[5] the singer of Love and of
Elsa does not believe that the universe of the heart and the soul
is reducible to the material conditions amidst which it arises,
and it was a Catholic poet who summed up the content of his
work with the one phrase "The Soul" (which is incidentally the
title of one of Elsa Triolet's novels) and who was led to remark
that it was ". . . a curious paradox that a writer who is so fully
committed politically and ideologically, should have been so
objective a discoverer of the human heart";[6] lastly, the philosopher who wants to integrate the spiritual preoccupations of
the individual, his anguish as well as his "projects", in his all-
embracing system is not, despite his intransigent atheism, a man
who can be accused of destroying the "metaphysical dimen-
sion".

"FIDELITY OF REPRESENTATION"

The central problem for a realistic writer is that life and
reality are infinitely more complex than any human representation of them. How can the writer impose shape on a
permanently moving and permanently changing material
without telling "lies", as Aragon would say? How is the artist
to achieve "fidelity of representation"? Committed literature
feels that the challenge can be met in four ways—the essence of
reality should be grasped and disclosed; the meaning of objectivity in literature must be clarified; the details selected have to
be characteristic and typical; and a new awareness of time is
required from the artist.

(i) *The essence of reality*

For Péguy, Aragon and Sartre, contradictions are the essence
of reality. They might not all put the matter in this way, but I
feel that it corresponds to their basic approach, particularly as
each of their respective philosophies stresses that the world is
not a collection of static objects, but that movement is the
fundamental law of nature. Aragon and Sartre, who are both
dialecticians, explain movement in terms of a struggle between
opposites. Does Péguy? One critic who knows him well
describes him as a man who always sees both sides of a problem

and transcends them, as "the man of 'dépassement' and synthesis".[a] The Sartrian approach is described in exactly the same terms by Albérès: "Sartre seeks synthesis, or more precisely, 'dépassement'."[7] This is more than mere coincidence, for the words in question, although they are sometimes loosely applied by superficial critics, have a very precise meaning. They both imply that there is always conflict in life, and that each new synthesis is a means of going forward. Moreover, the continuous changes which take place in nature spring from a fight between the old and the new, or between right and wrong. The concept of "littérature engagée", which involves a crusade to change the world, leads the writer to the disclosure and explanation of those contradictions so that they may be transcended. Such is the meaning of "dépassement".

As in all great literature, conflict is the dominant note in the works of Péguy, Aragon and Sartre. According to the Catholic poet, there is a conflict between the pagan soul and the Christian soul, but in order to reach true Christianity, there must be a fusion of the two, and not an attitude of superiority on the part of mind over matter, nor on the part of the spiritual over the temporal. Péguy thought that he was nearer to Jesus, that friend of publicans and sinners, than the orthodox theologian Laudet, because for him religion did not mean a comfortable solution to all difficulties, but a permanent effort to face the issues of life and to resolve them by reconciling all that is positive and discarding all that is negative. In the same spirit, Sartre emphasizes the conflict between nausea and action, but in order to reach true commitment, one must have experienced the feeling of nausea. The shadows alone give light its full blaze. One is strikingly reminded of Aragon's assertion that "there is no light without shadows". In the novels of the "Monde réel", the victory of light is the outcome of a conflict between individual destinies and history, and only a synthesis can save man: he must inscribe his personality into the movement of history. Most of the heroes fail to do this, and it is their own personal lives which are filled with misery as a result. Aragon's novels are not a series of edifying Communist sermons in which the uncommitted individual is condemned by the disapproval of

---

[a] Jean Roussel, *Charles Péguy*, p. 112. The French word "dépassement" literally means "going beyond". There is not, to my knowledge, an adequate English equivalent.

society, but moving human documents which reveal that love, the highest form of personal happiness, cannot be attained by selfish people. On the other hand, when Catherine Simonidzé falls in love with Victor in *Les Cloches de Bâle*, or Cécile with Jean in *Les Communistes*, they get progressively nearer the light because their quest for individual happiness is blended with concern for the happiness of others. It is worth stressing that in the latter novel Cécile's political progress springs from her love for Jean: the precarious nature of their happiness in a world at war makes her eager to join the battle against general misfortune. She learns from her own experience that "there is no such thing as a happy love"—under existing conditions.

All the characters created by committed literature are in a state of perpetual conflict. Péguy's Joan has to fight the enemies of France as well as the false friends of God within Christendom, and out of the conflict, the figure of a great saint emerges. In Aragon's earlier novels, the socialist moral is conveyed through the contrast among various characters; for example, in *Les Cloches de Bâle* and in *Les Beaux Quartiers*, Clara Zetkin and Armand Barbentane are the "positive heroes" respectively, but Diane and Catherine, on the one hand, and Edmond Barbentane, on the other, occupy the larger part of each novel. The positive heroes cannot be understood except by contrast with those who prepare them, as Catherine prepares Clara, or those who negate them, as Edmond is the antithesis of his brother. In the case of *La Semaine sainte*, although we are still in the "monde réel", it is the real world of 1815, where the issue of socialism was as yet premature. What history had put on the agenda was the issue of national independence. The oppositions among the vast diversity of characters in the novel serve to delineate each one of them with great precision and to disclose the relationship between their private lives and their country's fate. In particular, Marshal Berthier and Géricault stand in profound contrast, the former symbolizing the past when he commits suicide in his inability to see a way out, and the latter representing the future because he is seeking reasons to justify his existence. It is significant that when he describes another old officer on his deathbed, with young Théodore Géricault standing by, the novelist intervenes in order to enlarge upon the contrast between two individuals, and shows it as an illustration of the struggle between the old and the new:

Yes, these young people who are arising carry with them the hope of the world. What your eye, already vitrified, can see is not yourself, or that past which is past, but your son, your sons, the future. Reject once and for all the lying legends which make the ancestor greater than the grandson.[8]

In *La Mise à mort*, the story is dominated by the conflict between Alfred and his other selves and by his feeling of jealousy when he thinks of his wife's admirers.

The contrast of one character with another is also practised with great dexterity by Sartre. In *La Nausée*, Roquentin is opposed to the self-educated man, and he discovers the true meaning of life by realizing, among other things, the fragility and inauthenticity of bookish knowledge; in *Les Chemins de la liberté*, Mathieu's lack of commitment is all the more futile because there is before us the limited commitment of Brunet, but Mathieu's honesty, his only redeeming feature, is enhanced by the hypocritical respectability of his brother; in the plays, the action progresses almost exclusively on the basis of conflicts among various characters, in the best Racinian tradition—one example among many is *Les Séquestrés d'Altona* in which the father's wicked practice of setting the members of his family one against the other is the dramatic clue to an understanding of each one of them.

(ii) *Objectivity*

The question of objectivity is closely linked to the existence of contradictions in reality: for a synthesis to be possible and valuable, neither term of the antinomy must be neglected or ignored. This, according to Péguy, was the great lesson of Corneille's *Polyeucte*, in so far as it presented all opposing viewpoints with equal truthfulness; God Himself received no special favours in the play, but had to state His case like everyone else. Therefore, we must not expect to find heroes and villains, in the conventional, fairy-tale sense, when we read committed works of fiction. There are, of course, positive and negative characters, but they are not good or bad once and for all, and without faults or qualities. More often than not, the same characters are good *and* bad, and the story of their lives is the story of the struggle between the conflicting tendencies within themselves. The best example in Aragon's novels is probably himself as he appears in *La Mise à mort*. In showing how he is torn between his private and his public image, he strikes a final blow at the legend of the Communist hero who is endowed with positive qualities exclusively. Aragon's complete devotion to Communism is not in doubt, but he is not a robot: he has feelings and anxieties of his own, and he reveals them with embarrassing honesty. Sartre does the same in his autobiography. His fictional heroes (whom he creates in his own image, he said in *Les Mots*) are as complex as he is. Mathieu Delarue, in particular, has a dual personality, just as any character in Aragon's "Monde réel". Without it, he would be completely immersed in "mauvaise foi". It is a pity that we never learn what "last chance" the author had in mind for him. As for Péguy, he created few characters apart from Joan, but even she is not free from inner conflicts; she is a great sinner as well as a saint, she commits the gravest crime of all by doubting the infinite mercy of God, she is occasionally put in her place by Madame Gervaise, and not without the poet's approval, she makes mistakes, and her voices are no infallible guarantee against human failings. The permanent conflicts of the Péguyian hero inside the Church was a reflection of Péguy's own situation. Although much of his work is devoted to an attack on the "modern world" which he knew so well and whose illusions he had once shared, he is equally concerned with criticizing the Christians who do not live up to the teachings of their Master. He often said that the greatest obstacle to the conversion of the Infidels was to be found in the Christians themselves.

In addition to honesty towards oneself and one's friends, there must also be honesty towards the enemy. It would be idle to pretend that Péguy, Aragon and Sartre always achieve this, but their efforts in that direction are impressive. Péguy, although he was very unfair to the opponents who had crossed his path—his treatment of Jaurès is definitely unbalanced—always displayed great respect for the enemy's *ideas*, so long as they were honestly held. What he could not tolerate was the exploitation of a "mystique" for selfish ends. He was broadminded enough, however, to praise all genuine "mystiques", and the large number of Free Thinkers, Protestants and Jews among the contributors to the *Cahiers* bears testimony to his sincerity in this respect. Sartre made a valiant attempt to understand the mind of a Nazi criminal when he depicted the tormented soul of Franz von Gerlach; earlier, in *Le Diable et le bon Dieu*, he dealt with a character who was thoroughly wicked, or at least imagined himself to be—yet it was that general, drunk with power and delighting in sadism, who eventually decided to help the cause of the poor. A great number of Aragon's heroes are also drawn objectively. In *Les Communistes*, for example, one has to read four volumes before Cécile and Jean begin to behave in a way of which the author approves. In the same book, which is the most partisan of all his novels, it is impossible not to be struck by the objective description of non-Communists, including a right-wing Colonel, a Catholic priest, a Radical deputy, and the minister Paul Reynaud himself who is presented in such a way that Aragon had to confess he had received complaints from ". . . a few comrades who were accustomed to see him treated in quite a different way in *L'Humanité*".[9]

The problem of the writer's objectivity must also be examined in relation to Aragon's contention that a novelist is compelled to lie in a work of fiction. By lies, we have already seen that one should understand the inventive powers of the artist. The latter invents people and events and appears to be at perfect liberty to make anything happen. But is he? There is, inevitably, the need to remain within the bounds of what is plausible if he wants to be believed, but if, in addition, he has a committed purpose in mind, his characters must be sufficiently close to life so that their adventures may be meaningful to a modern reader. Mathieu, Jacques, Daniel and Brunet would cease to represent pre-war Frenchmen if they did not behave respectively as young teachers without any convictions, respectable middle-class businessmen, self-centred homosexuals and active Communists do in fact behave. The same applies to the heroes of Aragon's contemporary "real world". In dealing with the past, the committed novelist must also respect historical accuracy if he wishes us to learn anything from the experience of previous generations; for example, if he makes the officers of Louis XVIII behave as if they already possessed the knowledge of their descendants, this would be so incredible as to make little impact on the reader, whereas the latter is more likely to draw inspiration from the example of human beings tackling their own specific problems, or to learn from their mistakes when they fail to do so. Moreover, Aragon attaches such importance to precision in describing all the external aspects of reality, places, clothes, means of transportation, etc., that he gave up an attempt to write a novel with a twelfth-century background because he was too ignorant of the material conditions of life at that time.

Sometimes, the realistic writer's freedom is particularly restricted if he chooses to speak of people who really existed, Joan of Arc, Chamberlain and Daladier, generals and statesmen of the last war, Théodore Géricault. Here, the dangers of "lying" can be overcome either by an acute sympathy for the character concerned, or by a scientific attitude towards history. Péguy provides an excellent illustration of the former, because he recognized himself in Joan and could easily enter into her personality. His Joan is a living person because she is very much like her creator. It does not matter whether any of her remarks were indeed uttered by her, because we know that they are thoroughly in keeping with her character. To some extent, Aragon was no less successful when he tried to penetrate into Géricault's soul. This was not so easy for him as it had been for Péguy when he dealt with Joan, but it was possible because he had not forgotten his youth and could imagine the feelings of a young artist when he faced a world whose significance escaped him. The most important event in the novel, the secret meeting at Poix, which opened Théodore's eyes to the life of the common people, has its parallel in Aragon's first encounter with ordinary workers during the first world war, and he tells us so in the course of the novel, in order to put the incident in perspective. He revealed in an article significantly called *Secrets de fabrication* (Manufacturing Secrets)[10] that the meeting at Poix had never taken place in the way it is described in the novel and was a figment of his imagination. But many Republicans did in fact get together to determine their policy in relation to the Emperor and the monarchy, and there is nothing far-fetched in visualizing Théodore overhearing one or several of their discussions—his later paintings obviously show direct knowledge of his own people, and it is not improbable to assume that he acquired it in the course of a meeting or a series of meetings. Aragon, who loudly announces that he is writing a work of fiction, and not a history textbook, has the right to invent a meeting at Poix and to contrive Théodore's attendance.

He is all the more entitled to this imaginative licence in view of his great care in reproducing the life of the epoch in its various aspects. All critics have been struck by the splendid resurrection of the past which is achieved in *La Semaine sainte*. Aragon calls his method *scientific*: his lies are not only made in accordance with reality, they have a solid dose of reality for their background; they are a form of what he calls the "mentir-vrai"—truthful lying. It is in that sense that he could describe all his novels as historical, and yet protest that none of them is, strictly speaking, a historical document. They are works of art. Art brings reality to life because it can seize it in the depth of its being, a result which is denied to mere historians who remain on the surface. This, needless to say, does not amount to contempt for history as a useless science, but simply to a correct assessment of the unique possibilities which are available to artists. Their objectivity is of a special nature—it is coloured by their philosophy of life. The more that philosophy corresponds to reality, the greater the artist's objectivity. It is never complete and absolute, as far as committed writers are concerned, because that in itself is impossible. They reject the naïve belief that one can photograph events and remain in the background, and none of them would have said with Christopher Isherwood, "I am a camera." Isherwood himself did not succeed in reproducing life without any bias, and as a critic recently remarked, "nor does a camera . . ." for each one has a "different way of seeing the world".[11] The art of the novel is, in the words of Aragon, "*to know* how to lie".[12] For there are two sorts of lies in literature, those which impose on real life a pattern which corresponds to the author's wishes and prejudices, and those in which the writer's creative faculty has been kept in check by the "fren dell' arte" (the brake of art) of which Dante spoke when he said that he would not allow his imagination to run wild, so that it might be guided by the "law", or, in more modern terminology, by realism. To the first kind of lies belong edifying tales in which the reward of virtue desired by the author is brought about somewhat unconvincingly. Oscar Wilde summed up this type of literature very wittily when he made Miss Prism describe the novel she had written in her youth as a book in which the good end happily, and the wicked unhappily, and add for the benefit of her pupil, "This is what fiction means." The second sort of lies, although they are untrue in the sense that they did not really happen, take place in accordance with reality; they are not in glaring contradiction with it, they are highly credible because the author lies realistically, as it were.

(iii) *Selection of typical and characteristic details*

There is another aspect to the lies of the artist, for the selection of certain aspects of reality necessarily implies that others have been discarded, and is therefore a kind of lying. A work of art reflects reality up to a certain point; there are features which it either deliberately or unconsciously ignores. The committed writer believes that his task is to sort out the typical from the insignificant, and arrange his material in a way that gives reality a special meaning.

This raises a number of crucial questions. First, the place of details in art. Here again, Aragon's opinion is particularly instructive. He believes, quite simply, that no art can do away with details altogether.

> In non-realistic art of the past [he writes], detail represents that small part of reality from which the artist cannot escape.[a] You will find it in the curves and columns at Vézelay, in the description of heaven and hell . . . you will also find it in Breughel's fantastic scenes, *which are realistic from the point of view of details. . . .* The real debate in art has never been between pure invention, which does not exist, and observation, which one cannot do without, but between the significance of the work of art and its futility.[13]

Aragon agrees with R. L. Stevenson that under an excess of details one fails to see the wood for the trees, and furthermore that detail should never become, as it tended to do among French Naturalists, an end in itself—details should be selected because of their significance, because the artist feels they embody his view of reality. Aragon's own works provide numerous examples of this approach. One illustration among many is the way in which he summed up the horrors of war in a powerful image which compared man's fate in the Army with that of a pastry to be cut with a knife:

---

[a] Aragon actually speaks of "le bout du nez de la réalité".

I am not theirs because my human flesh
Is not a pastry to be cut with a knife[14]

A whole book could be written about Aragon's skill in finding
the significant detail and giving it poetic form. It is no exaggeration to say that the art of realistic poetry consists in this process.
One can also detect it in the poems of Péguy, in which ideas
always take a concrete form, and where a mass of successive
details all play their part in expressing the poet's "mystique".
Consider, for example, the remarkable sixty pages in *Eve* in
which stanza after stanza crystallizes in one or two striking
images, drawn from Péguy's observation of his contemporaries,
the vain efforts of mankind when it turns away from God; nearly
every stanza is constructed on the same pattern: the poet
selects a specific aspect of modern life, of which man is particularly proud, and asserts that it will be of little use to us when we
meet our Maker and Judge—money, status, science, art, what
will they weigh in the great balance of God? In the case of
Sartre, the significance of details is particularly evident in his
Chemins de la liberté trilogy; in Volume One, for example, the
futile details of Mathieu's own life have been selected *because* of
their futility, in order to make the point that uncommitted
freedom is vain.

The second issue is the way in which an artist selects what he
considers to be significant. Committed writers believe that the
selection is always guided by the author's philosophy of life, and
they see in this one of the many proofs of the inescapable
character of commitment. Once more, the problem, from their
point of view, is not to aim at a mythical impartiality, but to
take sides on the basis of a thorough, painstaking analysis of
reality, which endeavours to prevent any significant aspect
from being overlooked or under-estimated. There are two ways
of achieving this—to see all sides of a situation, and to discern
the seeds of the future within the past or the present. With
regard to the first point, the controversy between Sartre and
his Communist critics over his play *Morts sans sépulture* is not
without interest. Sartre's heroes are members of the Resistance
Movement, and a few hours before their death they seem more
preoccupied with their personal fate than with the future of
France. They refuse to betray their comrades by giving information about their leader's hiding place, but their refusal is

mainly due to a sense of pride. The whole thing is a wager for them.

> The important thing is to win. . . . There are two teams—one which wants to make the other talk. It's absurd.[15]

Communists objected at the time that the play slandered the Resistance, and they quoted as being more typical of the movement Aragon's description of *One who sang at the Stake*, whose last words were,

> I go to my death and O my friends
> You will know the reason why[16]

It is difficult to deny that there were many heroes who died in that noble fashion, but it is equally true that others were as self-centred as the characters in Sartre's play. A complete picture of the Resistance must include both attitudes, whilst stressing the one which is particularly representative. Sartre himself seems to have had second thoughts about his un-balanced presentation, and I have already mentioned the fact that he revised the last scenes in order to make one of the Underground fighters increasingly more positive.

For an understanding of the second point, and the difficulties involved in discovering the future within the present, one must return to Aragon's *La Mise à mort*. The author remarks that if realism is to avoid both a utopian embellishment of contempor-ary reality and lack of vision, ". . . it must be based, not, as was generally believed until now, on present reality, but on a reality which is yet to come; it must become, in other words, a realism of conjecture".[17] What Aragon is attacking here is the Stalinist interpretation of "socialist realism" which compelled artists to depict Soviet society as free from conflicts and diffi-culties. Even before Stalin's death, Aragon had forcefully rebelled against this caricature of realism. Thanks to the more enlightened climate which prevails in Communist ranks, he now denounces it as "one of the most surprising frauds in human history", and he can truthfully say, "It is not I who invoked [realism] arbitrarily in order to justify lies."[18] This time, we can speak of *lies* without inverted commas. Aragon's "lies", we already know, are a form of telling the truth, whereas Stalinist lies distorted reality and claimed to be the truth. The task of the socialist writer, according to Aragon, is not to run ahead of the present and "improve" it out of all recognition. His task is rather ". . . to depict the birth of tomorrow out of today, with all the attendant problems".[19] He is still entitled to look for the seeds of the future within the present, but he must not pretend that they are more than seeds and forget that they belong to a "reality which is yet to come". Aragon himself provided good illustrations of this approach in *La Semaine sainte* and in *Le Fou d'Elsa*. In the former, he carefully avoided assimilating the problems of 1815 to those of today, or making any of his characters premature socialists; yet the significance of the particular Easter week he was describing cannot be grasped without the numerous digressions which enable us to see how subsequent historical events, some of them referring to a very recent past, were affected by the choices and decisions which were made when King Louis XVIII was retreating before Napoleon. In *Le Fou d'Elsa*, with great poetic licence, a fifteenth-century "Medjnun" worships a twentieth-century woman, but he worships her as a creature of the future and does not delude himself with the belief that the "era of the couple" has already arrived. In both books, Aragon's task was comparatively simple, since the future from the characters' point of view was in fact the present as far as the author was concerned. In dealing with contemporary reality, the difficulties are incomparably greater, and Aragon, who is not a man to mince his words, calls them insurmountable. But this is not a defeatist approach; it is rather an urgent reminder that the main task is "to change the world" and not "the novelist's brain".

> The great difficulty of realism today [he writes], is not that its rules are absurd, but that they are not applicable. . . . *For its rules to become valid* [my italics], what is needed is . . . to change the world.[20]

Literature can contribute to the change if it never loses its *critical sense*, a point briefly touched upon in Chapter I, and to which one will have to return in discussing Aragon's contribution to the development of socialist realism.

Lastly, an interesting problem connected with the selection of significant details is that there are times when it is impossible to copy reality. Cubist painters were aware of this difficulty and thought of solving it with the help of what came to be known as "collages"—a colloquialism which literally means "sticking" because it describes the process by which an artist actually sticks external material on to his canvas, such as labels, bus tickets and even objects. By extension, Aragon considers as "collages" any additions to a work of art which seem to have no logical connections with it. He calls them a "detail of the first magnitude".[21] His life-long interest in the subject is illustrated by the essays and articles which he wrote between 1923 and 1965, some of which are gathered in a little book. In his preface to the collection, he stresses that the problem transcends the boundaries of painting and that it concerns all forms of art. The use of "collages" spotlights the impact of surrounding reality on the artist. Picasso, he points out, could not have used the colours of Félix Potin ". . . in a world in which there had not been a Félix Potin",[22] but he stresses that the painter's individual "decision" constitutes his personal reaction before the reality of his time. "For myself, I cannot imagine art outside its time. If I consider it as a product of the society in which it arises, I do not, for one minute, believe that this is enough to account for its miracle."[23] His collection of essays, he adds, does not claim to provide a satisfactory explanation of the "miracle", but merely to draw attention to an important problem, "the intrusion of reality" into art. Two extracts are particularly devoted to "collages" in the field of literature. The first one is a chapter from La Mise à mort which discusses the value of the "secondary theme" in the novel. Such a theme, which Elsa Triolet is fond of introducing in her books, adds perspective to the main one, and throws light on the characters' hidden thoughts, ". . . I would even say their hidden passions ('leurs arrière-passions') of which they themselves are the temporary, unconscious or semi-conscious bearers."[24] The second extract is taken from Aragon's recent preface to Les Beaux Quartiers.[a] He recalls the numerous trifling incidents of his personal life which he transposed in the novel, commenting that the process was one of the manifestations of his newly-found realism, although ". . . for a Cubist or a Dadaist, the use of 'collages' was already the expression of a realistic trend, the acknowledgement that there is an objective reality existing independently of the painter or the writer."[25]

[a] The preface was written for the volume of the Œuvres romanesques croisées which includes Les Beaux Quartiers.

(iv) *The problem of time in works of fiction*

"The problem of time," Aragon told Francis Crémieux, "is closely related to the philosophy of the novel."[26] For committed literature, the issue is not purely technical and we have already seen how Aragon, for example, makes his readers aware of the past in order to inspire them to fight for the future. It is, however, very hard to give an adequate idea of the passage of time in a work of art, and there are two aspects to the difficulty. On the more elementary level, both reader and writer are aware of the artificial device which consists in describing events which take place over hours, days, months or years in the course of a few minutes; in a novel, for example, there seems to be no apparent reason for making six months or ten years elapse between one chapter and another; in a play, there is an obvious contrast between the two or three hours of the actual performance and the time taken by the unfolding of the plot. With regard to this last point, the seventeenth-century French Classics believed that the famous twenty-four-hour rule, according to which there should not be more than a single day between the first and the last scenes, reduced the gap between the two times and satisfied the spectator's requirement that a play must be "plausible". Why twenty-four hours, one wonders, and not the time of the performance itself? This, at least, would be entirely logical! But these remarks do not yet take us to the heart of the matter. The real difficulty for an artist is to reveal the motion of time without petrifying it. Any description inevitably over-simplifies that which is complex, interrupts that which is continuous, and petrifies that which is alive. Great art transcends these limitations to a considerable extent, but it does not altogether make them vanish.

Péguy, Aragon and Sartre do not solve the problem in the same way, but they all refuse to be imprisoned by "spatial time", or, as Sartre calls it, "the time of the clock".[27] A striking similarity between Péguy and Aragon is that they both believe in the power of poetry to express the living flux of existence. The poet's images, being a "short-cut" view of reality, can espouse the actual flow of time without bringing it to a stop, and they experience the passage of time from the inside, transcending mechanical divisions into units. Péguy, who shared Bergson's belief that words never adequately describe living duration, felt, however, that the music of a poem was the nearest reproduction of the symphony of continuously moving Time that man is capable of. Péguy's great complaint against Clio, the muse of history, is that it misses the essence of the past, and forgets that it was once a living present. The poet, on the other hand, can restore the freshness of time. Aragon is not a Bergsonian, but he is no less struck than Péguy by the inability of ordinary language to grasp "life in motion", and he suggests that a new tool is needed—what he calls the "radar"[28] of poetry.

In his novels, he still approaches life as a poet, and for this reason he is one of the few great writers who, according to Pierre de Lescure, ". . . show, in the whole of his work, that preoccupation with the passage of time, and make us aware of that great river which carries us forward".[29] One of his favourite devices is that he takes considerable liberties with his material, comparing his own experience in the twentieth century with that of characters belonging to another age, not in the belief that one can mechanically assimilate different epochs, but in order to convey the living continuity of time, and show that, in the case of human phenomena, years and whole centuries matter less than the interrelations which link us with our predecessors as well as with our unknown descendants; or alternatively, he interrupts his tale in order to select a significant detail in the past or future life of one of his characters, which throws unexpected light on his present behaviour. The whole of La Semaine sainte is constructed in this way, and the events which are encompassed within the one Holy Week in 1815 are seen in their true perspective thanks to the process. For example, although the death of Marshal Berthier occurred three months after the week in question, it is fully described in advance, because the presence of an old officer among Louis XVIII's retinue acquires an entirely different aspect when we realize that the same officer, who reluctantly followed his king abroad, committed suicide a few months later as he could not reconcile himself to the presence of foreign troops on French soil.

Another means at Aragon's disposal for rendering the fluidity of time is his handling of language. Lescure compares his style to a "song which proceeds by musical intervals . . . pointing to the prolonged resonance of the striking hour without making the clock appear", and he feels it is by means of the "discontinuity of language" that Aragon succeeds in expressing "the instantaneity of the present which is linked to the past and which already contains the future".[30] This last expression could have been used word for word by Bergson and Péguy.

Sartre approaches the problem in a different way. In his theoretical writings, he suggests that one way of making reader and character share the unique experience of the living moment is to use the present tense exclusively, a piece of advice which he himself does not always follow, but which has inspired the authors of the "new novel" in France, although they, too, do not spurn the past tense. "To relate the present in the past tense is to resort to something artificial,"[31] writes Sartre in an article on Dos Passos. The logic of the argument, in my opinion, is somewhat abstract and overlooks the fact that there is always "something artificial" in all fiction; a condemnation of all "contrivances" (Sartre uses the word "artifice") amounts to a condemnation of all literature. This is perhaps what "new novelists" have in mind when they claim to write "anti-novels" and to show the limitations of the novel form by using the medium itself. Another of Sartre's requirements is to let the characters remain unpredictable, so that the discovery of their deeds and their thoughts should come as a common surprise to both author and public. In that way, instead of being presented with living experiences which have been "thought over" ("du vécu déjà repensé"),[32] we find in the novel events which have not lost their "unvarnished freshness" ("brutale fraîcheur").[32] Sartre's practice does not always match his own advice. Many critics have drawn attention to the fact, but it is unfair to conclude that the Sartrian principles are necessarily incapable of application. A Robbe-Grillet or a Michel Butor seems to prove the opposite. Perhaps Sartre himself was not so successful because he was less concerned with the technique of writing and was more eager to convey his philosophical and moral message. One could speak of a "sacrifice" on the altar of commitment, and I would agree, but the "sacrifice" is due to Sartre's personal impatience rather than to the requirements of commitment. Neither Péguy nor Aragon felt that they were "wasting time" in considering, with almost meticulous care, the presentation of their material, as we shall have occasion to see when we discuss the issue of poetry in the next chapter. To be fair, Sartre is by no means contemptuous of technical problems, and his use of simultaneity in *Le Sursis*, and partly in *La Mort dans l'âme*, is a case in point which has already been briefly touched upon. In his latest play, he makes extensive use of the "flash-back" device in order to throw light on Franz's character. This is part of his general attempt to apply Brechtian principles to the theatre, and deserves brief examination.

REALISM IN THE THEATRE

It was Bertolt Brecht, the Marxist playwright and theorist, who first thought of exploiting the artificiality of drama in a realistic manner with a view to fulfilling the purpose of commitment. His theory of "Verfremdung" (which is better rendered by "distanciation" rather than by the more commonly used term "alienation") amounts to treating the play as a problem rather than as a story in which we readily believe. The spectator should be made to *think* instead of becoming emotionally involved in the characters' fate. Brecht did not suggest that we should be completely divorced from the feelings which are expressed on the stage, but rather that we should remember the "distance" between drama and real life. The playwright's task consists in finding all sorts of tricks to keep the spectator at a distance, a responsibility which he shares with the producer. Brecht himself was both playwright and producer, and he attached considerable importance to such aspects as lighting, modern costumes for a period play, introduction of an unexpected poster (a form of "collage" perhaps?), etc. As a dramatist, he felt that reasoned argument must replace emotional suggestion.

The above principles, which are obviously based on a committed conception of the theatre, are by no means the only ones available to the committed dramatist, and many Marxist playwrights do not accept them. One could mention, in particular, the Moscow Art Theatre under Stanislavsky, which relies on a "participationist" method. As far as Sartre is concerned, there is little evidence of Brecht's influence in the plays he wrote before *Les Séquestrés d'Altona*, unless one were to consider the introduction of Zeus in *Les Mouches* and of Hell in *Huis clos*, in which the author obviously does not believe literally, as methods of achieving the "distanciation" effect. After *Altona*, however, Sartre mentioned in an interview that he had tried to apply some of Brecht's principles. The "flash-back" was one of the devices he used to make us feel at a distance from his main character: as we pass from the present to the past, we are increasingly aware that what is happening on the stage is not real, that the whole thing is symbolic and should make us think. Similarly, Franz's unnatural "sequestration" introduces greater distance between him and the spectator. Lastly, his speech to a crowd of Crabs is sufficiently artificial not to be taken too seriously, and should remind us that the main point is to think of our own responsibility, as a twentieth-century audience, before posterity.

SOCIALIST REALISM

Socialist realism is one of the most controversial literary issues of our time. In an essay devoted to committed literature, it is impossible to avoid a brief discussion of it, partly because it is undoubtedly *one* of the many forms of commitment, and partly because Aragon has untiringly proclaimed his attachment to it.

I shall endeavour to present his viewpoint as objectively as possible and in the way in which he himself would choose to do it. This does not mean that I am in full agreement with him, but in dealing with a subject which has aroused so much passion, and has been responsible for so many unbalanced pronouncements on both sides, I feel that there is room for a short, unpretentious account of the position as it is seen by a particularly authoritative representative of socialist realism. I do not claim that the following pages provide a substitute for further reading and further enquiry into the matter; I rather hope that they will stimulate them.

The expression "socialist realism" was coined by Gorky at the first Congress of Soviet writers in 1934. The Grand Old Man of Soviet letters meant it to describe the essential difference between the critical realism of the nineteenth century and the new realism which draws upon the experience of the first socialist society. Unlike their predecessors, he claimed, contemporary realists need not confine themselves to criticism of bourgeois society, but can depict the birth of a new civilization; and even in their criticism, they are in a position to make use of the historical perspective which scientific socialism analyses and outlines. Granted the two basic assumptions that Marxism is the scientific explanation of human history and that the

October Revolution of 1917 ushered in a new epoch, the epoch of socialism, there was nothing outrageous in Gorky's new expression. It was merely an assertion of his belief in the superiority of Marxism and of the Soviet system and an appeal to *like-minded* artists that they should observe and describe reality in the light of the changes taking place around them and of their socialist convictions. It was the natural form for commitment to take, and I do not think Gorky ever meant it to amount to the imposition of specific themes, a specific style or a specific method. Soon, however, the concept became one of the unquestioned dogmas of Soviet orthodoxy, and when it was endorsed by no less a person than the great Stalin himself, it acquired the value of a categorical imperative. Socialist realism was no longer considered desirable, it became compulsory, and instead of representing a challenge to the creative artist, it sank to the level of conformist art. Worse was to follow. At a time when all those who did not think like Stalin were branded as "enemies of the people" and were summarily jailed or shot, so-called "offenders" against socialist realism were shown up as "traitors" to the Soviet motherland, and administrative measures were taken against them. The notorious decisions associated with the name of Zhdanov amounted to direct and unwarranted intervention on the part of the state. Instead of merely reminding writers that they have a social responsibility, a perfectly legitimate reminder for any state to issue, Zhdanov placed before them the correct style they had to adopt (it was a mechanical transposition of nineteenth-century "critical" style, adapted to modern times), he told them what themes were worthy of them and which they ought to ignore, he took them to task for daring to suggest that there could be conflicts in Soviet society, and if they showed any inclination to experiment with new artistic techniques, not officially approved, they were accused of a new crime, specially invented and dug out for their benefit—the crime of "formalism". There was no place for tragedy, no place for criticism, no place for personal lyricism; the function of literature and art was the mass production of "positive heroes", i.e. of characters, no matter how unreal, who could typify the virtues thought desirable by the state. Fortunately for the Soviet Union, the picture was not as black as might have been expected in the face of such ludicrous excesses. In spite of Stalin and Zhdanov, some fine books were written, some beautiful pictures were painted, and some great music was composed. How much more would have been possible if administrative measures had not stifled creative genius, is anybody's guess.

There was a partial reaction against "dogmatism" and "schematism" at the second Congress of Soviet writers in 1954. Aragon's intervention at the Congress was noticeable for its emphasis on the *French* character of socialist realism in his country and for its assertion that poets in particular could learn from the achievements of the past without in any way becoming servile imitators. The idea that other, non-Russian sources could be found for socialist realism was more than a question of prestige; it was part of the general process of freeing the concept from excessive one-sidedness. A positive feature at the Congress was also the rejection of the theory that Soviet society was already free from conflicts. On the whole, the reaction against Zhdanovism had begun, but it was too early yet to expect the spectacular criticism of former state truths which was made possible after Khrushchov's denunciation of the famous "personality cult". Not that everything is now perfect and sensible in Soviet art and in Soviet cultural policy: it is difficult to rid oneself of a heavy and negative legacy in a short time. What the future holds, and what further developments are desirable and possible, are matters which are outside the scope of this essay on commitment in modern French literature. I felt, however, that a very brief historical outline was indispensable before attempting to understand the impact of socialist realism on Aragon.

It may not be out of place to add a word or two about recent cultural changes in the policies of the French Communist Party. In March 1966, its Central Committee devoted a whole three-day session to "ideological and cultural problems", and readers might be interested in the following short extract from the final resolution adopted by the meeting:

Artistic creation cannot be imagined without research, without trends, without various schools, and without confrontation among them. The Party appreciates and supports the diverse ways in which creative artists contribute to human progress on the basis of the free development of their imagination, their personal taste and their originality. It expresses the wish that they will understand and back up the ideological and political standpoint of the working class.[33]

Aragon, who presided over the drafting of the resolution, described it as a "compromise . . . in the honourable sense of the word" among various trends, and expressed his satisfaction that it was not "a complete document", adding that

We have produced too many complete documents which we were the only ones to read.[34]

We must now examine how Aragon interprets socialist realism and how he illustrates it. In order to understand his position, I think it is possible to distinguish between the nature of the theory and the general method it involves. Socialist realism is conceived by Aragon as a special form of realism in so far as it is opposed to naturalism: the objective significance of reality which the naturalist denies and which every realist asserts is, from the point of view of socialist realism, that the onward march of mankind leads to socialism. Such a belief, which is the core of Marxism, is not a messianic idea—Marx always stressed that he had arrived at the conclusion on the basis of a factual analysis of an existing process, and that the trend towards socialism and a classless society was not just desirable, but inevitable. By "inevitable", he did not mean that men need not fight for it or that capitalism would automatically collapse under the strain of its own contradictions, but rather that those contradictions were bound to arouse, sooner or later, the subjective desire for change among the widest sections of the people; then, and then only, would conditions for a revolution be ripe.[a] The Marxian economic analysis tends to prove that the present level of productive forces is in glaring contradiction to the private ownership of the means of production, but it is not until human beings become aware of this that social change can take place. "It is men who make history," said Engels, "but they make it in certain conditions which are not of their own choosing."[b] In the light of these

[a] Marx himself admitted that he had often been unduly optimistic concerning the time required for revolutionary awareness to spread to the masses, but he never doubted the final outcome.

[b] There is a striking similarity between Engels's approach and Sartre's description of the relationship between freedom and situation.

guiding principles, Aragon would define socialist realism as ". . . the realism of our time, which takes into account the historical perspective of the future or of the present, according to each country, in other words, of socialism".[35]

With regard to the general method of socialist realism, Aragon believes that a writer who is equipped with Marxist philosophy has two advantages—he can relate individual details to the historical evolution of the times, and he is in a better position to look for what is significant in the complex situation he observes. How he communicates his experience and the results of his research, what formal means he uses in the way of structure, style and genre, what aspect of the world he explores—all these factors are part of his personal responsibility and depend on his temperament, background, preferences, etc. . . . It is ludicrous to legislate in this field, and Aragon once laughingly remarked that socialist realism was not a Trade Union and that there were no special rules for the game. One does not become a socialist realist to order, one naturally applies the general method because it is the concrete form of commitment for a writer who has found in Marxism the "Weltanschauung" that it claims to be. His definition is worth quoting because it is sufficiently broad not to imprison Communist artists in a strait-jacket.

> Socialist realism [Aragon writes], is the organizing conception of *facts* in literature, of *detail* in art, which interprets the detail, gives it significance and force, and integrates it into the general movement of history.[36]

On the whole, it can be said that Aragon openly acknowledges that socialist realism is the special "bias" of a Marxist, but states also that it avoids one-sidedness and distortion precisely because Marxism is an expression of the truth and an all-embracing philosophy. One need not be a Marxist in order to grant that it is an honest position, and that it merely applies the principle which is common to all committed literature—namely, that no work of art can avoid taking sides and that the real issue is to be as honest as possible in deciding on which side of the fence one is going to be.

This is not to say that socialist realism has always been interpreted in such a broad way. The truth, as we have seen, is that the reverse did in fact take place, and that in the Stalinist period the expression often took on a ridiculous, and even a criminal aspect. It is to Aragon's credit that he was most vocal in denouncing the excesses, but in view of his special position in the French Communist Party—he has been a member of its Central Committee since 1950—I do not think it is enough for him to say, as he did recently, that he is ". . . surprised that a study [of Stalinist crimes in relation to literature] should not yet have been undertaken".[37] One feels tempted to suggest that, perhaps, no one is better placed than Aragon himself to make such a truthful study! It would be a fitting climax to the battle he has been waging for some time, long before Stalin's death, in favour of sanity and common sense.

If one were now to summarize his special contribution to the interpretation and development of socialist realism, six features would have to be mentioned. First, he stands for an *open* conception:

> I demand an open realism [he said at the University of Prague when he received an honorary degree], a non-academic realism, . . . which is capable of modifying itself as it goes along . . . , a realism which helps to change the world, a realism which is not meant to reassure us, but to rouse us, and which occasionally, because of that very feature, disturbs us.

The most important characteristic of this open conception is that Aragon firmly believes that socialist realism is not the only fruitful method in art, although he naturally feels it is the best. He creatively applies his party's line on the danger for a "vanguard" to cut itself off from the rest of the people, and untiringly reminds the most sectarian of his friends—there are many of them—that the future of literature in France and in the world is the common concern of ALL writers. His articles in *Les Lettres françaises*, particularly in recent years, have generally been heavily biased in favour of new literary experiments, new approaches to the novel and to poetry, and at times he has not been afraid of praising a book "without the slightest 'social' justification".[38] Love stories, in particular, never leave him cold, for he is fond of ". . . that wonderful love of young people, with its novel curiosity".[39] In 1963, he wrote a preface to Roger Garaudy's book *D'un réalisme sans rivages* (Realism without

Limits) in which the author analyses the work of three artists, Picasso, Saint-John Perse[a] and Kafka, two of whom at least can hardly be called "realists". Both Garaudy and Aragon were accused of having stretched the concept of realism to the point where it does indeed cease to have any limits, but also any significance. The reproach would be valid if Kafka, for example, had been presented as a realist, whatever the cost; in fact all that is asserted is that Kafka was not "a decadent petty-bourgeois", but that he managed to create "... a mythical world which is the expression of the real world".[40] (I do feel, however, that Garaudy is not always very careful in defining his terms, and that his commendable approach would have gained if he had clearly distinguished between the lack of conscious realism of some very great artists and the possibility for realist critics to appreciate their work.)

Secondly, Aragon stresses that socialist realism need not be confined to the Soviet Union and other socialist lands. It is also available to writers living in capitalist countries, with the difference that they base themselves on the future whereas their Soviet colleagues can draw upon the experience of the present. This view was strongly criticized in Russia, but Aragon firmly held to it and openly defended it in Moscow, both before and after Stalin's death. It is now generally accepted by most Communists, and Aragon's part in extending the concept beyond the borders of the Soviet Union was not inconsiderable. For him, French socialist realism is the heir to the nineteenth-century critical realism of writers like Stendhal. It is interesting to notice that his praise for Stendhal is one of the numerous instances of his reaction against mechanical repetition of Marxist formulae. For it had long been fashionable among Marxists to admire Balzac rather than Stendhal on the strength of a few comments by Marx and Engels on *La Comédie humaine* in which the realistic descriptions of the contemporary scene give the lie to the author's "reactionary" views. Aragon ironically reminded the parrots that Marx never praised Stendhal, for the simple reason that he had not read him! What was needed, he claimed, was to apply Marx's broadminded approach to other writers. This was particularly important,

[a] Saint-John Perse is the literary pseudonym taken by Alexis Léger, a permanent civil servant in the French Ministry of Foreign Affairs between the two world wars, who wrote lyrical poetry in his spare time.

because in each country socialist realism must continue and extend national traditions if it does not want to become a meaningless and lifeless label.

I do not think Aragon would agree with Lukacs that the distinctive characteristic of socialist realism is that it describes ". . . the forces working towards socialism *from the inside*"[41] (Author's italics). This, for Aragon, is too restrictive a view, as it implies that the new artistic method can only flourish after the Revolution. Certainly, it requires the existence of at least one socialist society, otherwise it would be utopian and not scientific, but the significance of October 1917 is that it has put socialism on the agenda throughout the world:

> We are the writers of the epoch of socialism. . . . We necessarily reflect our time. . . . Whether we want to, or whether we don't.[42]

Thirdly, Aragon rejects the view that socialist realism cannot find inspiration except in the present, allegedly because there were no socialists before Marx and Lenin. This is a variant of the theory that the method cannot exist outside the Soviet Union. It was given up by Soviet writers themselves in the early fifties, and Aragon's own contribution was his novel *La Semaine sainte*, written, he insisted, ". . . from the point of view of socialist realism".[43] He presented the national tragedy of 1815 as a landmark in the struggle between the old world and the new forces unleashed by the French Revolution. The book is by no means the story of Géricault or of Marshal Berthier. Its real hero is the people of France, grappling with the issue of national independence at a time when the idea of patriotism had just begun to mean something for them. The significance of the novel is that the quarrel between Napoleon and the Bourbons is seen in historical perspective, as an episode in the birth-pangs of the bourgeois republic, without which there could never have arisen a socialist and working-class movement in France.

Fourthly, Aragon believes that socialist realism does not have to be openly didactic. His novels and his poems hardly resemble the type of propaganda literature in which one always feels that the author has an axe to grind and that the moral is predetermined in advance. In two cases at least, with *Aurélien* and with *La Semaine sainte*, a number of well-intentioned readers,

Communists and non-Communists, have been left wondering whether the works in question had anything to do with socialist realism, or whether the author was not treating himself to a short holiday, as it were. The truth is that Aragon does not think that the task of literature is to preach a sermon—there are enough pulpits for that purpose! Its function is to depict a real living situation and let it tell its own story. The example of *Aurélien* is particularly instructive in this respect, if only because the author has always looked upon it as his favourite child. The sub-title of the novel could well have been "Love in the bourgeois world", although it is difficult to find any passage where capitalism is directly attacked. Aurélien Leurtillois is, first of all, a ". . . man who is thrown back into civilian life, into a world which has changed without him".[44] He represents the generation whose youth was spent in the first world war and who acquired in the armed forces the habit of passive obedience to their superiors. Being a man of independent means, Aurélien cannot find in daily work a substitute for idleness, and his civilian life is dominated by dawdling—he lounges about all day long and feels quite detached from everyone and from everything. In this last respect, he closely resembles Mathieu Delarue, but Aragon goes one stage beyond Sartre—he traces the aloofness displayed by so many Frenchmen before 1939 to the first world war. Aurélien's only hope, however, is to be saved by love. When he finds Bérénice, a woman who believes in the total devotion of each partner in a couple, his life takes on a different meaning—from now on, there is something to live for, as far as he is concerned. Unfortunately, he is separated from Bérénice by a "gulf"—the living habits of his class, or rather, as Aragon puts it, of his "world". It is significant that the word "class" is not used, as the novelist effaces himself behind his two characters, neither of whom is likely to resort to Marxist terminology. All that Bérénice notices is that the man she once thought she loved because he was "different" is really very much like others in his "world", idle, aimless, incapable of providing her with anything more inspiring than high society evening parties or dinners at expensive restaurants:

She would just be Mrs Aurélien Leurtillois. A feeling of nausea came over her at the thought.[45]

The word "nausea" naturally brings to mind another Sartrian character, Antoine Roquentin, who experienced the same feeling when he encountered the absurdity of the world. The tragedy of Aurélien is the same as Roquentin's, as both men desperately want to find a sense of purpose, but what Aragon's hero looks forward to, and eventually fails to achieve, is fulfilment through love. It is piquant that the Communist novelist should seem more concerned with individual solutions than the existentialist, but Aragon cannot imagine a world without love. He told Jean Sur that "every novel proposes a solution . . . the solution is love".[46] It is because Aurélien does not come up to Bérénice's expectation that his love fails. Such is the message of the book, and in its lack of open didactic approach it probably *teaches* more than would appear at first sight.

Closely linked with the previous point, the fifth feature of Aragon's socialist realism is that it cannot be reduced to the echoing of Party slogans. Here, it is enough to quote from his speech to the 13th Congress of the French Communist Party:

A great national art cannot be created to last a couple of days, despite the opinion of some comrades who think that what matters is that books should support their viewpoint on some topical issue which is being debated during a particular week. Or should seem to support it. A great national art requires a long-term perspective, which is that of the nation. . . .[47]

Lastly, Aragon insists that socialist realism should never lose its critical aspect. It should be able to criticize, not only society, not only the mistakes of its friends, but its own assumptions, and it should frequently re-examine its own tenets. The outstanding illustration of this critical approach on Aragon's part is *La Mise à mort*, which destroys a number of hitherto accepted notions among Communists, most of which have already been mentioned in the course of this essay. It is necessary to add two more books in the same connection, *Les Poètes* and *Le Fou d'Elsa*. In the former, Aragon criticizes the naïve optimism which he once partly shared and stresses that one must have the courage to look at reality without rosy spectacles, and remember that the "victory of the angels" is not likely to be round the corner:

I do not say this to demoralize people One must look at
complete darkness
Face to face in order to overcome it Song is no less beautful
when it is a descant[a]

In the same book, Aragon develops at great length his idea that
conflicts will not automatically disappear after the establishment of socialism, that there will always be "a war" for young
people to take part in—the war against routine, conventions,
die-hard dogmas, and that technological advances, of which
we should be rightly proud, will never kill the need for art and
beauty. Poetry, he feels, will not become "automated", and
he sees it as ". . . the ultimate challenge of man to himself."[48] So
long as "man is accountable to man",[49] the last word will never
be said. Such a tone and such courageous warnings have been
all too absent in the works of a number of so-called "socialist
realists".

With regard to *Le Fou d'Elsa*, which is also a poem written
in the light of Aragon's philosophy,[b] the poet's critical sense is
illustrated by his treatment of history. First, there is a small
entry in the Glossary provided at the end, to which not enough
attention has been paid so far, in my opinion; it reads as follows:

History: a word which *everywhere* means a supposedly scientific justification of the interests of a particular human
group. . . .[50]

This is hardly veiled criticism, not only of the way Spanish
Catholic historians describe the fall of Granada and the
character of King Boadbil, but of recent Soviet distortions of
history. It is Aragon himself who stresses the word "everywhere" in the above quotation. He goes on to express the hope
that, some day, history will become a truly scientific discipline.
Secondly, the privileged place given to subjective elements in

---

[a] Je ne dis pas cela pour démoraliser Il faut regarder le néant
En face pour savoir en triompher Le chant n'est pas moins beau
quand il décline
(op. cit., p. 212.)
[b] Aragon described it as an example of "realism" in poetry, again in the
sense that realism interprets facts instead of merely registering them. The
background to the poem, and indeed one of its main themes, is the fall of
Granada.

viewing historical developments is itself a critical reaction against many so-called Marxists, past and present, who forget that humanism and not economism is the essence of Marxism. We have already seen how the assertion that "Woman is the future of Man" is a conscious echo of Marx, but it is part of Aragon's creative originality that he does not merely repeat his Classics—he extends their thoughts. Marx, he feels, was perfectly right to stress that man's fight for the future consists in creating the conditions for a truly human existence, but this was a general statement, requiring application to a wide variety of fields. Aragon's chosen province is concrete human relations, and he sees in the genuine couple of tomorrow the finest embodiment of the new spirit which he expects from socialism and communism. Similarly, his remark about putting mysticism "back on its feet" is more than a neat reproduction of the terms used by Marx when he described Hegelian dialectic as "walking on its head"; it is both an assertion of materialism, since a woman of flesh and blood is substituted for a supernatural Being as the proper subject worthy of complete self-sacrifice which is associated with mysticism, and an attack on vulgar materialism which rejects the whole of idealism root and branch, inasmuch as it wants to retain what is positive, and indeed very noble, in the mystics' form of love.

NOTES

1. *Que peut la littérature?*, p. 126.
2. Preface to Garaudy's *D'un réalisme sans rivages*, p. 14.
3. op. cit., p. 403.
4. Jean Roussel, *Charles Péguy*, p. 48.
5. *Œuvres poétiques complètes*, p. 813.
6. Jean Sur, op. cit., pp. 192–93.
7. R. M. Albérès, *Jean-Paul Sartre*, p. 35.
8. *La Semaine sainte*, p. 580.
9. *J'abats mon jeu*, p. 156.
10. Ibid., pp. 45–70.
11. *Tribune*, 30.9.1966.
12. *J'abats mon jeu*, p. 48.
13. Ibid., pp. 159–60.
14. Poem in *Le Crève-cœur*, translated by Malcolm Cowley.
15. *Théâtre*, p. 218.
16. Poem in *La Diane française*, translated by Rolfe Humphries.
17. op. cit., p. 404.

18. *Les Collages*, p. 22.
19. E. Fischer, *The Necessity of Art*, p. 112.
20. *La Mise à mort*, pp. 403–4.
21. *Les Collages*, p. 23.
22. Ibid., p. 13.
23. Ibid., p. 13.
24. Ibid., p. 101.
25. Ibid., p. 115.
26. *Entretiens avec Francis Crémieux*, p. 74.
27. *Les séquestrés d'Altona*, p. 153.
28. *Les Poètes*, p. 187.
29. *Aragon romancier*, p. 66.
30. Ibid., p. 65.
31. *Situations I*, p. 19.
32. *Situations II*, p. 254.
33. *Cahiers du communisme*, May–June 1966, p. 279.
34. Ibid., p. 263.
35. *J'abats mon jeu*, p. 80.
36. Ibid., p. 173.
37. *Les Collages*, p. 22.
38. Article reproduced in *J'abats mon jeu*, p. 39.
39. Ibid., p. 32.
40. op. cit., pp. 154 and 241.
41. Georg Lukacs, *The Meaning of Contemporary Realism*, p. 93.
42. *J'abats mon jeu*, p. 173.
43. Ibid., p. 91.
44. Ibid., p. 144.
45. op. cit., p. 349.
46. op. cit., p. 22.
47. *J'abats mon jeu*, p. 213.
48. op. cit., p. 171.
49. Ibid., p. 212.
50. op. cit., p. 438.

CHAPTER VI

POETRY AND COMMITMENT

W E H A V E A L R E A D Y seen that one of the opening statements of Sartre's *What is Literature?* is that prose alone can be committed and poetry cannot. The author bases this curious theory on the belief that the poet is the slave of words, whereas the prose writer uses them as tools. As the aim of commitment is to clarify the issues, and as poetry tends to obscure them, there is, we are told, an absolute incompatibility between the two. There is good reason to believe that Sartre would no longer subscribe to this view, because since dismissing all arts apart from prose as incapable of commitment, he later described the painter Lapoujade as fully committed. It is worth, however, examining how the example of Péguy and Aragon disproves the contention made in *What is Literature?* that poetry and commitment cannot mix.

It may not be out of place to start by recalling that some of the greatest works in which the issue of human destiny is faced and *clarified* were written in verse, and the names of Dante, Shakespeare, Milton and Racine suggest themselves automatically. Furthermore, prose and poetry cannot be considered as two entirely different forms of expression. Benedetto Croce, for example, stresses that poetic devices are not, as Sartre believes, ends in themselves, but that they play their part in expressing reality.[1] This applies particularly to rhythm and rhymes. It is true that all poetry is rhythmical and that prose writers do not clothe what they have to say in the mould of a special metre. But what a poor idea we would have of poetry if we thought that metre was a brake on the free expression of ideas! This may be so for the mere versifier. For a real poet, however, metre is not a meaningless adornment, it is something which helps to concretize his thoughts. It does not lull the consciousness of the reader or the hearer, but rather fixes his attention and heightens his consciousness. Is it possible, then, to seek in rhymes the proof that the poet is enslaved by his devices, instead of being, like the prose writer, their master? The first objection to this view is that rhyming is not indispensable in poetry, and that in some of the finest verse it does not occur at all. But even when it does, it helps to give ideas a special form and to make a more forceful impact on the audience. Aragon claims that rhymes manage to reveal certain aspects of reality, that they belong to "the real world, and [are] the link between objects and song, that which helps objects to sing".[2] It follows that if the differences between prose and poetry are not so clear-cut and fundamental as Sartre would have us believe, one is compelled to probe deeper into the issue and ask oneself: What is poetry?

WHAT IS POETRY?

In the absence of a thorough investigation of the genesis of poetry, which has yet to be made,[a] it is reasonably safe to say that poetry, as different from other kinds of literature, achieves its effects by the use of images, that it relies on imagination, and that it is, in one way or another, a form of "song", of what Aragon calls the "bel canto". That images are an essential part of poetry will hardly be disputed. Even in ordinary speech, we say that an expression is poetical because of its imagery. What committed writers like to stress is that images, no matter how fanciful, have their basis in reality and derive their force from the concentrated view of reality which they give. They are not technical devices for expressing the world, they are the form in which reality unfolds itself to the poet. In other words, the latter expresses things differently, because he *sees* them differently. For example, Péguy's imagery is his own way of apprehending the world: his poetic vision detects the depths of human destiny which are revealed in temporal conflicts, such as the Dreyfus Affair. Unlike Aragon, he sees the invisible hand of God everywhere, but divine intervention is not mysterious, it is experienced by men in their daily lives. Péguy's conception of the "supernatural" being itself "carnal" is nowhere more evident than in his poetry. Saint Joan and Saint Geneviève are shown by him in their complete humanity, and it is the performance of their human tasks which reveals to them the inner reality of the world which, according to the poet, is its spirituality. By communicating this experience and by singing the songs of the Christian soul, Péguy's verse, no less than his prose, leads to action.

[a] In this country, the works of George Thomson and Christopher Caudwell constitute a Marxist attempt to tackle the issue, but both authors would agree, I think, that they have by no means exhausted the subject.

One of the best ways of illustrating the close relationship between images and reality in Aragon's poetry is to use the method which he himself applied to the study of Victor Hugo, i.e. to compare his poems with his prose. For example, the theme of *Les Lilas et les roses* is the same as that of Volume IV of *Les Communistes*. The latter describes at greater length what the former condenses with the help of imagery. Such a test shows that, in great poetry, images are a "short-cut" view of reality, to return to Aragon's own expression. There is therefore little justification for Sartre's false opposition between words as "signs" and as "images". The truth of the matter is that images are not divorced from reality, but rise above it. They make us visualize what our senses alone cannot grasp, and they appeal to our imagination.

This leads straight to the next question: if imagination is so important, is poetry the realm of dreams? Here, it is unfortunate that, under the influence of neo-Freudians, the word "dreams" should have acquired a psycho-analytical connotation and that poetry should be seen as the expression of the subconscious. This is not the way in which committed literature understands the part played by dreams in poetic creation. I mentioned in the previous chapter that committed dreams equip us for action. They infuse into our whole being the burning desire to improve the world,

> For everything brings man back to the battlefield
> Be it the detour of some milky way[a]

Aragon believes that man's struggles would be poorer, narrower without dreams; not just dreams of a better society, but also the dreams of personal happiness and aesthetic enjoyment. The poet's dreams make us appreciate that life is worth living, and so, gently surrounded in imagination by trees, plants, mountains, lakes, rivers, by the whole of Nature, we begin to dream of a world in which we can appreciate these simple pleasures without having them clouded and spoilt by the material worries of the present. We emerge from the dream stronger to face the battle and not numbed into passivity. We are committed body and soul.

[a] Car tout ramène l'homme au cœur de la bataille
Serait-ce le détour de quelque voie lactée
(*Les Yeux et la mémoire*, p. 44.)

Lastly, poetry is, in the words of Aragon, "le bel canto"—
the poet is a singer and the music of his poem is inseparable
from its content. In the essays he collected under the title of
Chroniques du Bel Canto, Aragon develops two main ideas. He
stresses, first, that all poetry is dictated by "circumstances",
an idea which was already put forward by Goethe. By that,
he means that a poem owes its inspiration to an aspect of
reality which made an impact on the artist and aroused certain
feelings in his soul. Not to know the "circumstances" is to
miss the significance of the poem altogether; that is why Aragon
felt it necessary to include many explanatory notes at the end
of *Les Yeux et la mémoire*, *Le Roman inachevé*, and *Le Fou d'Elsa*.
If such notes are absent from *Les Poètes*, it is probably because
the text itself refers directly to the background of the work,
particularly at the end, where the poet reveals his "manufacturing secrets" and describes in detail the genesis of his
poem—we detect with him the part played by Elsa as well as
by contemporary scientific and social reality. Aragon's second
point is that poetry is not at all mysterious, except in so far as
the origins of song and its effects are still imperfectly known.
The whole "mystery" of poetry lies in song, but that "mystery"
is already "well on the way out" ("en passe de réduction").[3]
Besides, if song represents the mysterious aspect of poetry, it is
also, according to Aragon, what provides it with an objective
character: it is through the medium of song that the poet
communicates with other men, it is song which enables "circumstances" to take on a body as it were and to be recognized by
singer and audience alike as a bond between them. By insisting
on the non-mysterious character of poetry, Aragon does not
deny its magical powers and he speaks of the "bel canto" as
"that *mysterious* power of resonance, which makes glasses
vibrate on the table and insensitive people quiver"[4] (my
italics). He is the last person who would reduce poetry to
"circumstances"; all he asserts is that there is a close link
between them. If poetry is particularly fitted to voice the
message of commitment, it is both because it is based on the
world which the poet and the reader share as a common
experience, and because it adds something to the world.

In *Les Poètes*, Aragon further develops his ideas on song and
shows that the singer is not alone. He starts by borrowing the
voice of the great poets who came before him. They all had

their special "secrets" and, like novelists, were often compelled "to lie" in order to reveal the truth:

> The sun of truth
> Yields before the moon of lies[a]

But the basic task of poetry is to give more light. Without despising his predecessors, whose limitations and shortcomings Marxism has taught him to understand and *respect*,[b] he is conscious of his superiority and in a mood of fearless confidence, he goes on to exclaim:

> To hell with moonlit beauty
> And with age-long darkness
> . . . .
> Let there be full light on the modern world
> Full light on our neon souls
>
> Full light on the darkness of dreams
> Full light on the art of lying
> Shine everlasting summer
> Shine from our human blaze
> And let our hands bring back in all directions
> The great sun of Truth[c]

[a] *Les Poètes*, p. 82.
> Le soleil de la vérité
> Cède à la lune du mensonge

[b] No Marxist would describe the past as "a heap of abuses, errors and crimes" as Voltaire did. The men of each age, according to Marxism, are historically limited, and they deserve our respect when they go as far as their time allows them to.

[c] op. cit., pp. 113-14.
> Au diable la beauté lunaire
> Et les ténèbres millénaires
>
> . . . .
> Plein feu sur l'univers moderne
> Plein feu sur notre âme au néon
>
> Plein feu sur la noirceur des songes
> Plein feu sur les arts du mensonge
> Flambe perpétuel été
> Flambe de notre flamme humaine
> Et que partout nos mains ramènen
> Le soleil de la vérité

This is the proud accent of a twentieth-century poet who is not afraid of the truth, as he lives in an age when man is beginning to see clearly the real nature of the world and his own place in it. The "secret" of man gradually ceases to be a secret at all, and from all sides the old mysteries are rapidly melting away under the burning heat of light. The artist is increasingly a discoverer of the world, and thanks to the special *radar* at his disposal, the radar of poetry, he can say,

> Mystery is compelled to lie down at my feet [a]

and also,

> I am the man who brings order into the great dwelling-place of men
> Who mows digs stones and weeds the realm where they pass
> The roads I take explain the world. . . . [b]

We are far indeed from Sartre's contemptuous assertion that poetry cannot fulfil the committed aim of clarifying issues. Aragon insolently replies that there is method in the poet's madness and that he, at any rate, goes a long way to *explain* the world. What Sartre seems to have overlooked is that feelings, as well as intelligence, contribute to the clarification of human problems. There are times when powerful ideas cannot be expressed in prose but need the music of poetry, a music in which the whole soul of a people is expressed. Poetry then becomes ". . . human thought at the height of its intensity".[5] It represents a remarkable blending of "musical invention" and "scientific imagination", and the poet himself is the man "who creates with the help of a hypothesis—the image", and who discovers in reality "relationships hitherto unperceived".[c]

With regard to Péguy, whose commitment was based on a

---

[a] op. cit., p. 187.
> Le mystère à mes pieds terre à terre se couche

[b] op cit., p. 153.
> Je suis celui qui met de l'ordre dans la demeure énorme des hommes
> Celui qui fauche défriche empierre et sarcle l'empire traversé
> J'explique par des chemins le domaine. . . .

[c] op. cit., p. 194. ". . . celui qui crée au moyen d'une hypothèse image aperçoit à partir de la réalité un rapport jamais vu par un chemin qui est celui de l'invention musicale à la fois et de l'imagination scientifique. . . ."

religious view of the world, the point at issue is not whether
Sartre would recognize the value of Christianity—he probably
would not!—but whether it is possible for him to deny that
Péguy's poetry makes sense only in the light of his Christian
commitment. This is what Alexander Dru stresses in his excellent study, and as it is the only analysis of Péguy's poetry to have
appeared in English so far, I take the liberty of summarizing
his views. He sees a striking similarity between Coleridge's
theory of the imagination in the *Biographia literaria* and the
remarks which Péguy ". . . hurriedly dictated to Lotte over a
glass of beer, and which most of his French critics make no
attempt to interpret. . . ."[6] "In both cases," writes Mr Dru,
"the ideas in question are linked to the act of conversion," and
he adds,

> Both of them are attempting to describe the poetic power as
> the fruit of harmony and unity of vision, in which not one
> faculty alone is active, but the whole soul of man.[7]

The power of poetry is based on imagination, which Coleridge
carefully distinguishes from fancy. The "primary imagination"
as he calls it is a "repetition in the finite mind of the eternal act
of creation" and it is this essentially spiritual faculty which is
echoed in poetry and gives it the power to lead to action.
Whether one agrees with the Christian interpretation or not,
the relevant point, as far as Péguy is concerned, is that he
considered himself as having received from God the gift of
reflecting with particular force the creative spark which can
be found in every man, and that his duty was to communicate
his vision, to stir our emotions and *make us act*. It is the Christian
view of "littérature engagée". Far from poetry being looked
upon as a process in which "emotion has become a thing",[8] as
Sartre says, it represents the supreme medium for expressing
Péguy's emotions and his "mystique". It is the ideal tool for
conveying his deeper spiritual commitment, and it is significant
that the "deepening" of his mind—since he always rejected the
word "conversion"—coincided with his newly-found poetic
genius.

The commited character of his poetry comes out in two striking ways: First, in its close association with French tradition,
a feature which reminds one of Aragon's point about the

national character of great poetry. For Péguy, patriotism, Christianity and poetry are three facets of the same reality, and one critic describes his return to Christ as a manifestation of his patriotism.[a] What his poems reveal above all is the temporal character of the saints he admired, the fact that they were *French*.

"For that great saint," he says of Joan, "was a girl from home."[b] It is no exaggeration to assert that it was not so much Our Lady whom he worshipped, but Our Lady *of Chartres*, the Virgin Mary on French soil. God Himself is described as a "good Frenchman" in Péguy's verse! His poetry is, above all, an act of love dedicated to the land of France for which he died. It is an appeal to his countrymen, urging them to defend "la patrie en danger" and continue its glorious traditions.

Secondly, the choice of metre, rhymes and sounds is always subordinated to the idea Péguy wants to express. When he renders the word of God, in its beautiful simplicity, he uses blank verse, as in the "Mysteries". In the *Tapisseries* and in *Eve*, he finds that the solemnity of the subject requires the alexandrine, always a favourite metre with French poets, particularly when their theme is noble and uplifting. The *Quatrains* are based on the alternation between hexasyllabic and four-syllable lines in order to give greater speed and liveliness to the ideas and to avoid rhetoric. As for rhymes and sounds, a whole book could be filled with significant examples of careful selection. Here is how, in the *Tapisserie de Sainte Geneviève*, he opposes Jesus and Satan:

> Les armes de Jésus c'est la belle marraine
> Et c'est le beau baptême et c'est la belle étrenne
> Et l'avoine et le seigle et c'est la bonne graine
>
> . . . .
>
> Les armes de Satan, c'est une gagerie,
> C'est sa fortanterie et son effronterie,
> Et c'est le philologue et sa quincaillerie.[c]

---

[a] Dom Charles Poulet, "Le retour de Péguy au Christ se présente comme une modalité de son patriotisme." (*La Sainteté française contemporaine*, vol. II, p. 198.)

[b] "Mais cette grande sainte était une fille de chez nous."

[c] As the purpose of this quotation is to illustrate Péguy's handling of rhymes and sounds, I do not think a translation is required. (*Œuvres poétiques complètes*, pp. 639–41.)

The sounds "aine", "ême" and "oine" are pleasant and light; they remind one of the prophet who said that his yoke was easy, whereas the sounds "rie", "aillerie" and the "f" alliteration [a] describe the eternal tempter, the showman who tries to ensnare and beguile the unwary. These remarks bring us to the issue of poetic form, which I intend to examine very briefly with regard to Aragon, as he does not simply illustrate his views, but often formulates them theoretically.

POETIC FORM—ARAGON'S POSITION

Aragon's position about the relationship between form and content can be expressed as follows: Form is the tool through which a new content must be communicated. This attitude leads him to make a serious attempt to develop form, to experiment with all the possibilities available in French prosody, to suit his metre to the various moods he wishes to convey, to make rhymes tell their own story, and generally speaking, to make such a thorough study of poetic language that it can be handled by him as a scientist handles a complex piece of machinery whose technical secrets he has completely mastered.

His conception can best be understood by seeing it as a dialectical process in which the first step is the assertion of the poet's freedom to choose the form he likes; the second step is the apparent negation of that freedom (insistence on the labour required for good poetry); whereas the third one is the "negation of the negation", i.e. liberty on a higher level, which combines the freedom of selection and of inspiration with supreme workmanship. The guiding thread of the poet throughout these various steps is that poetry is language, a means of communication.

Aragon's freedom is the antithesis of the so-called freedom of the surrealists. Freedom does not consist in opposing all traditional forms in poetry, because that in itself soon becomes a dogma and, in the end, represents the same kind of tyranny as the need to confine oneself to alexandrines and to conventional rhyming patterns. For a poet, real freedom is "to be able to say all" ("Pouvoir tout dire"),[b] to refuse to be

---

[a] The sound "f" in French often conveys the idea of hypocrisy—witness "Tartuffe", "félon", "faux", etc.

[b] The expression is Eluard's.

imprisoned by theories about form, no matter how revolutionary they sound, and to start with the idea that a poet has
something to say and is speaking to the people. Such concern for
content and public is the essence of "littérature engagée". It
led Eluard and Aragon to break with the surrealist "free
verse"—Aragon much more than Eluard—and return to more
traditional forms. They found that with those they could speak
directly to their countrymen and be understood by them. In
later poems, however, Aragon went back to free verse, particularly when he chose to describe his surrealist youth.

Aragon's second step concerns the mastery of technique,
for a poet must strive after perfection. This is not an intellectual
pastime for its own sake, but a necessary consequence of
commitment: if the nature of the message determines the choice
of form, its importance requires the poet to tackle his verse in
such a way that it yields the best of itself. The paradoxical
result is thus reached that "littérature engagée", or rather,
despite Aragon's dislike for the phrase, "poésie engagée"
demands perfection of form on behalf of "engagement" itself:

> Poetry is in the ideas. . . . It becomes perfect only when
> clothed in the grace and majesty of verse. [9]

We therefore find the poet laboriously at work in front of his
writing desk, handling his poetic devices as the craftsman his
tools or the artist his paint-brushes. From *Le Crève-cœur* to *Le
Fou d'Elsa*, there is hardly a line of his left to chance. All his
poems reveal an increasing mastery of poetic technique,
achieved as a result of painstaking effort. But it is not enough to
work hard in order to produce great poetry: the poet's genius
consists in making one forget all the labour involved. Lombroso
once said that genius involves ninety-nine per cent of perspira-
tion and one per cent of inspiration, but it is the one per cent
which matters and which alone should be noticed.

The important feature of devotion to form in the name of the
message it conveys, is particularly well illustrated in Aragon's
wartime poetry. It might be thought that between 1940 and
1944 conditions were far from ripe for elaborate theories about
poetic technicalities, but Aragon felt he was a soldier of the
Resistance and had no more right to neglect his special weapon
than a soldier his rifle. Ten years later, he reminded a Moscow
audience that

Discussions about the technique of verse are not at all some kind of Byzantine affair. Writers have a weapon which is language, . . . and the rules concerning its use are of considerable importance if it is to be handled effectively.[10]

Form, however, is but a means to an end, and we now reach the third step of the dialectical process, which is the synthesis between freedom and hard work, both of which are needed in order to give commitment a human content adequately expressed. In this light, obedience to rules becomes real liberty. Just as Racine found the rules of Classicism a help rather than a fetter because the content of his tragedies admirably suited those rules, so Aragon proves his freedom by selecting the metres and rhymes which best correspond to his ideas and makes them fulfil their role in conveying his message. There is a science of poetry, and if a writer does not want to master that science, he is perfectly free not to become a poet or to choose other means of expression; but if he is spontaneously led to choose poetry, he does not give up his freedom by working at his poem and by making his instrument as effective as possible—he rather establishes his freedom on a solid basis.

Aragon's use of the most diverse metres has already been briefly referred to. With regard to rhymes, two features should be mentioned. First, his endeavour to introduce more flexibility into French rhyming patterns in order that poetry should reflect the new world in which we live, that its language should express the scientific and technological revolution of our time, whilst still remaining musical. In order to achieve this, Aragon believes that new rhymes must be found, and he suggests in particular the modern "rime enjambée" (now known as the "Aragon rhyme"), in which a sound is carried over from the end of one line to the beginning of the other (for example:

> . . . J'écoute mon cœur BATTRE
> . . . .
> . . . Que fait-elle là-BAS
> Trop proche et trop lointaine . . .

where "battre" of line one rhymes with "bas tr" of lines three and four), and the "complex rhyme" which allows one word to rhyme with many others, (for example, "ivresse" with "vivre est-ce"). The whole object is to achieve an effect of surprise, which is not to be despised since it arrests the reader's attention, and mainly to prevent the poet from rejecting certain words which are important from the point of view of the theme, but which could not find their place at the end of a line according to conventional rules. Moreover, the discontinuity of the above rhymes is particularly suited to express the realities of the twentieth century. Secondly, together with novelty, Aragon believes in tradition because it represents a link between the national past and the present. In this respect there is a striking similarity between his approach and Péguy's. They are almost alone among modern poets to have used so many rhymes which recall the mediaeval epoch, the glorious period of Classicism and the early Romantics.

NOTES

1. Cf. pp. 30 et passim of Croce's *Estetica* (ed. Lateza, Bari, 1958).
2. *La Rime en 1940*, in *Le Crève-cœur*, p. 76.
3. op. cit., p. 258.
4. Ibid., p. 10.
5. *J'abats mon jeu*, p. 193.
6. A. Dru, op. cit., p. 54.
7. Ibid., pp. 55–56.
8. J. P. Sartre, *Situations II*, p. 69.
9. Aragon, *Hugo poète réaliste*, p. 54.
10. *J'abats mon jeu*, pp. 189–90.

CONCLUSION

SOME CONCLUSIONS

THIS BRIEF STUDY should enable us to single out some of the common features in the path followed by Péguy, Aragon and Sartre in their quest for commitment. The first striking similarity among them is their continuous obedience to the voice of truth as it revealed itself to them under the influence of a changing world, even when this involved dramatic reversals of attitude or contradictions. Their spiritual evolution is one of permanent "deepening" and "enrichment", and can be characterized as a form of *constancy through change*. They were never more faithful to their ideals than when they had the courage to change sides and bring with them the basic values of the men they had left or the philosophies they had transcended. Péguy gave up his membership of the Socialist Party, not because he had ceased to believe in socialism, but in the name of a higher conception of socialism; he embraced Christianity, not in order to renounce the temporal battle, but rather so that he could go on waging it with greater strength and confidence. Aragon broke with the surrealists, not in order to return to the path of convention, but because he wanted to attack the very roots of convention in the "real world"; more recently, he threw away a narrow interpretation of socialist realism so that socialism should gain by looking at the whole truth, however unpleasant, and realism be enriched by the exploration of subjectivity. When Sartre discarded some of his original existentialist tenets, because life itself was compelling him to revise his views, he merely applied the basic existentialist principle that "existence precedes essence"; he bravely denounced the limitations of his early approach to commitment, not in order to take shelter behind passive neutrality, but so that the lucidity required by his commitment should be complete and free from self-deception. What Garaudy says of Aragon alone is true of all these writers—they are the men "of exemplary fidelity". Throughout their lives, they have remained intellectually and morally honest with themselves. This is the greatest lesson of commitment, and it is illustrated by Péguy's insistence that one should at all times "bawl out the truth", by Aragon's description of himself as a man "who says what he thinks", and by the merciless attack which Sartre launches on all forms of "mauvaise foi".

An important aspect of their intellectual honesty is their refusal to be taken in by what they consider false values. Péguy's unorthodox use of current words was intended to show that there is another side to most of the comforting concepts which we take for granted; the "modern world", for example, is not just the era of material progress and civilization, but the world of money and of sterile intellectualism. Aragon denounces what he calls "cant" when he fights, inside his own party, against stereotyped slogans and when he ridicules mechanical repetition of lifeless formulae; a good illustration is the way in which he rebukes those Communists who imagine that the class struggle explains everything and that it dispenses the artist from analysing real men and women, with their complexities and their idiosyncrasies. Sartre considers that one of the advantages of commitment is that it prevents the writer from being "tricked by his time"; for example, it helps him to denounce the fallacy of abstention from the struggle, which is just a cowardly way of taking sides; or to draw a clear distinction between the "rebel", who wants the world to remain as it is so that he may enjoy striking it with the force of his invective, and the "revolutionary", who is anxious to change it. What unites Péguy, Aragon and Sartre, in spite of their diversity, is that they never remain satisfied with superficial appearances and soothing illusions, but that, at the risk of jeopardizing their most cherished beliefs, they always endeavour to get at the *roots* of the issues which they tackle. Theirs is, literally, a radical approach. Because the roots of human life are the concrete and the present, they declare war on abstractions and on the view that the "eternal" can ever be divorced from the "temporal". It is not only Aragon who wants to put the "mystique back on its feet", but also, in his own special way, the Catholic poet for whom Christianity was always a guide to action, and the existentialist philosopher who puts existence before essence.

Lastly, Péguy, Aragon and Sartre all believe that literature is not a futile form of entertainment, but that it is *useful*—in the broadest and best sense of the word. Without any false modesty, they earnestly hope that their own work and their own example will benefit their fellow men. Péguy sacrificed everything, his health, his money and his career, to the success of the *Cahiers* in which he saw a platform for those who wanted to tell the truth. "Ye shall know the truth, and the truth shall make you free." Aragon has always fought that "monstrosity which one calls individualism", and made the principle of helping others the golden rule of his life:

> I gave my all so that you might know better
> The road which must be taken[a]

Sartre is never weary of stressing that the writer has a duty, and when he recently discarded the idea of a literary "mandate", he was not thinking of finding excuses for irresponsible detachment, but simply of doing his duty without feeling proud about it. Commitment is not a writer's glorious ministry—it is his daily task.

It now remains to sum up very briefly the chief characteristics of "littérature engagée" and to bring out one or two lessons which are implied in this literary conception. The committed outlook rests above all on the recognition that an artist is part of his environment—the society in which he lives, the ideologies of his time, and the public for whom he creates. No modern writer is free from these influences, and the greater his understanding of them, the greater his commitment will be. Péguy, Aragon and Sartre are men whose evolution was vastly different, but their militant crusade always brings them back to three or four central ideas—action, co-operation, responsibility and hope. They tried to grasp being in its totality, and nothing human was foreign to them.

In a sense, few people have done more than our three "engagés" to "debunk" literature and, so to speak, put it in its proper place. They have reminded writers with some vehemence that the illusions of absolute freedom, complete independence and the unfathomable mystery of art are just this—illusions! But if, in the words of the philosopher, freedom is the knowledge of necessity, they have performed a great service to literature by showing what its function is and where its true greatness lies. It cannot be sufficiently stressed that, despite early excesses and exaggerations, "littérature engagée" does not despise other forms of art, and it was Sartre who stated,

---

[a] Moi j'ai tout donné pour que vous sachiez mieux
La route qu'il faut prendre

at the time when his committed mood was most intransigent, that the artist's disclosure of an aspect of reality *always* has a liberating effect. "Littérature engagée" does not claim that it is necessarily more realistic than other kinds of literature, but simply that it is consciously so. This, in turn, leads it to portray *all* aspects of reality and to bring out what it thinks is the objective significance of the world around us. Since the writer is not, as we have seen, an inanimate mirror passively reflecting his surroundings, his interest in the world is dominated by a desire to change it. We touch here upon the most original characteristic of "littérature engagée", repeatedly emphasized throughout this essay: it is militant and active.

Can English writers learn from the French example? I believe they can, provided there is no attempt at servile imitation. It is as men of their time that Péguy, Aragon and Sartre achieved greatness, and all that one can hope for is that English writers in the second half of this century will also achieve greatness by being men of their land and their age. There are many signs that this is already taking place and there is a growing recognition that the two challenges contained in *What is Literature?* cannot be evaded—namely, "Why does one write?" and "For whom does one write?" As commitment is a living concept, it is sure to alter considerably in the years to come, and I personally welcome the prospect as proof of its vitality.

SELECT BIBLIOGRAPHY

SELECT BIBLIOGRAPHY

Unless otherwise stated, the place of publication is Paris in the case of French books, and London in the case of English books. Where more than one edition is mentioned, the one I have used is marked *.

PÉGUY

Main works by Péguy

Most of Péguy's work appeared in the *Cahiers de la Quinzaine*, the complete edition of which (1900–14) can be found at the Bibliothèque Nationale in Paris. After his death, Gallimard published his complete works in twenty volumes under the title *Œuvres complètes* (1916–55). I have used this edition in one case only (cf. p. 65). Otherwise, reference is always to the following three volumes of the Pléiade edition (N.R.F.):

Œuvres poétiques complètes,	1941
	1948*
Œuvres en prose (1898–1908),	1959
Œuvres en prose (1909–1914),	1957

The following English translations may be found useful:

A. Dru: *Temporal and Eternal*, 1958 (extracts from *Notre Jeunesse* and *Clio*)
A. and J. Green: *Basic Verities*, 1943
— *Men and Saints*, 1947 (both are anthologies of prose and poetry)

Main works written on Péguy—
English studies
Yvonne Servais: *Charles Péguy, The Pursuit of Salvation*, 1953
Alexander Dru: *Péguy*, 1956
Marjorie Villiers: *Charles Péguy, A Study in Integrity*, 1965
N. Jussem-Wilson: *Charles Péguy*, 1965

French studies
Romain Rolland: *Péguy* (2 volumes), 1944
André Rousseaux: *Le Prophète Péguy* (2 volumes), 1945
Jean Roussel: *Mesure de Péguy*, 1946
— *Charles Péguy*, 1952

Albert Béguin: *L'Eve de Péguy*, 1948
Félicien Challaye: *Péguy socialiste*, 1954
Georges Cattaui: *Péguy, témoin du temporel chrétien*, 1964

In 1948, "L'Amitié de Charles Péguy" started the publication of a regular Bulletin which gives details of the poet's life and works and reviews books written about him.

ARAGON

Main works by Aragon—
Poems
Feu de joie, 1920
Le Mouvement perpétuel, 1925
La Grande Gaîté, 1929
Persécuté Persécuteur, 1931
Hourra l'Oural, 1934
Le Crève-cœur, 1941
      1946*
Les Yeux d'Elsa, 1942
Le Musée Grévin, first published under the pseudonym of
    François La Colère, 1943

En francais dans le texte, 1943   ⎱ Gathered under the title of "*En étrange*
Brocéliande,   1943   ⎰ *pays dans mon pays lui-même*"

Les Yeux et la mémoire, 1954
Le Roman inachevé, 1956
Elsa, 1959
Les Poètes, 1960
Le Fou d'Elsa, 1963
Voyage de Hollande, 1964
Elégie à Pablo Neruda, 1966

Novels
Anicet, ou le panorama roman, 1921
Le Paysan de Paris, 1926
Les Cloches de Bâle, 1934
Les Beaux Quartiers, 1936
Les Voyageurs de l'impériale (written in 1939), 1943
                    1947*

Aurélien, 1944
Les Communistes (6 volumes), 1949–51
La Semaine sainte, 1958
                    1959*
La Mise à mort, 1965

  The Editions Robert Laffont recently started the publication
of all the novels written by Aragon and Elsa Triolet under the
title of *Œuvres romanesques croisées d'Elsa Triolet et d'Aragon.* The
work, which includes prefaces written by each author, is
available on subscription only.

Essays
Le libertinage, 1924
Une Vague de rêves, 1924
Traité du style, 1928
Pour un réalisme socialiste, 1935
Chroniques du Bel Canto, 1947
L'homme communiste, Tome I, 1946
                       Tome II, 1953
Avez-vous lu Victor Hugo? (an anthology, with comments), 1952
Hugo, poète réaliste, 1952
L'Exemple de Courbet, 1952
La Lumière de Stendhal, 1954
Journal d'une poésie nationale, 1954
Littératures soviétiques, 1956
Introduction aux littératures soviétiques, 1956
J'abats mon jeu, 1959
Entretiens avec Francis Crémieux, 1964
Les Collages, 1965
  Aragon has also written a number of articles, mostly in the
Lettres Françaises, a weekly journal of which he is the editor.
Unpublished manuscripts of his can be found in the Biblio-
thèque Jacques Doucet, Paris.

History
Histoire parallèle des U.S.A. et de l'U.R.S.S., André Maurois and
    Louis Aragon (4 volumes), 1962, English transl.: Aragon,
    History of the U.S.S.R. (1 volume), 1963

English translations
The following English translations of Aragon's novels may be found useful:

The Bells of Basel, 1937
Residential Quarter, 1938
Passengers of Destiny, 1947
Aurélien, 1961
Holy Week, 1961

Main works written about Aragon
Hannah Josephson and Malcolm Cowley, *Aragon, Poet of Resurgent France*, 1946. (Includes a selection of Aragon's prose and poetry. The poems are translated by English and American poets, including Louis MacNeice and Stephen Spender)
Claude Roy, *Aragon*, 1945, revised ed., 1962
A. Gavillet, *La Littérature au défi: Aragon surréaliste*, 1957
Pierre de Lescure, *Aragon romancier*, 1960
Hubert Juin, *Aragon*, 1960
Roger Garaudy, *L'Itinéraire d'Aragon*, 1961
Georges Raillard, *Aragon*, 1964
Jean Sur, *Aragon, le réalisme de l'amour* (with marginal comments by Aragon), 1966
Charles Haroche, *L'idée de l'amour dans le 'Fou d'Elsa' et l'œuvre d'Aragon*, 1966
Georges Sadoul, *Aragon*, 1967

SARTRE
Main works by Sartre
Philosophical works
L'Imagination, 1936
Esquisse d'une théorie des émotions, 1939
L'Imaginaire, 1940
L'Être et le Néant, 1943. English transl.: *Being and Nothingness*, 1957
L'Existentialisme est un humanisme, 1946. English transl.: *Existentialism and Humanism*, 1948
Critique de la raison dialectique (Tome I), 1960. English transl.: (Introduction only): *The Problem of Method*, 1964

Essays
Situations I
      II (includes *Qu'est-ce que la littérature?*)
      III
      IV (political and aesthetic essays)
      V (articles on colonial problems)
      VI ⎫
      VII ⎬ (articles on Marxism)

English transl.: *Literary and Philosophical Essays*, 1955 (extracts from Volumes I, II and III). *What is Literature?*, 1951
Réflexions sur la question juive, 1947. English transl.: *Anti-Semite and Jew*, 1948
Baudelaire, 1947. English transl.: *Baudelaire*, 1949
Saint Genêt, comédien et martyr, 1952. English transl.: *Saint Genêt, actor and martyr*, 1964
Les Mots, 1964. English transl.: *Words*, 1964

Novels and short stories
La Nausée, 1938. English transl.: *The Diary of Antoine Roquentin*, 1949. U.S.: *Nausea*
Le Mur (short stories), 1939. English transl.: *Intimacy* and other stories, 1949
Les Chemins de la liberté—
   Vol. 1: *L'Age de raison*, 1945. English transl.: *The Age of Reason*, 1947
   Vol. 2: *Le Sursis*, 1945. English transl.: *Reprieve*, 1947
   Vol. 3: *La Mort dans l'âme*, 1949. English transl.: *Iron in the Soul*, 1950
   Vol. 4 (unfinished): *La Dernière Chance*. (Extracts only have appeared so far in *Temps modernes*, November and December, 1949)

Film scripts
Les Jeux sont faits, 1946. English transl.: *The Chips are Down*, 1951
L'Engrenage, 1946. English transl.: *In the Mesh*, 1954

Plays
Théâtre (includes: *Les Mouches, Huis clos, Morts sans sépulture* and *La Putain respectueuse*), 1947. English transl.: *The Flies* (Les Mouches) and *In Camera* (Huis clos) in *Two Plays*, 1946. *Men without Shadows* (Morts sans sépulture) and *The Respectable* (*!*) *Prostitute* (La Putain respectueuse) in *Three Plays*, 1949.

Also: *The Victors* (Morts sans sépulture) and *The Respectful Prostitute* (La Putain respectueuse) in *Three Plays*, 1949
Les Mains sales, 1948. English transl.: *Crime passionel* in *Three Plays*, 1949
Also: *Dirty Hands* in *Three Plays*, 1949
Le Diable et le bon Dieu, 1953. English transl.: *Lucifer and the Lord*, 1953. U.S.: *The Devil and the Good Lord.*
Kean (adapted from Alexandre Dumas), 1954. English transl.: *Kean*, 1954
Nekrassov, 1956. English transl.: *Nekrassov*, 1956
Les Séquestrés d'Altona, 1960. English transl.: *Loser Wins*, 1960
Also: *The Condemned of Altona*, 1961

Main works written about Sartre
English studies
Iris Murdoch: *Sartre, Romantic Rationalist*, 1953
Alfred Stern: *Sartre: His Philosophy and Psychoanalysis*, 1953
Philip Thody: *Jean-Paul Sartre: A Literary and Political Study*, 1960
Maurice Cranston: *Sartre*, 1962
Anthony Manser: *Sartre—A Philosophic Study*, 1966

French studies
Francis Jeanson: *Le Problème moral et la pensée de Sartre*, 1947; new revised edition: 1966
— *Sartre par lui-méme*, 1954
Marc Beigbeder: *L'Homme Sartre*, 1947
R. M. Albérès: *Jean-Paul Sartre*, 1954

GENERAL

It is impossible to mention all the important books which deal with the issues raised in this essay, as there are too many of them. I should just like to draw readers' attention to four French periodicals which are particularly useful:
Esprit (a Catholic monthly)
Les Lettres françaises (a left-wing literary weekly; published many articles by Aragon)
Temps modernes (an independent left-wing monthly, edited by Sartre; published many of his articles)
La Nouvelle Critique (a Communist cultural monthly)

INDEX

INDEX